I0019135

THE COMPLETE GUIDE TO CYBERSECURITY FOR SMALL BUSINESS OWNERS

Maxine Rhodes

Reactive Publishing

CONTENTS

COPYRIGHT © 2025 REACTIVE PUBLISHING. ALL RIGHTS RESERVED.

No part of this book may be reproduced, stored in a retrieval system, or transmitted in any form or by any means—electronic, mechanical, photocopying, recording, or otherwise—without prior written permission of the publisher, except for brief quotes used in reviews or articles.

Published by Reactive Publishing

The information provided in this book is for educational and informational purposes only. The author and publisher assume no responsibility for errors, omissions, or contrary interpretation of the subject matter herein.

PREFACE

In today's digital age, every small business owner stands at the crossroads of opportunity and risk. As you steer your enterprise toward growth, you may have already noticed how technology can transform operations, boost customer engagement, and open doors to new markets. Yet, beneath these promising possibilities lies an ever-evolving landscape of cyber threats that can challenge your business's very foundation. This book is your companion— a comprehensive guide designed specifically to empower you, the small business owner, to master the art of cybersecurity.

When I first encountered the harsh realities of cyber breaches, I realized that the traditional notion that "cybersecurity is just for big corporations" was a dangerous myth. Your business, no matter how modest in size, is a valuable target. Each customer's data, every transaction record, and even your proprietary processes are at risk. This guide was born out of a commitment to demystify cybersecurity and to arm businesses like yours with the knowledge, strategies, and practical tools needed to secure your digital future.

What sets this guide apart is not just its depth and breadth, but the way it speaks to the heart of what small businesses endure. We understand that each decision you make has real consequences—both opportunities and potential setbacks. That's why the book doesn't just offer theoretical knowledge. It provides you with step-by-step procedures, real-life examples, and interactive tools designed to instill confidence and create a proactive security culture within your organization.

Imagine this guide as your personal roadmap through a challenging yet navigable terrain. Whether you're just beginning to consider your cybersecurity options or are already in the process of implementing defenses, you will find thoughtful advice that recognizes your limited resources yet harnesses your indomitable entrepreneurial spirit. We delve into the technical aspects when needed but always circle back to what matters most: protecting your business, preserving your reputation, and ensuring the trust of your valued customers.

As you embark on this journey, remember that cybersecurity is not a destination but an ongoing pursuit. The digital threats of today evolve, and so must your strategies. This text will not only guide you through current best practices but will also encourage a mindset of resilience and perpetual improvement. The strategies, checklists, policies, and resources in these chapters are designed to reassure you that, no matter what challenges come your way, you are never alone in this fight.

Thank you for choosing to invest time in fortifying your business's digital fortress. In the pages that follow, may you find inspiration, practical guidance, and the empowerment to transform potential cyber vulnerabilities into robust defenses. Together, we can build a future where security is an enabler of growth, innovation, and peace of mind.

Welcome to the journey toward a secure and thriving small business.

INTRODUCTION

U nderstanding cybersecurity goes beyond technical jargon or keeping up with the latest software updates. It requires recognizing the intrinsic value of your business's data—from customer details to proprietary processes—and acknowledging that each piece of information is a potential target for malicious actors. As you navigate this guide, consider how these vulnerabilities could impact your organization directly. The stakes are high; safeguarding your enterprise is not merely hypothetical—it's essential for its survival and growth in an increasingly hostile environment.

This book aims to achieve two key objectives: equipping you with actionable strategies and nurturing a proactive mindset toward cybersecurity. Think of it as your toolkit for establishing a robust security framework that not only protects your assets but also fosters confidence among clients and stakeholders. Each chapter will draw upon best practices, real-world examples, and actionable insights specifically designed for small business owners like you.

Navigating the complexities of cybersecurity can feel overwhelming, especially when you're juggling multiple responsibilities. However, breaking down these concepts into manageable steps allows for effective implementation without disrupting your daily operations. Together, we will explore methods to assess your current security posture, identify protection gaps, and implement changes that can yield significant benefits with minimal disruption.

You may wonder why focusing on cybersecurity matters beyond mere compliance or basic safety measures. The answer lies in the broader context of trust—trust from customers who expect their information to be secure and from partners who rely on your integrity. When security becomes ingrained in your business culture, it evolves from a simple obligation into a competitive advantage.

Throughout this guide, we will delve into essential areas such as risk management strategies tailored for small businesses, data protection protocols—including encryption techniques and backup solutions—and effective responses to incidents when they occur. By building an understanding across these domains, you will not only mitigate risks but also foster an organizational ethos that prioritizes security at every level.

This introduction marks the beginning of your journey toward cybersecurity competence and confidence—a journey that will reshape your approach to risk management within your organization. Embrace this opportunity to turn challenges into strategic advantages that protect what you've built while positioning you favorably in the market. Your commitment to learning will ultimately enhance your operational resilience and cultivate a culture rooted in awareness and adaptability.

· Importance of Cybersecurity for Small Businesses

Every small business owner must face the stark reality that cyber threats are not a distant concern; they pose an immediate risk that can jeopardize years of hard work. As businesses become more reliant on technology, the opportunities for cyberattacks increase, making robust cybersecurity measures more crucial than ever. Protecting your data goes beyond safeguarding information; it encompasses the overall integrity of your enterprise. With the rise of remote work and online transactions, the potential for breaches has expanded, placing even the most vigilant companies at risk.

The impact of a cyber incident on a small business can be devastating. Research indicates that nearly 60% of small companies close their doors within six months of a cyberattack. The fallout extends beyond immediate financial loss; it often includes reputational damage that can take years to mend. Customers expect their data to be handled securely, and losing their trust can result in decreased loyalty and dwindling sales. An attack can ripple through your operations, affecting everything from employee morale to supplier relationships.

Recognizing that cybersecurity is not merely a technical issue but a business imperative is vital. Your cybersecurity strategy should align seamlessly with your broader business objectives and risk tolerance. This alignment ensures that your security measures facilitate growth rather than obstruct it. For example, investing in strong cybersecurity infrastructure can enable smoother transactions and foster trust with clients, ultimately driving sales and enhancing customer loyalty.

Also, cybersecurity intersects with various business functions, from marketing to finance. Take this example, finance teams rely on secure payment systems, while marketing departments depend on customer data analytics to create effective campaigns. By treating cybersecurity as an integral part of your business model, you empower every department to contribute to a collective defense strategy.

Training employees in cybersecurity awareness is another essential component directly influencing your organization's resilience. Each team member should understand their role in preventing incidents—whether that involves recognizing phishing attempts or adhering to secure password practices. Alarmingly, human error accounts for a significant percentage of breaches, underscoring the necessity for comprehensive training programs. Regular workshops and simulations can foster a culture where security is prioritized at all levels.

Given these considerations, developing a robust cybersecurity framework is not just prudent—it's essential for survival in today's digital landscape. High-profile breaches involving companies like Target and Equifax remind us that no business is immune; these cases underscore the importance of being proactive rather than reactive.

Effective risk management strategies tailored specifically for small businesses will be invaluable as you navigate this complex landscape. Identifying critical assets—such as client databases or intellectual property—is a crucial first step in strengthening your security posture. Once these assets are identified, assessing vulnerabilities becomes more manageable, allowing you to prioritize areas that require immediate attention.

As we delve into various aspects of cybersecurity throughout this guide, you will gain insights into developing policies tailored specifically to your needs as a small business owner. This journey is not solely about compliance or reacting to current threats; it's about committing to an ongoing security strategy that evolves with emerging risks and technological advancements.

To wrap things up, the significance of cybersecurity goes beyond mere protection; it's about building a resilient business model anchored in trust and integrity. Embrace this responsibility by investing time and resources into creating a secure environment for your company and its stakeholders. The stakes are high, but with the right strategies in place, you can navigate this landscape with confidence, ensuring that your business thrives despite the challenges ahead.

 • **Overview of Cybersecurity Threats and Landscape**

Navigating the cybersecurity landscape is essential for small business owners, as they face a multitude of threats in an increasingly digital world. While the online realm offers vast opportunities, it also introduces significant risks. Cyber threats manifest in various forms—such as ransomware, phishing, and data breaches—each targeting different vulnerabilities within an organization. As attackers employ increasingly sophisticated tools and techniques, staying informed about these threats becomes crucial for effective business protection.

Ransomware attacks have become particularly prominent in recent years. This type of malware encrypts data and demands a ransom for its release. A notable example is the 2021 attack on Colonial Pipeline, which severely disrupted fuel supplies across the eastern United States. This incident not only had serious financial repercussions but also underscored the vulnerability of critical infrastructure. Many small businesses mistakenly believe they are not attractive targets for cybercriminals due to their perceived lack of robust security measures. However, these businesses often hold valuable data and intellectual property that make them appealing targets.

Phishing attacks represent another significant threat in the cybersecurity landscape. These deceptive attempts typically involve emails or messages that appear legitimate but are intended to steal sensitive information or deploy malware. Take this example, an email might impersonate a trusted vendor or partner, prompting employees to click on malicious links or provide login credentials. By understanding the mechanics of phishing, employees can learn to recognize warning signs and reduce the likelihood of falling victim to such tactics.

Data breaches remain a persistent concern, occurring when unauthorized individuals gain access to confidential data. Breaches can result from external hacking efforts or internal errors. For example, in 2019, Capital One suffered a breach that affected over 100 million customers due to a misconfigured firewall—illustrating that even large corporations can be vulnerable if their security configurations are not properly managed. Small businesses must prioritize the protection of sensitive data, such as customer information and proprietary assets, to mitigate the risks associated with breaches.

In addition to recognizing various threats, it is vital to understand the evolving nature of cybersecurity. Attackers continuously refine their strategies, often utilizing artificial intelligence and machine learning to automate and enhance their attacks. This evolution calls for a proactive approach; waiting for an incident to occur before taking action can be disastrous for recovery efforts.

Regulatory compliance adds another layer of complexity to the cybersecurity landscape. Various regulations dictate how organizations should manage sensitive data, and non-compliance can lead to hefty fines and legal consequences. Familiarizing yourself with regulations like the General Data Protection Regulation (GDPR) or the Health Insurance Portability and Accountability Act (HIPAA) is essential for ensuring compliance while also maintaining customer trust.

Emerging technologies present both opportunities and challenges in the realm of cybersecurity. The rise of remote work has introduced new vulnerabilities, as employees may connect to unsecured networks when accessing company resources. Implementing virtual private networks (VPNs) can secure these connections, but they require proper configuration and ongoing maintenance.

The relationship between technology and human behavior further complicates cybersecurity efforts; employees are often the first line of defense against cyber threats. As previously noted, human error accounts for many breaches. Regular training on cybersecurity awareness is crucial for cultivating a culture where every team member understands their role in maintaining security.

An effective cybersecurity strategy combines awareness of these threats with robust safeguards tailored to your specific business needs. Identifying critical assets early enables you to prioritize risk management efforts effectively. Conducting regular assessments can reveal vulnerabilities in your systems or processes that need immediate attention.

Agility and adaptability are paramount in this landscape; what worked yesterday may not suffice tomorrow as new threats continually emerge. Cultivating a mindset geared toward continual improvement ensures that your cybersecurity measures evolve alongside technological advancements and shifting threat vectors.

 by gaining a comprehensive understanding of the current cybersecurity landscape—its threats and complexities—you position yourself as an active defender of your business's future rather than a passive participant. Engaging with these concepts equips you to develop targeted strategies that enhance your organization's resilience against cyber threats while fostering a culture of security awareness among your team members. Your commitment today will pave the way for a more secure tomorrow.

- **Objective of the Book**

Understanding the objectives of this book is essential for navigating the complex world of cybersecurity, especially tailored for small business owners. Our goal extends beyond mere information; we aim to empower you with practical knowledge and strategies that can be applied immediately to your specific situation. This guide transcends theoretical concepts, providing actionable steps you can implement right away.

At the heart of this book is a commitment to demystifying cybersecurity. Many small business owners feel overwhelmed by the technical jargon and intricacies involved in protecting their digital assets. To alleviate this, we break down complex ideas into clear, digestible information using relatable examples. By bridging the gap between technical details and real-world applications, we strive to create a resource that feels approachable rather than daunting.

Recognizing the unique challenges faced by small businesses compared to larger corporations is another focus of this guide. Budget constraints and limited resources often necessitate prioritizing certain security measures. We provide guidance on identifying which actions will yield the highest return on investment for your specific context. Whether it's establishing a cost-effective data protection plan or utilizing free tools for monitoring network traffic, our emphasis is on strategies that deliver results without straining your finances.

Throughout the text, real-world case studies serve as both cautionary tales and sources of inspiration. These examples highlight successful security implementations as well as devastating breaches encountered by similar organizations. By learning from others' experiences, you can avoid common pitfalls while adopting best practices tailored to your industry.

In addition to addressing current threats, this guide also explores emerging challenges in the cybersecurity landscape. The rapid pace of technological advancement means cybercriminals are constantly adapting their methods. Therefore, staying ahead requires continuous learning and adaptation. We encourage you to adopt an agile mindset toward security—regularly reassessing risks and updating practices based on new information or changing circumstances.

Compliance with regulatory requirements relevant to your industry is another critical aspect we emphasize. Understanding these regulations is vital—not just for avoiding potential fines but also for maintaining customer trust in an era where data privacy is paramount. Integrating compliance into your broader security strategy ensures that your business operates within legal parameters while effectively safeguarding sensitive information.

our objective is straightforward yet significant: to empower you as a small business owner with the knowledge and tools necessary to defend against cyber threats effectively. By fostering an environment where cybersecurity becomes a shared responsibility among all employees, you enhance resilience against potential attacks while creating a culture rooted in vigilance and proactivity.

As you explore this guide further, remember that every step taken toward improving your cybersecurity posture not only protects your business assets but also strengthens trust with customers and partners alike. The journey toward robust cybersecurity might seem intimidating at first glance; however, with each chapter offering new insights and actionable strategies, you'll be well-equipped to navigate this complex landscape with confidence and clarity.

- **Structure and Format**

Understanding the structure and format of this guide is essential for maximizing your engagement with its content. Each section is carefully designed to flow seamlessly into the next, enabling you to grasp the complexities of cybersecurity without feeling overwhelmed. The narrative style goes beyond mere information consumption; it immerses you in practical knowledge that you can readily apply to your business.

Each chapter begins with a targeted focus, delving into a specific aspect of cybersecurity relevant to small business owners. Take this example, one chapter may explore the intricacies of network security, while the following one connects these concepts to data protection strategies. This interconnected approach enhances your learning experience, illustrating how various elements of cybersecurity interact and support one another, much like assembling a puzzle where each piece contributes to a comprehensive picture of a secure business environment.

To promote clarity and retention, we've integrated actionable steps and guidelines throughout the text. Each key point comes with straightforward instructions or checklists for immediate implementation. For example, when discussing how to conduct a risk assessment, you'll find a step-by-step walkthrough that clarifies not just what needs to be done but also how to do it effectively. This practical approach transforms complex concepts into manageable tasks.

Real-world case studies peppered throughout each chapter provide context and relatability. These narratives highlight successful initiatives as well as cautionary tales from businesses similar to yours. By closely examining these cases, you gain valuable insights into what works and what pitfalls to avoid. Take this example, one compelling example may showcase how a small retail business successfully implemented an employee training program on phishing attacks, leading to a notable reduction in security incidents. Such stories serve as both motivation and guidance as you develop your own strategies.

Visual aids also play a crucial role in enhancing comprehension. Diagrams, charts, and infographics accompany many sections, breaking down complex information into easily digestible formats. Take this example, a flowchart might illustrate the incident response process step-by-step, making it easier for you to understand critical actions during a cyber event. These visuals complement the text by reinforcing key concepts through visual learning.

As you progress through the chapters, you'll notice an emphasis on continuous improvement—an agile mindset toward cybersecurity is vital in today's fast-changing digital landscape. Each chapter concludes with reflective questions or prompts that encourage you to consider how the material applies specifically to your organization. This introspective approach fosters deeper engagement and cultivates a proactive stance toward security challenges.

Another fundamental aspect of this guide is its focus on compliance with industry regulations. Throughout various sections, you'll find references to relevant laws such as GDPR or HIPAA, along with practical advice on integrating compliance into your overall cybersecurity strategy. This dual focus ensures that safeguarding sensitive information goes hand in hand with meeting legal obligations—an essential consideration for any small business navigating today's regulatory environment.

 this guide's structure is crafted not only for ease of navigation but also for fostering actionable insights that empower you as a small business owner. Each component—from case studies and visual aids to reflective prompts—enriches your understanding while emphasizing that cybersecurity is integral to your business strategy.

By fully engaging with this guide's format and leveraging its resources, you'll be well on your way toward establishing robust cybersecurity practices that protect both your assets and your reputation in the marketplace. Though the journey may seem daunting at first, each thoughtfully structured section brings you closer to mastering the essentials of cybersecurity tailored specifically for your needs as a small business owner.

CHAPTER 1: UNDERSTANDING CYBERSECURITY BASICS

Definition of Cybersecurity

Cybersecurity encompasses a wide range of practices, technologies, and processes aimed at protecting digital data from unauthorized access, theft, or damage. At its essence, it focuses on ensuring the integrity, confidentiality, and availability of information in the digital world. For small business owners, grasping this concept is crucial; it lays the groundwork for establishing a strong security posture capable of withstanding various online threats.

Consider the everyday activities involved in running a business online. Whether managing customer data or processing transactions, every interaction carries potential vulnerabilities. Cybersecurity addresses these risks by implementing multiple layers of protection, which can include firewalls, antivirus software, and employee training programs designed to recognize phishing attempts. Each of these components is vital to building a comprehensive security framework.

Breaking down cybersecurity into key domains reveals its complexity: network security, application security, information security, operational security, and end-user education. Network security aims to protect the integrity of networks and data during transfer. Application security focuses on securing software applications throughout their lifecycle. Information security safeguards sensitive data from unauthorized access or alteration. Operational security involves processes and decisions for managing and protecting data assets. Finally, end-user education underscores the importance of training employees to identify potential threats and respond effectively.

Real-world examples highlight how these domains interact within daily business operations. Take this example, a small e-commerce retailer might implement network security measures like firewalls to defend against intrusions while also adopting application security protocols to secure their checkout process from attacks. Additionally, regular training sessions can help employees recognize scams that could jeopardize customer data.

As businesses grow in their digital capabilities, the understanding of cybersecurity expands beyond mere protection; it embraces resilience. A resilient cybersecurity strategy not only prevents attacks but also prepares for swift recovery in the event of an incident. This includes having an incident response plan—an essential element for businesses seeking to minimize damage from cyber incidents and maintain customer trust.

Recognizing the dynamic nature of cybersecurity is also vital. New threats emerge continuously—malware evolves, phishing tactics become more sophisticated, and regulatory landscapes shift. This ever-changing environment demands that businesses adopt a proactive approach rather than relying solely on reactive measures. Regular assessments of current practices are crucial to ensure alignment with emerging threats.

As you navigate the complexities of cybersecurity, remember that it is not just a technical challenge; it is an organizational one that requires commitment from all levels—from leadership to every employee. By embracing cybersecurity as a core component of your business strategy, you cultivate a culture where everyone understands their role in safeguarding sensitive information.

With this foundational understanding of cybersecurity and its implications for your small business in mind, you are well-prepared to explore specific areas such as risk assessment and network defense strategies. As we delve into these specialized topics, keep in focus that each element builds upon this comprehensive definition—creating a cohesive strategy tailored to your unique business landscape.

Cybersecurity vs. Information Security

Cybersecurity and information security are closely related yet distinct disciplines within the broader framework of protecting digital assets. Cybersecurity is primarily concerned with defending networks, devices, and data from external threats. It encompasses a range of strategies designed to shield systems from cyber attacks, including malware, phishing scams, and unauthorized access attempts. In contrast, information security focuses on ensuring the integrity and confidentiality of data itself, regardless of where it resides. This discipline aims to protect sensitive information from being accessed or altered by unauthorized individuals.

To better illustrate this difference, consider a small business that processes customer transactions online. Cybersecurity measures would involve protecting the entire network supporting those transactions—this might include implementing firewalls to prevent intrusions or using secure protocols for data transmission. On the other hand, information security would center on safeguarding the sensitive customer information stored in databases, ensuring that data is encrypted during storage and transfer, while also establishing strict access controls to restrict unauthorized personnel from viewing it.

Small business owners often find themselves navigating the intersection of these two domains. Many may assume that securing their network is sufficient; however, without robust information security practices, they leave themselves exposed. For example, if an employee accesses customer data on an unsecured device or network, they not only jeopardize their own system but also put the entire business at risk for data breaches and identity theft. A comprehensive approach that integrates both cybersecurity and information security is essential for creating a strong defense mechanism.

The difference in focus between the two areas also leads to varying methods of implementation. Cybersecurity strategies frequently employ technology-driven solutions such as intrusion detection systems and antivirus software that operate in real time to counter threats as they arise. Conversely, information security methodologies involve developing policies and procedures for handling sensitive information responsibly. This includes creating comprehensive data classification schemes and conducting regular audits on data access practices.

Additionally, the evolving regulatory landscape underscores the importance of compliance with requirements related to both cybersecurity and information security. Laws such as GDPR impose strict regulations regarding data handling and privacy protections, significantly impacting how businesses must approach these areas. Noncompliance not only endangers customer data but can also lead to serious legal consequences.

Engaging employees is crucial in bridging these two areas effectively. Training initiatives should aim to foster a culture of awareness, helping employees understand how their actions can impact both cybersecurity and information security. Take this example, sessions focused on recognizing phishing emails can directly enhance both the network's defenses (cybersecurity) and the protection of sensitive customer information (information security).

gaining a thorough understanding of both cybersecurity and information security empowers small business owners to protect their operations more effectively. By integrating proactive measures from both fields, you can establish an infrastructure that not only defends against immediate threats but also builds long-term trust with your customers through responsible data management practices.

As you explore cybersecurity concepts tailored to your business needs, keep in mind the interplay between safeguarding your technological infrastructure and securing your valuable data assets. This dual focus lays a solid foundation for developing actionable strategies that align with your business goals while enhancing overall resilience against emerging threats.

Common Cyber Threats

In the world of cybersecurity, small business owners must prioritize recognizing and understanding common cyber threats. These threats manifest in various forms, each presenting distinct challenges that require specific responses. By identifying these risks, you can better equip your organization and develop effective strategies to mitigate their impact.

One of the most prevalent threats is malware, which includes a wide range of malicious software designed to harm or exploit devices and networks. From viruses and worms to ransomware and spyware, malware can compromise sensitive information, disrupt operations, and result in significant financial losses. Ransomware is particularly notorious for locking users out of their files until a ransom is paid. The infamous WannaCry attack in 2017 serves as a stark reminder of this threat, affecting thousands of businesses worldwide and illustrating how vulnerable even established organizations can be.

Phishing attacks represent another serious concern for small businesses. These often take the form of seemingly legitimate emails that deceive employees into revealing sensitive information or clicking on harmful links. Take this example, a cybercriminal might impersonate a trusted vendor in an email requesting payment details. When employees fall for such schemes, they inadvertently jeopardize the organization's financial security and expose confidential data. The financial repercussions of data breaches stemming from successful phishing attempts can be staggering, often reaching millions of dollars for a single incident.

Denial-of-service (DoS) attacks introduce yet another layer of complexity to cybersecurity challenges. In these scenarios, attackers inundate a business's network with excessive traffic, overwhelming resources and rendering services inaccessible to legitimate users. This disruption can paralyze operations for hours or even days, leading to lost revenue and damaging customer relationships. Small businesses, in particular, may lack the infrastructure needed to defend against such overwhelming assaults.

Insider threats also present significant risks that are frequently underestimated. Whether intentional or unintentional, insiders—employees or contractors with access to sensitive data—can inadvertently or deliberately cause data breaches. A disgruntled employee might leak proprietary information, while negligent actions like using weak passwords or sharing access credentials can expose systems to vulnerabilities. Regular training on security protocols is essential for mitigating these risks by fostering awareness among staff about potential insider threats.

Social engineering attacks exploit human psychology rather than technical vulnerabilities. In these cases, attackers manipulate individuals into divulging confidential information by building trust or instilling fear. For example, an attacker might pose as IT support and request an employee's login credentials under the pretense of routine maintenance. Educating employees about these tactics is crucial for reducing vulnerability.

Additionally, advanced persistent threats (APTs) have emerged as a growing concern. In these situations, attackers infiltrate a network undetected over extended periods to steal data or monitor activities. While APTs often target high-value industries like finance or healthcare, any organization handling sensitive information is at risk.

Recognizing these common cyber threats is the first step toward developing a comprehensive cybersecurity strategy tailored to your business needs. Cultivating a culture of awareness within your organization and implementing robust security measures—such as regular employee training sessions on threat recognition and response—creates an environment where vigilance becomes second nature.

And, integrating technology solutions like firewalls, intrusion detection systems (IDS), and consistent software updates significantly enhances your defense against these threats. Each layer of protection you add decreases the likelihood of a successful attack while empowering your team to respond swiftly should one occur.

As you navigate this complex landscape of cyber threats, keep in mind that proactive measures far outweigh reactive responses. By preparing for potential challenges, you not only protect your digital assets but also safeguard your business's reputation and trustworthiness in the eyes of clients and stakeholders alike.

Cybersecurity Terminology

Understanding cybersecurity terminology is crucial for small business owners who want to navigate the digital landscape effectively. Just as mastering the language of finance or marketing is vital for success, grasping fundamental cybersecurity terms and concepts empowers you to communicate clearly with IT professionals and make informed decisions about your organization's security posture.

One essential term to know is "threat." In cybersecurity, a threat represents any potential danger that could exploit a vulnerability in your system, leading to unauthorized access or damage. By recognizing various types of threats—such as malware, phishing, or insider attacks—you can proactively anticipate and mitigate risks. For example, knowing that ransomware is a form of malware can inform your strategies for data backup and employee training focused on recognizing suspicious activity.

Closely related to threats are vulnerabilities, which are weaknesses in your system that attackers can exploit. Vulnerabilities may arise from outdated software, misconfigured systems, or even human error. Regularly updating operating systems is crucial; neglecting this can leave you exposed to exploits that vendors have already patched. Conducting regular vulnerability assessments helps identify and address these weaknesses before malicious actors can take advantage of them.

Another key term in the realm of cybersecurity is "firewall." Firewalls serve as barriers between trusted internal networks and untrusted external ones, such as the internet. They filter incoming and outgoing traffic based on predefined security rules, acting as a critical first line of defense against cyber threats. Understanding how firewalls function—whether as hardware devices or software applications—will help you configure them effectively for your organization.

Encryption" is another important concept. It involves transforming data into a code to prevent unauthorized access during transmission or storage. For small businesses managing sensitive customer information, implementing encryption protocols ensures that even if data is intercepted, it remains unreadable without the correct decryption key. Familiarizing yourself with encryption standards like AES (Advanced Encryption Standard) can guide you in selecting secure communication channels for your operations.

The idea of "access control" is also significant in cybersecurity. Access control mechanisms determine who can access specific resources within your organization. By implementing strong access control policies—such as role-based access control (RBAC)—you ensure that employees only have access to the information necessary for their job functions. This practice minimizes the risk of accidental data exposure or intentional breaches from within.

For dealing with cybersecurity incidents, "incident response" refers to the systematic approach taken when an incident occurs. Understanding this concept allows you to prepare an incident response plan outlining steps for detecting, responding to, and recovering from breaches or attacks. A well-defined incident response strategy can significantly reduce recovery time and mitigate damage following an event.

And, "malware" encompasses various types of malicious software designed to harm devices or networks. Being familiar with forms of malware—such as viruses, worms, and trojans —can help you identify potential threats early and implement effective antivirus solutions tailored to combat them.

In addition to these terms, understanding "phishing" is vital. Phishing exploits human psychology rather than technical vulnerabilities by masquerading as legitimate communications from trusted sources. These attempts aim to trick individuals into revealing sensitive information like passwords or financial details. Raising awareness among employees about recognizing phishing attempts can drastically reduce the likelihood of successful attacks.

By cultivating a robust understanding of these foundational cybersecurity terms and concepts, you lay the groundwork for effective strategies within your organization. This knowledge fosters an environment where all team members contribute to maintaining security standards—a crucial aspect in today's threat-laden digital world.

With this vocabulary and insight into key principles like risk management and data protection measures, you position yourself not just as a passive consumer of technology but as an active participant in safeguarding your business against cyber threats. Integrating cybersecurity language into daily operations enhances communication among teams and establishes a culture of vigilance essential for navigating today's complex digital ecosystem.

Importance of Cyber Hygiene

Cyber hygiene is an often-overlooked yet essential element of maintaining a secure business environment. Just as personal hygiene is crucial for health, practicing good cyber hygiene keeps your digital landscape clean and safeguarded against potential threats. It goes beyond merely installing the latest security software or implementing a robust firewall; it involves cultivating habits that promote ongoing vigilance and proactive management of your systems.

One cornerstone of effective cyber hygiene is regularly updating software. When you receive notifications about software updates, they should not be dismissed as mere annoyances; these alerts indicate vulnerabilities that need immediate attention. Each update typically includes patches for known security flaws, and neglecting to install them can expose your systems to exploitation. A stark reminder of this occurred in 2020, when a vulnerability in Microsoft Exchange Server was widely exploited. Organizations that delayed or overlooked these updates faced significant breaches, resulting in data loss and reputational damage.

Password management is another critical aspect where cyber hygiene plays a vital role. A weak password can serve as an open invitation for cybercriminals. To enhance security, implement strong password policies that require complex combinations of letters, numbers, and symbols, along with regular password changes. Utilizing tools like password managers can help create and securely store unique passwords for each account, significantly reducing the risk of unauthorized access. This not only mitigates potential threats but also encourages employees to adopt better practices without the stress of remembering multiple complex passwords.

Employee training is key to fostering good cyber hygiene practices within your organization. Regularly educating staff about current threats—such as phishing scams—can significantly strengthen your defenses. Conducting simulated phishing attacks can be an effective exercise to test employees' ability to recognize suspicious emails. Research shows that such training can reduce successful phishing attempts by over 30%. When team members are equipped to identify phishing signs, they become active participants in your cybersecurity strategy rather than passive observers.

Data management also plays a crucial role in cyber hygiene. Regularly backing up important files ensures that you have access to vital information even during a ransomware attack or system failure. Establishing a routine backup schedule— whether daily, weekly, or monthly—should align with your business's operational needs. Using a combination of cloud storage solutions and local backups provides redundancy, enhancing data protection and recovery options in case of disaster.

Additionally, device cleanliness is often overlooked. Just as dust and clutter can hinder the performance of physical equipment, malware and unwanted software can accumulate on devices if not monitored properly. Implementing regular scans with reputable antivirus software allows for the timely identification and removal of potential threats. Educating employees on recognizing suspicious downloads or unfamiliar applications further contributes to maintaining device integrity.

Conducting regular audits of your cybersecurity practices serves as a vital checkpoint for assessing your current status and identifying areas for improvement. By reviewing security protocols, assessing vulnerabilities, and ensuring compliance with established policies, you cultivate an environment where cyber hygiene is prioritized. Utilizing checklists or engaging external experts for thorough assessments can provide unbiased insights into your security posture.

Establishing a culture of accountability around cyber hygiene within your organization empowers all team members to take ownership of their roles in maintaining security. Encouraging open communication regarding cybersecurity issues and promoting the reporting of suspicious activity without fear of repercussions fosters resilience within your organization, enabling swift responses to emerging threats.

Cyber hygiene is not a one-time effort; it demands continuous commitment and adaptation to the ever-evolving challenges of the digital landscape. By embedding these practices into the daily operations of your business, you create a robust defense against potential attacks while nurturing an organizational culture rooted in security awareness.

 recognizing the importance of cyber hygiene lays the groundwork for implementing more advanced cybersecurity measures in the future. When every member of your organization understands their role in safeguarding assets and maintaining data integrity, you foster an environment where proactive measures become second nature—a crucial component for success in today's interconnected world.

Cybersecurity Regulations and Compliance

Understanding the landscape of cybersecurity regulations and compliance is crucial for small business owners who want to protect their organizations from both threats and legal repercussions. Regulations are not merely bureaucratic hurdles; they provide essential frameworks that guide businesses in managing sensitive data and defending against cyber threats. By complying with these regulations, businesses not only safeguard themselves but also foster trust with customers who expect their personal information to be handled responsibly.

One significant piece of legislation in the cybersecurity realm is the General Data Protection Regulation (GDPR). Enacted by the European Union, GDPR establishes strict requirements for data protection and privacy. Even if your business operates outside Europe, you may still be affected if you handle data belonging to EU residents. Take this example, a small online retailer in the U.S. that sells products to European customers must comply with GDPR provisions, which require that personal data be processed lawfully, transparently, and only for specified purposes. Non-compliance can lead to hefty fines —up to 4% of annual global revenue or €20 million, whichever amount is higher.

Another important regulation is the Health Insurance Portability and Accountability Act (HIPAA), which dictates how healthcare organizations manage patient information. For small medical practices or any business dealing with health-related data, understanding HIPAA's requirements is essential. Implementing proper encryption methods when transmitting patient data not only ensures compliance with

HIPAA standards but also protects sensitive information from unauthorized access.

The Payment Card Industry Data Security Standard (PCI DSS) sets the standard for organizations that handle credit card transactions. Compliance involves adhering to a series of security measures designed to protect cardholder data from theft and fraud. Small businesses that accept credit card payments must conduct regular self-assessments and maintain secure networks to ensure compliance. A notable example of the consequences of non-compliance occurred when a small restaurant chain failed to meet PCI standards, resulting in a significant data breach that exposed thousands of customer credit card details.

However, compliance goes beyond simply adhering to laws; it's about fostering a culture of security within your organization. Establishing policies and procedures that align with regulatory requirements sets clear expectations for how your team approaches cybersecurity. Regular training sessions on regulatory compliance can keep employees informed about their responsibilities regarding data protection.

In addition to these major regulations, many industries have specific compliance requirements that can impact small businesses based on their operational focus. The National Institute of Standards and Technology (NIST) offers guidelines through its Cybersecurity Framework—a flexible structure that can be customized according to your unique needs and resources.

When audits—whether internal or external—occur, having thorough documentation can greatly simplify compliance efforts. Keeping records of security measures implemented, employee training conducted, and incidents reported serves as proof of due diligence should questions arise during an audit or investigation.

Investing in compliance also means staying ahead of evolving regulations as technology rapidly advances. Regulatory bodies frequently update guidelines to address new risks posed by emerging technologies such as cloud computing or artificial intelligence. Regularly reviewing regulatory changes ensures your business adapts proactively rather than scrambling after changes take effect.

Understanding cybersecurity regulations isn't solely about avoiding penalties; it's also about enhancing your organization's credibility in the eyes of clients and stakeholders. When clients observe you actively engaging in compliance efforts, they are more likely to view your organization as trustworthy—a vital component for building long-term relationships.

By incorporating these regulatory frameworks into your cybersecurity strategy, you can transform them from mere obligations into proactive measures that strengthen your overall security posture. Aligning your business practices with recognized standards creates a solid foundation for ongoing security efforts while minimizing risks associated with non-compliance.

Embracing cybersecurity regulations requires commitment but ultimately fosters an environment where compliance and security thrive together—ensuring longevity and resilience in an ever-evolving digital landscape.

The Cost of Cyber Incidents for Small Businesses

The financial consequences of cyber incidents for small businesses can be staggering, often surpassing initial estimates in both immediate costs and long-term impacts. For many small business owners, the mere thought of a cyber breach stirs anxiety—not only for the sensitive data at stake but also for the financial stability of their entire operation. Cyber incidents bring with them a range of expenses that can quickly disrupt even the most carefully crafted budgets.

To begin with, let's examine the direct costs associated with a data breach. These costs include forensic investigation fees, essential for determining how the breach occurred and what data has been compromised. Engaging cybersecurity professionals for this investigation can range from thousands to tens of thousands of dollars. For example, a small law firm facing a data breach may incur expenses exceeding (15,000 just to assess the extent of their exposure.

Once the investigation concludes, businesses must grapple with additional costs such as notifying affected customers and providing credit monitoring services. If lawsuits arise, legal fees can add to the financial burden. The California Consumer Privacy Act (CCPA) requires businesses to notify consumers about breaches within specific timeframes, complicating matters further for those who fail to comply promptly. Ignoring these regulations can lead to fines that exacerbate existing losses.

The long-term effects of cyber incidents can be even more damaging. A business may suffer significant reputational harm, as customer trust is notoriously hard to rebuild once lost. Research shows that nearly 60% of small companies close within six months of a cyberattack due to customer attrition and declining revenues. A mid-sized retail chain serves as a cautionary tale: after experiencing a breach, they saw sales plummet by 30% in the following year as loyal customers sought alternatives.

And, insurance premiums typically rise dramatically following a data breach. When filing a claim for such an incident or system downtime, insurers may categorize your business as higher risk, resulting in increased premiums or even cancellation of your policy. This situation compounds existing challenges as companies face rising operational costs alongside dwindling revenue streams.

Given these realities, investing in cybersecurity before an incident occurs is essential—not only as a protective measure but also as a long-term cost-saving strategy. By proactively enhancing security protocols through firewalls, employee training on phishing detection, and multi-factor authentication, businesses can significantly lower their chances of falling victim to an attack.

Take this example, consider a bakery in Chicago that implemented employee training programs focused on recognizing phishing attempts and other social engineering tactics. Over two years, this bakery reported no incidents while its peers faced multiple breaches during the same period due to a lack of awareness.

Investing in robust cybersecurity tools—such as intrusion detection systems (IDS) or endpoint protection solutions—can yield substantial returns by preventing costly breaches before they happen. These preventive measures function much like insurance policies: although they require initial investment and commitment upfront, they ultimately save businesses from potentially crippling expenses down the line.

Beyond financial considerations, compliance with regulations and industry standards is crucial for safeguarding against incidents and their associated costs. Non-compliance with regulations such as GDPR or HIPAA can result in hefty fines and expose your organization to increased risks due to inadequate protections against breaches.

The equation becomes clear: while implementing cybersecurity measures necessitates upfront costs and effort—be it through technology investments or employee education—the potential savings far outweigh these expenses when compared to the catastrophic impact of cyber incidents.

understanding both the immediate and long-term costs associated with cyber incidents empowers small business owners to make informed decisions about their cybersecurity strategies. The challenge lies not just in reacting to threats but in adopting proactive measures that build resilience against future attacks—a journey where every dollar invested today paves the way for safeguarding tomorrow's success.

CHAPTER 2:
ASSESSING YOUR
SMALL BUSINESS
CYBERSECURITY
RISKS

Identifying Assets and
Data of Value

Identifying valuable assets and data within your small business is the essential first step in establishing a strong cybersecurity framework. This process goes beyond a simple inventory; it serves as a crucial assessment that influences how effectively you can protect what matters most. Start by considering everything that contributes to your operation's success—financial records, customer information, intellectual property, and proprietary software. Each of these elements is vital not only for your business's functionality but also for its reputation.

Begin with a thorough audit of all your digital and physical assets. A structured approach can be particularly helpful; consider using an asset management tool or a spreadsheet to keep track. Organize your findings into columns that include asset type, location (digital or physical), owner, and sensitivity level. As you compile this information, pay special attention to customer data, such as names, addresses, social security numbers, and payment details. This kind of sensitive information is frequently targeted by cybercriminals due to its high resale value on the dark web.

Next, assess the importance of each asset to your daily operations. Not every piece of data holds the same weight; some are critical for your business continuity while others, though sensitive, may be less urgent. Prioritize these assets accordingly. For example, in a small e-commerce store, customer payment data might be classified as critical, whereas employee training materials could be considered less pressing but still deserving of protection.

Once you've identified your assets, it's important to understand how they are stored and transmitted within your organization. Are sensitive data points encrypted? Are appropriate access controls in place? Map out how information flows through your business—from collection to storage or deletion. This mapping exercise can help you uncover potential vulnerabilities; for instance, if customer data travels through multiple unencrypted channels before reaching secure servers, you've identified an area that requires immediate attention.

Additionally, consider the implications of using cloud services. Many small businesses depend on third-party platforms for data storage or application hosting. Evaluate which of these services handle sensitive information and ensure they adhere to industry security standards. Request documentation from these providers outlining their security protocols and breach history to assess their reliability.

To illustrate the importance of this identification process, let's consider a real-world example: a small healthcare provider suffered a ransomware attack because they had not thoroughly assessed their digital assets. They lost access to unencrypted patient records that were inadequately backed up, resulting in significant operational downtime and damage to their reputation. Had they conducted a comprehensive asset identification process beforehand—recognizing the sensitivity of patient data—they could have implemented stronger security measures like regular backups and encryption protocols.

Don't overlook external risks that may impact your organization's data value. Third-party vendors can introduce vulnerabilities without you even realizing it. For example, if you hire an external marketing firm with access to customer lists but insufficient cybersecurity practices, they could unintentionally become a gateway for cyber threats.

Involve your employees in the identification process by encouraging open communication about the sensitivity of various assets and the associated risks. Training sessions that highlight the importance of protecting specific types of data can foster an informed workforce ready to respond to potential threats.

By diligently identifying valuable assets within your business —and understanding their significance—you lay a solid foundation for effective cybersecurity measures tailored to those critical elements. This proactive approach not only enhances protection but also cultivates a culture where every team member recognizes their role in safeguarding essential organizational resources against ever-evolving cyber threats.

Threat Identification and Analysis

Understanding the types of threats your business faces is not merely a precaution; it is a vital step toward establishing effective cybersecurity. Every small business, regardless of its industry, is vulnerable to a variety of cyber threats that can compromise sensitive data, disrupt operations, and tarnish its reputation. As the landscape of these threats continues to evolve, staying informed and prepared becomes increasingly essential.

To begin, it's helpful to categorize threats into three primary types: malware, social engineering, and insider threats. Each type presents unique challenges and requires tailored strategies for mitigation.

Malware** encompasses various forms of malicious software, including viruses, worms, trojans, ransomware, and spyware. Ransomware, for instance, encrypts files and demands payment for their release. A notable example is the WannaCry ransomware attack in 2017, which affected organizations worldwide, including the UK's National Health Service. To effectively combat malware threats, it's crucial to implement robust antivirus solutions and keep them updated regularly. Additionally, educating employees about the dangers of downloading suspicious attachments or clicking on dubious links is essential.

Social engineering**, on the other hand, exploits human psychology rather than software vulnerabilities. Phishing emails are a common tactic in this category; attackers impersonate trusted sources to steal credentials or financial information. Consider a small accounting firm that fell victim to such a scheme when an employee clicked on a link disguised as an invoice—this led to unauthorized access to sensitive financial records. Training your team to recognize phishing tactics can be effective; encourage them to verify communications through secondary channels before acting on requests for sensitive information.

Insider threats** arise from current or former employees who misuse their access privileges either maliciously or negligently. For example, a disgruntled employee might leak sensitive data out of spite, while another may inadvertently expose it through careless actions. To mitigate this risk, implementing strict access controls is key—granting permissions based solely on job responsibilities. Regular audits of user access can help identify potential insider threats early on.

Beyond categorizing these threats, it's important to conduct a thorough threat analysis tailored to your specific business operations. Engage in threat modeling exercises that simulate various attack scenarios relevant to your organization's structure and data assets. Take this example, consider the consequences if your customer database were compromised: what financial losses or regulatory penalties might you face? Assessing potential fallout allows you to prioritize defenses accordingly.

Utilizing tools like the MITRE ATT&CK framework can further enhance your threat identification efforts. This framework offers a comprehensive matrix of known adversarial tactics and techniques that you can use to map out potential attack vectors against your systems and identify security gaps.

To apply these concepts practically, consider developing an incident response playbook tailored specifically to the identified threats relevant to your business context. This playbook should outline procedures for quickly detecting incidents and responding effectively. For example, if an employee inadvertently exposes credentials due to phishing, include steps like immediate credential revocation and thorough investigation processes.

Regular engagement with cybersecurity resources—such as industry reports and threat intelligence feeds—is also vital for refining your threat analysis process. Subscribing to sources like the Verizon Data Breach Investigations Report (DBIR) will help you stay informed about current trends in cyberattacks that are particularly relevant to businesses like yours.

Fostering a culture of vigilance within your organization is crucial for successfully navigating this complex threat landscape. Encourage employees at all levels to report suspicious activities or security incidents without fear of reprisal; promoting transparency fosters proactive defense mechanisms.

By diligently identifying and analyzing threats specific to your operations, you empower yourself and your entire team to act decisively against emerging risks. Each step taken builds resilience into the very fabric of your organization's security strategy—so when threats do arise (and they inevitably will), you're not just prepared to respond but also positioned to rebound even stronger than before.

Vulnerability Assessment

Vulnerability assessment is a fundamental component of any small business's cybersecurity strategy. While identifying threats lays the groundwork for understanding potential risks, a vulnerability assessment goes further by examining your systems, processes, and policies to uncover weaknesses that cybercriminals could exploit. This proactive approach not only safeguards sensitive data but also strengthens the entire organization against possible breaches.

The first step in conducting a vulnerability assessment is to create an inventory of your assets. This includes everything from hardware and software to data and user access points. Knowing what you have is essential, as each asset can serve as an entry point for cybercriminals. For example, consider a local retail store using outdated point-of-sale (POS) systems. If these systems aren't regularly updated with security patches, they become prime targets for attackers aiming to steal credit card information. Regular network scans to compile a comprehensive asset list can reveal overlooked vulnerabilities.

With an inventory in hand, the next step is to conduct vulnerability scans using automated tools designed for this purpose. Solutions like Nessus or Qualys can provide valuable insights by scanning for known weaknesses, outdated software versions, and misconfigurations. Take this example, running a Nessus scan might uncover that one of your web servers is still running an outdated version of Apache, leaving it vulnerable to known exploits. The scanner will not only identify this vulnerability but also recommend corrective actions, such as updating the software or adjusting specific security configurations.

Alongside these technical assessments, it's crucial to review internal policies and procedures to uncover non-technical vulnerabilities. Take this example, if employees are allowed to use personal devices without sufficient security protocols, this creates potential entry points for malware. Establishing clear policies around Bring Your Own Device (BYOD) practices can significantly mitigate these risks. Consider developing a BYOD policy that requires the use of mobile device management (MDM) software to secure personal devices used for work.

Once vulnerabilities are identified through scans and policy reviews, prioritize them based on their risk severity and potential impact on the organization. The Common Vulnerability Scoring System (CVSS) can assist in this process by providing a standardized method for rating vulnerabilities according to their exploitability and effect on business operations. For example, if you find a high-risk vulnerability that exposes customer data on your website, addressing it should take precedence over lower-risk issues, such as minor design flaws.

The next critical step is remediation, which involves systematically addressing the identified vulnerabilities. This may include applying patches, altering configurations, or enhancing security protocols across systems. Creating a vulnerability management plan can streamline this process by establishing timelines and responsibilities for remediation efforts. Take this example, if several critical patches are needed across multiple systems during an assessment, assigning specific team members to address each issue with clear deadlines ensures accountability.

To maintain resilience against future vulnerabilities, it's essential to integrate continuous monitoring into your cybersecurity strategy. This means conducting regular vulnerability assessments rather than treating them as one-time tasks. Automated tools can schedule scans and alert you to new vulnerabilities as they arise, keeping you one step ahead of potential attackers.

Incorporating feedback from remediation efforts can also refine future assessments. After fixing vulnerabilities, it's important to revisit those areas periodically to confirm that the fixes are effective and that no new issues have emerged as a result of the changes made during the remediation process.

Lastly, fostering a culture of security awareness throughout the organization complements technical measures in vulnerability management. Engaging employees in training sessions on recognizing phishing attempts or understanding basic cybersecurity hygiene can significantly reduce human-related vulnerabilities. An illustrative example comes from a small law firm that implemented monthly security workshops; this initiative not only reduced incidents of phishing attacks but also nurtured a security-first mindset among staff members.

By systematically assessing vulnerabilities within your organization's infrastructure and culture, you enhance your defenses against ever-evolving cyber threats. Each identified and addressed vulnerability brings you closer to securing not just your business but also the trust of your customers—an invaluable asset in today's digital landscape where confidence can be as critical as technology itself.

The Role of Risk Tolerance in Security Strategy

Understanding risk tolerance is crucial for shaping a small

business's cybersecurity strategy. At its essence, risk tolerance indicates the level of uncertainty a business is willing to accept regarding potential security threats. This concept is not merely theoretical; it has tangible implications that affect everything from resource allocation to incident response planning.

Several factors influence a small business's risk tolerance, including its industry, size, and the specific data it handles. Take this example, a healthcare provider dealing with sensitive patient information may adopt a very low risk tolerance due to stringent regulatory requirements and the severe consequences of data breaches. In contrast, a small tech startup might exhibit a higher risk tolerance, motivated by the need for rapid innovation and competitiveness in a fast-paced market.

To assess your organization's risk tolerance, begin by identifying your assets and the types of data you collect. This encompasses everything from customer information and intellectual property to proprietary software systems. By understanding what is at stake, you can better evaluate how much risk your organization is prepared to assume. A company that manages highly sensitive data must prioritize its security measures significantly more than one handling less critical information.

After defining your assets, consider the potential impact of various threats. What would happen if customer data were compromised? What if your website experienced downtime due to a cyberattack? Engaging stakeholders in discussions about these scenarios helps clarify acceptable levels of risk. For example, a small retail business might conclude that while it cannot afford to invest heavily in every conceivable security measure, it should prioritize protecting payment information to avoid financial loss and reputational damage.

A clear understanding of acceptable risks enables businesses to implement tailored cybersecurity strategies without overextending their resources. Take, for instance, an e-commerce business that decided to focus on securing its payment processing systems rather than distributing its investments evenly across all areas of IT infrastructure. This strategic choice allowed them to maintain essential operations while minimizing costs associated with more comprehensive security solutions.

Once you establish your risk tolerance framework, it's vital to align it with your overall cybersecurity strategy. This involves determining which vulnerabilities require immediate attention and which can be monitored over time. A robust risk assessment process is invaluable in this context; for instance, you might discover that certain legacy systems are vulnerable but pose little immediate threat due to low usage rates. In such cases, monitoring these systems while directing resources toward more pressing vulnerabilities can be an effective approach.

Keep in mind that risk tolerance is not static; it can evolve based on changing business conditions or emerging threats. Regular reviews of your cybersecurity strategy are essential for adapting to these shifts. Creating a feedback loop where past incidents inform future decisions enhances resilience over time. For example, a local marketing firm reassessed its approach and updated its risk tolerance levels after experiencing a phishing attack, applying lessons learned from that incident.

Integrating training and awareness programs is also critical for aligning employee behavior with organizational risk tolerance. When employees grasp the rationale behind specific security measures—such as the importance of reporting suspicious emails or adhering strictly to password policies—they are more likely to comply with protocols designed around accepted risks. An accounting firm that implemented regular training sessions observed a significant decrease in security incidents following the introduction of targeted awareness programs tailored to their specific risks.

To wrap things up, clearly defining and understanding your business's risk tolerance is not just an academic exercise; it is a vital component of building a robust cybersecurity posture. By evaluating what risks are acceptable within the context of your operational environment and aligning your strategies accordingly, you empower your organization to manage threats effectively while fostering a culture that prioritizes security at every level. This proactive approach transforms how your organization navigates the complexities of today's digital landscape—making it not only reactive but strategically resilient against future challenges.

Prioritizing Risks

To enhance your cybersecurity framework, the next crucial step is to prioritize the risks identified during your assessments. While understanding risk tolerance lays a solid foundation, prioritization ensures that your limited resources are directed toward areas where they can make the most significant impact. This involves evaluating each risk based on its potential impact and likelihood of occurrence, allowing for informed decisions about which vulnerabilities require immediate attention.

Start by creating a risk matrix that categorizes threats along two key dimensions: the severity of their potential impact and their probability of occurrence. For example, a data breach that could compromise sensitive customer information may be classified as high impact and high probability, while a rare natural disaster affecting your data center might be categorized as low probability but high impact. This visual mapping helps you quickly identify which risks should take precedence.

Consider the case of a small online retailer that uncovers vulnerabilities in its payment processing system. Given the potential for significant financial loss and reputational damage from a breach in this area, it becomes a top priority for immediate remediation. In contrast, an outdated software version used internally may pose a lower risk since it doesn't directly handle customer transactions. Although it still requires attention, it does not demand the same urgent response as the vulnerabilities in the payment system.

Next, engage stakeholders across your organization to gather insights on how various risks might affect different business areas. This cross-functional dialogue encourages collaboration and reveals perspectives that may not surface in isolated discussions. Take this example, a marketing team might highlight risks related to client data exposure due to lax access controls, prompting a reassessment of access policies alongside technical security measures.

As you prioritize risks, it's essential to consider context. Cyber threats evolve rapidly; what was once deemed low priority can shift in importance as new threats emerge or as your business grows. Regularly revisiting your risk assessment helps maintain an up-to-date understanding of which areas require focus. For example, a small healthcare provider might initially prioritize patient record security but later find that enhancing cybersecurity for telehealth services becomes necessary following increased usage during public health emergencies.

Once you've identified and prioritized risks, allocate resources strategically. Develop plans that encompass both preventative measures and responsive actions. A comprehensive strategy should include implementing security controls to mitigate high-priority risks while establishing protocols for monitoring and responding to incidents related to lower-priority risks.

A notable illustration of this approach can be found in a financial advisory firm that invested heavily in intrusion detection systems (IDS) after identifying vulnerabilities in their network infrastructure. They prioritized this investment because they recognized that any breach could lead to severe financial consequences and loss of client trust. Concurrently, they implemented routine security audits for less critical systems to ensure ongoing monitoring without detracting from addressing more pressing issues.

Documentation plays a pivotal role in prioritizing cybersecurity efforts. Establish clear policies outlining how you assess and respond to various risks over time. This transparency fosters accountability across teams and allows new employees to quickly grasp existing protocols. Additionally, maintaining comprehensive records of past incidents and responses can reveal patterns that inform future prioritization efforts.

Incorporating lessons learned from previous incidents further refines your prioritization strategies. If an attack on an employee's personal device led to unauthorized access within your organization, recognize this as a risk factor needing attention—perhaps by shifting focus toward strengthening endpoint security or enhancing awareness training around BYOD policies.

 prioritizing cybersecurity risks is an ongoing process rather than a one-time task. As your business evolves, so too should your strategies for effectively managing threats. Regular reviews ensure continuous alignment between business goals and security needs while fostering an organizational culture where security remains a top priority at every level—leading to more resilient practices against emerging threats.

This proactive approach lays the groundwork for establishing robust incident response protocols aligned with prioritized risks, ensuring preparedness not only for potential breaches but also for navigating the complexities of managing them effectively when they arise. Each step taken today not only addresses immediate concerns but also strengthens your organization's long-term resilience against future cyber threats.

Developing a Risk Management Plan

Creating a risk management plan is a crucial step that turns theoretical assessments into practical strategies. Once you've prioritized the risks identified in your assessments, the next phase involves developing a structured approach that details how your organization will tackle these vulnerabilities. This plan not only protects your assets but also aligns with your business objectives, ensuring that security measures support rather than hinder operations.

Start by outlining the key components of your risk management plan. Essential elements should include risk identification, assessment methodologies, response strategies, and communication protocols. A well-organized structure streamlines the process and makes it easier to update as your business environment changes. For example, if phishing attacks have been prioritized as a significant risk, specify how you will educate employees about these threats and implement technical controls like email filtering.

Next, link specific actions to each identified risk. Take this example, if outdated software poses a significant threat due to its potential for exploitation, your plan could outline regular update schedules and automated patch management solutions. This direct connection between risk identification and actionable steps ensures you stay focused on what matters most.

Consider the example of a small manufacturing company that faced escalating cybersecurity threats from remote access vulnerabilities. In response, they developed a risk management plan that included immediate employee training on secure remote access practices and investment in VPN technology. By detailing these actions within their plan, they set clear expectations for both employees and IT staff.

Involving various stakeholders during the development phase can strengthen your risk management plan. Collaboration fosters a more comprehensive understanding of how different risks affect various departments and promotes shared ownership of security initiatives. Consider organizing workshops or meetings where teams can voice concerns or share insights related to risks specific to their functions. Take this example, finance teams might raise issues regarding unauthorized access to sensitive data, leading to additional security measures designed to protect financial information.

As you refine your risk management plan, it's vital to integrate metrics for success. Establish key performance indicators (KPIs) that enable you to assess the effectiveness of your implemented strategies over time. Metrics such as reductions in phishing click rates or improvements in incident response times can provide valuable insights. Regularly reviewing these metrics not only reveals how effective your strategies are but also helps maintain organizational momentum toward achieving cybersecurity goals.

Documentation plays a critical role during this phase. Create a centralized repository where all aspects of the risk management plan are stored and easily accessible to relevant team members. Ensure this repository is regularly updated to reflect changes made in response to evolving threats or shifts in business strategy, such as incorporating new technologies or compliance regulations.

Another vital aspect is establishing clear communication protocols regarding cybersecurity risks and responses throughout your organization. It's essential that everyone understands their role in executing the risk management plan —from executive leadership to entry-level employees who may encounter phishing emails. Regular communication fosters an environment where security remains a priority for all team members.

Incorporating feedback loops into your risk management process is essential for ongoing improvement. After any incident or near-miss event, conduct post-incident reviews to analyze what worked well and what didn't within your response framework. This reflective practice allows you to refine future strategies based on real-world experiences rather than relying solely on theoretical models.

Lastly, remember that developing a risk management plan isn't just about addressing current vulnerabilities; it's also about preparing for future uncertainties. As cyber threats continually evolve, maintaining an adaptive culture within your organization is crucial. Encourage employees to view security as an integral part of their daily responsibilities, fostering resilience against future challenges.

In summary, crafting a comprehensive risk management plan is a pivotal step toward enhancing your organization's cybersecurity posture. By linking clear actions to prioritized risks, engaging stakeholders, implementing effective documentation practices, and embracing continuous improvement measures, you're laying the groundwork for sustained security success amidst ever-changing digital landscapes. Each element you implement today not only addresses current challenges but also strengthens your organization against future adversities—transforming cybersecurity from a reactive necessity into a proactive advantage for growth and innovation.

Tools for Risk Assessment

Identifying the right tools for risk assessment is crucial for strengthening your cybersecurity strategy. Once you've established a risk management plan, selecting and implementing tools that effectively evaluate and mitigate potential vulnerabilities is essential. These tools streamline your efforts, enabling you to prioritize and respond to risks while enhancing your overall security posture.

Begin with automated risk assessment tools that provide a comprehensive overview of your organization's vulnerabilities. Platforms like Nessus and Qualys can scan your network for weaknesses, such as outdated software or misconfigured devices. Not only do these tools identify risks, but they also offer insights into effective remediation strategies. By automating the scanning process, you save time and resources while ensuring regular assessments that keep pace with emerging threats.

In addition to automated tools, consider threat intelligence platforms. These systems collect and analyze data on potential threats from various sources, offering contextual information that supports informed decision-making. Services like Recorded Future and ThreatConnect aggregate data on malware signatures and attack patterns, enabling you to proactively adjust your defenses in response to current cyberattack trends. This intelligence empowers you to stay ahead of potential threats rather than merely reacting after an incident occurs.

Vulnerability management solutions are also vital components of your toolkit. Tools such as Rapid7 or Kenna Security prioritize vulnerabilities based on risk exposure instead of simply categorizing them by severity. They assess the likelihood of exploitation within the context of your specific environment and business operations, allowing you to focus on remediating those vulnerabilities most likely to impact your organization significantly.

Regular security audits play an equally important role in this process. Engaging third-party auditors provides an objective perspective on your security posture and risk assessment practices. These professionals can conduct penetration testing simulations that mimic real-world attacks, helping you understand how well your defenses stand against sophisticated threats. This external viewpoint not only identifies blind spots but also validates the effectiveness of your existing security measures.

Team collaboration is another key aspect of effective risk assessment. Utilize collaborative platforms like Jira or Trello to track vulnerabilities identified across departments. By maintaining a shared space where team members can log findings and updates, you promote transparency and foster a culture of collective responsibility toward cybersecurity. This approach encourages active participation from everyone in the organization in identifying potential risks.

Don't overlook the importance of employee input in this process; they often have insights into operational challenges that may not be apparent from a purely technical perspective. Conducting regular surveys or feedback sessions can reveal perceptions of risk that guide adjustments in tool selection and risk management strategies.

Once these tools are in place, it's vital to establish a continuous improvement cycle for assessing their effectiveness. Regularly reviewing metrics from automated scans or vulnerability assessments will help determine whether you're closing security gaps over time. Tracking key performance indicators (KPIs), such as the average time taken to remediate identified vulnerabilities, provides clarity on progress and highlights areas needing attention.

Documentation should be an ongoing part of this process as well; ensure that results from every assessment tool are recorded alongside remediation actions taken. This creates a historical reference that informs future assessments and aids in trend analysis over time—an invaluable resource when adapting strategies to counter evolving threats.

Finally, clear communication regarding the usage of these tools throughout your organization is essential. Regular training sessions should be held so that all relevant personnel understand how these tools function and their roles in the risk assessment process. When employees grasp the significance of these tools in safeguarding their work environment, they become more engaged participants in maintaining cybersecurity practices.

Integrating robust risk assessment tools into your cybersecurity framework transcends mere technology; it fosters a proactive mindset throughout your organization where security becomes everyone's responsibility. By leveraging automated assessments, utilizing threat intelligence platforms, engaging third-party audits, encouraging team collaboration, and continuously improving processes based on documented results, you're not just managing risks—you're cultivating an organizational culture poised to face whatever challenges arise in the digital landscape ahead.

Regular Risk Reviews

Establishing a routine for regular risk reviews is essential for maintaining an effective cybersecurity posture. Cyber threats are constantly evolving, often at a pace that can catch even the most prepared organizations off guard. By conducting periodic assessments, you can ensure that your defenses keep pace with these changes, allowing you to identify new vulnerabilities and adjust your strategies accordingly.

Begin by setting a clear schedule for your risk reviews. Conduct these assessments at least quarterly, though in rapidly changing environments, monthly reviews may be more appropriate. This frequency helps your team stay ahead of potential threats while also integrating lessons learned from recent incidents or industry developments. Regularly scheduled reviews create an environment of vigilance, making security a priority rather than an afterthought.

During these reviews, gather and analyze data from the tools you've implemented in your risk assessment strategy. For example, if you're using automated scanning tools like Nessus or Qualys, take a close look at their findings. Look for patterns in vulnerabilities: Are certain types recurring? Understanding these trends can reveal systemic issues in your security practices or highlight areas that require additional focus.

Incorporating feedback from employees is equally important in this process. As the first line of defense, employees can provide valuable insights into how well security measures are functioning in practice. Consider conducting brief surveys or focus groups to gather their perspectives on existing policies and any challenges they encounter. Take this example, if multiple staff members report difficulties with multi-factor authentication processes, this could indicate a need for further training or adjustments to the system.

During each review session, engage your cybersecurity team in brainstorming discussions aimed at identifying potential future risks. Encourage them to think beyond current vulnerabilities and assess the broader threat landscape. Are there emerging technologies being adopted by competitors that could pose risks? This proactive approach ensures that you're not just reacting to today's threats but also preparing for tomorrow's challenges.

Documentation plays a crucial role throughout this process; maintain detailed records of each risk review's findings and subsequent decisions. This historical data becomes invaluable for future reference, enabling you to track progress over time and demonstrate compliance with regulatory requirements as needed. Take this example, if an external auditor requests evidence of your ongoing risk management efforts, this documentation will provide tangible proof of your diligence.

Involving upper management in these reviews is another effective strategy. Their participation not only emphasizes the importance of cybersecurity at all levels but also fosters accountability across departments. Present clear metrics derived from your risk assessments—show how identified vulnerabilities have been mitigated over time or highlight instances where timely action has prevented potential breaches.

After each review cycle concludes, it's crucial to communicate findings transparently throughout the organization. Share both success stories and areas needing improvement with all employees; this cultivates a culture of collective responsibility toward security practices. When everyone understands the current threat landscape and the organization's response strategies, engagement levels typically rise.

Finally, foster an agile mindset within your cybersecurity framework that allows for adaptation based on insights gained during regular reviews. If a particular control proves ineffective over several assessment cycles, consider whether it's time to replace it with a more robust solution better suited to counter identified risks.

Regular risk reviews are not merely checkpoints; they are integral components of an adaptive security culture that values continuous improvement and collective vigilance against threats. By systematically assessing vulnerabilities, involving employees meaningfully, documenting actions taken, and ensuring transparent communication across the organization, you empower every team member to contribute proactively toward safeguarding your business against evolving cyber risks.

Case Studies of Small Business Risks

Understanding the landscape of small business cybersecurity often becomes clearer through real-world experiences. Each case study presents a unique narrative that sheds light on the challenges small businesses face and the effective risk management strategies they can adopt. Let's explore several notable examples that illustrate both the vulnerabilities these businesses encounter and the valuable lessons learned from their experiences with cyber threats.

Take, for instance, a small marketing agency that fell victim to a phishing attack. Employees received emails that appeared to come from a trusted client, containing a link to a document for review. The email was so convincing that one staff member clicked the link, unwittingly downloading malware onto the network. This incident escalated into a significant data breach, exposing sensitive client information and costing the agency not only financially but also in terms of trust and reputation.

This example underscores the critical need for robust employee training programs focused on recognizing phishing attempts and verifying communications before taking action. In response to the incident, the agency implemented regular security awareness workshops and simulated phishing tests to reinforce their training. This investment in ongoing education paid off; subsequent phishing attempts were quickly identified by vigilant employees who had learned from their earlier mistakes.

Next, let's consider an online retail business that faced a distributed denial-of-service (DDoS) attack during peak shopping season. The attack rendered their website inaccessible for several hours, leading to lost sales and frustrated customers. In light of this crisis, the company made strategic changes: they invested in DDoS protection services and collaborated with their hosting provider to enhance server resilience against future attacks.

Additionally, they established a contingency plan that included clear communication strategies for customers during downtime. This proactive approach not only mitigated backlash but also reassured clients of their commitment to service continuity. The experience taught them the importance of preparedness and responsiveness in managing customer relationships during crises.

Another compelling case involves a small law firm that

neglected proper data backup procedures. After falling victim to ransomware, they found themselves unable to access critical case files without paying a hefty ransom. Fortunately, they had some data backed up, but it was outdated and incomplete. This costly oversight prompted them to completely revise their data protection protocols.

In response, they implemented automated backups with cloud solutions that offered versioning capabilities—ensuring recent copies of files were always accessible. They also established an incident response plan detailing steps to take in the event of another ransomware attack, including effective communication with clients whose data might be affected.

A particularly illustrative example comes from a family-owned restaurant that sought to modernize its payment systems by adopting digital point-of-sale (POS) technology. Unfortunately, they overlooked basic security measures during implementation, leading to cardholder data being compromised over several months before detection. The aftermath was devastating; not only did they face fines from regulatory bodies for non-compliance with PCI DSS standards, but they also suffered significant reputational damage within their community.

Learning from this experience, the restaurant revamped its cybersecurity policies by implementing end-to-end encryption for transactions and conducting regular vulnerability assessments of their payment systems. They enlisted third-party cybersecurity firms to help fortify defenses against future breaches—a necessary expense that ultimately safeguarded customer trust and ensured business continuity.

These narratives highlight fundamental principles applicable across various sectors: employee training is paramount, robust incident response plans are essential, and proactive measures can make all the difference when confronting cyber threats. Small business owners must internalize these lessons: fostering a culture where cybersecurity is prioritized at all levels can significantly enhance overall resilience against evolving threats.

Each incident not only reveals vulnerabilities but also illuminates pathways for improvement—creating frameworks for stronger security practices through actionable insights gleaned from past experiences is invaluable. As you reflect on these stories, consider how your organization can implement similar strategies tailored specifically to your unique operational context. Resilience isn't built overnight; it is crafted through continuous learning and adaptation in an ever-changing digital landscape.

Building a Security Culture

Building a culture of security within your organization is not just an operational necessity; it's a vital aspect of your business's core values. This security culture permeates every level of the organization—from the executive suite to entry-level employees—shaping interactions with technology and sensitive information. By fostering this cultural shift, you create a robust defense against cyber threats.

The journey towards a security-first mindset begins with leadership. When executives prioritize cybersecurity, they establish a standard for the entire organization. Take, for example, a small accounting firm that embedded cybersecurity into its mission statement. The leaders consistently communicated their commitment to protecting client data, weaving discussions about cybersecurity into team meetings and strategic sessions. This proactive approach not only demonstrated leadership buy-in but also instilled a sense of ownership among employees, encouraging them to be vigilant.

Equally important is employee engagement in nurturing this security-conscious environment. Implementing regular training programs that extend beyond mere compliance is a crucial strategy. Engaging sessions can incorporate gamification elements—like quizzes or interactive scenarios —to make learning about security practices enjoyable and memorable. Take this example, a small tech startup initiated monthly "cyber hygiene" workshops featuring real-life scenarios relevant to their work. Employees participated in role-playing exercises where they identified phishing attempts and discussed data protection strategies for the project management tools they used daily.

Fostering open lines of communication further enhances this culture. Employees should feel safe reporting suspicious activities or potential breaches without fear of repercussions. One retail business, for example, created an anonymous reporting system that allowed staff to voice concerns about security practices or incidents without risking their positions. This transparency promoted proactive behavior and cultivated an environment where everyone took responsibility for security.

Recognition is also key in reinforcing positive cybersecurity behaviors. Small businesses can implement incentive programs to reward employees who identify vulnerabilities or successfully thwart phishing attempts. A recent initiative by a nonprofit organization illustrates this well; they introduced "Security Champion" awards to honor employees who excelled in protecting sensitive information or educating their peers on best practices.

Integrating cybersecurity into everyday business processes is crucial as well. Take this example, teams should conduct risk assessments as standard practice when launching new projects or implementing new technologies, rather than treating them as an afterthought. This proactive approach highlights the importance of cybersecurity and ensures that potential vulnerabilities are addressed before they escalate into issues.

Providing resources and tools empowers employees to adopt good cybersecurity habits independently. Implementing password managers enables staff to create complex passwords without the hassle of memorizing them all, while regular reminders about software updates help maintain system security. A small law firm adopted these measures after experiencing a breach due to outdated software—by equipping employees with practical tools, they significantly reduced future risks.

Ongoing engagement is equally important; initial training must be reinforced with refreshers and updates on emerging threats. Regular briefings on new types of cyber threats keep security top-of-mind for everyone. For example, a manufacturing company began hosting quarterly "threat intelligence" briefings where IT staff shared insights on recent attacks affecting similar industries and discussed preventive measures being implemented within their organization.

Transitioning towards a robust security culture takes time and requires concerted effort across multiple fronts—leadership commitment, employee engagement strategies, integrated processes, and ongoing education—but the investment pays off. As organizations increasingly confront sophisticated cyber threats daily, those with strong security cultures will find themselves better equipped to withstand attacks and recover swiftly when incidents occur.

 fostering a sense of collective responsibility regarding cybersecurity changes how employees perceive their roles within the organization. They become not just individuals performing tasks but integral parts of a cohesive defense system working together to safeguard business interests and client trust alike. As you consider these strategies for cultivating your organization's security culture, remember: resilience springs from continuous learning, open dialogue, and committed action at all levels of your enterprise.

CHAPTER 3:
BUILDING A CYBERSECURITY STRATEGY

Setting Cybersecurity Goals

Establishing clear cybersecurity goals is crucial for any small business striving to build a strong security framework. These goals provide a roadmap for navigating the complexities of cybersecurity and help ensure your organization remains vigilant against ever-evolving threats. It all begins with a clear understanding of what you want to achieve—whether that involves protecting sensitive customer data, ensuring compliance with regulations, or minimizing downtime during incidents.

The first step in setting effective cybersecurity goals is to assess your current security landscape. This assessment involves taking inventory of your existing systems, processes, and policies. Conducting a comprehensive audit of your IT infrastructure is essential. Identify the assets most critical to your operations and evaluate their vulnerabilities. Take this example, a local retail company discovered during an internal audit that its point-of-sale systems were outdated and vulnerable to breaches. This insight prompted them to prioritize technology upgrades as part of their cybersecurity objectives.

After assessing your current state, it's important to align your cybersecurity goals with your broader business objectives. Consider how effective cybersecurity can support growth initiatives or enhance customer trust. For example, if you plan to expand your online presence, implementing strong security measures will not only safeguard your data but also reassure customers about the safety of their information. A web development firm that recently expanded its e-commerce services set a goal of achieving PCI DSS compliance within six months to build trust among potential clients.

When formulating these goals, specificity is key. Instead of making vague statements like "improve security," define measurable targets such as "reduce the number of phishing attempts that reach employees by 75% within one year." This allows you to track progress through regular assessments and adjust strategies as needed. The aforementioned web development firm utilized metrics from simulated phishing tests to monitor employee awareness over time, providing concrete evidence of improvements and highlighting areas still needing attention.

Engaging team members in the goal-setting process fosters buy-in and accountability across the organization. Consider hosting workshops where employees can share ideas based on their experiences or concerns regarding cybersecurity challenges they encounter daily. This collaborative approach not only enhances commitment but also uncovers valuable insights that might otherwise go unnoticed.

Next, ensure that each goal is realistic and achievable given your available resources—both financial and human capital.

While it may be tempting to pursue rapid transformation, incremental changes often lead to better long-term results. Take this example, rather than implementing comprehensive security software organization-wide all at once, consider rolling it out in phases based on priority needs identified during your initial audit.

Another important aspect is integrating cybersecurity training into your goal-setting framework. Establish benchmarks for training, such as achieving 100% employee participation in annual security awareness programs or conducting quarterly simulations of potential cyber incidents. These benchmarks keep everyone engaged while fostering a proactive mindset toward security.

Once you've defined these goals, develop action plans detailing how you intend to achieve them. Assign specific responsibilities within your team; designating individuals or departments accountable for various aspects of your cybersecurity strategy ensures clarity and promotes ownership over progress.

Regularly monitoring progress is equally vital. Schedule periodic reviews to assess whether you're on track toward meeting these goals or if adjustments are necessary due to emerging threats or changing business dynamics. Utilizing tools like dashboards that provide real-time analytics on relevant metrics enables agile decision-making when new risks arise.

setting clear cybersecurity goals transforms abstract concepts into actionable steps that resonate throughout your organization. Each milestone achieved not only strengthens defenses against cyber threats but also reinforces a culture where security becomes everyone's responsibility—a collective effort aligned with the overarching mission of safeguarding both business interests and customer trust in an increasingly digital world.

As you embark on this journey toward enhanced cybersecurity maturity, remember that clarity in your objectives lays the foundation for resilience amid uncertainty—an essential element for thriving in today's rapidly evolving landscape.

Creating a Security Policy

Creating a security policy is a foundational step that builds on the cybersecurity goals your organization has already established. This policy acts as a guiding document, outlining your commitment to safeguarding assets and managing risks effectively. A well-crafted security policy translates strategic objectives into practical, actionable measures tailored to your specific operational environment.

Begin by clearly defining the purpose of your security policy. Outline its scope—what it covers and whom it affects. Take this example, does the policy apply solely to IT staff, or does it extend to all employees? A small accounting firm, for example, decided early on that their policy would encompass everyone, including part-time workers and interns, thereby fostering a comprehensive security culture throughout the organization.

Next, identify and categorize the sensitive data your business handles. Consider customer information, financial records, and proprietary company data. Each category may require different protection measures based on its sensitivity level. An educational institution, for example, categorized student records as highly sensitive, which necessitated stringent access controls and encryption protocols for both storage and transmission.

With a clear understanding of your data landscape established, outline specific security practices within the policy. Address key areas such as password management, data encryption standards, acceptable use of company resources, and guidelines for remote work scenarios. To ensure these practices resonate with your staff, incorporate real-world examples; for instance, share case studies of organizations similar to yours that experienced breaches due to inadequate password practices.

Defining roles and responsibilities related to cybersecurity is another critical element of your security policy. Establishing accountability clarifies who is responsible for implementing various aspects of the policy across the organization. For example, you might assign specific roles such as a Chief Information Security Officer (CISO) to oversee overall strategy or designate team leads in each department responsible for compliance with security measures.

Including incident response procedures within your policy is also essential. Clearly describe the steps employees should take if they suspect a breach or encounter suspicious activity—this might include reporting incidents to IT personnel or isolating affected systems. A restaurant chain, for instance, developed an easy-to-follow flowchart detailing these procedures, empowering staff at all levels to respond quickly in crisis situations.

To bolster engagement with your policy, regular training is paramount. Make participation in training sessions a requirement for all employees to reinforce the principles outlined in the document. Consider incorporating interactive elements like quizzes or role-playing scenarios that allow employees to practice their responses in simulated situations; this not only strengthens knowledge retention but also builds confidence in addressing potential threats.

It's important that your security policy remains dynamic rather than static. As technology evolves and new threats emerge, so too should your approach. Establish a timeline for reviewing and updating the policy—consider quarterly assessments as well as updates prompted by significant changes within your organization or industry regulations.

Regularly collect feedback from employees about the effectiveness of the policy and any challenges they encounter while adhering to it. Create an open channel for dialogue where staff can suggest improvements based on their firsthand experiences with cybersecurity measures in daily operations; this promotes a sense of ownership among employees.

Finally, disseminate the finalized version of your security policy widely throughout your organization. Ensure it's easily accessible and prominently displayed on internal platforms like intranets or employee handbooks. Include periodic reminders about its importance during team meetings or through company newsletters.

In summary, crafting a robust security policy transforms abstract cybersecurity goals into concrete actions tailored specifically for your business environment. By engaging every level of staff—from executives to entry-level positions—you cultivate an organizational culture where cybersecurity is viewed not as an isolated function but as an integral part of everyday operations.

As you take this significant step toward fortifying your organization against cyber threats, remember that an effective security policy not only protects valuable assets but also empowers employees by providing clear guidance on maintaining vigilance within their roles—a crucial factor in today's ever-evolving threat landscape.

Defining Roles and Responsibilities

Defining roles and responsibilities is crucial for the effective implementation of your security policy. This clarity not only establishes accountability but also ensures that every member of the organization understands their specific contributions to maintaining cybersecurity. Without this understanding, even the most comprehensive security measures can fall short, leaving potential vulnerabilities exposed.

To begin, identify who will take on primary cybersecurity responsibilities within your organization. A common strategy is to appoint a Chief Information Security Officer (CISO), who serves as the backbone of your cybersecurity framework. The CISO is tasked with crafting and updating the security policy, overseeing training initiatives, and coordinating incident response efforts. Take this example, in a mid-sized financial services company, the CISO worked closely with departmental leaders to adapt security protocols to each team's unique processes while ensuring overall consistency.

In addition to appointing a CISO, it's essential to define specific roles for team members across different departments. Each department has unique functions and data types that require tailored cybersecurity approaches. For example, in a marketing department that manages sensitive customer information, designating a lead marketer as the Data Protection Officer helps ensure compliance with regulations like GDPR or CCPA. This role allows for guidance on securely utilizing customer data in marketing campaigns while promoting best practices for privacy maintenance.

To enhance engagement further, clarify day-to-day operational responsibilities related to cybersecurity for all employees. Everyone should understand their role in safeguarding organizational assets—what actions they must take or avoid to uphold security standards. In an e-commerce environment where employees regularly handle financial transactions, it may be necessary for all staff involved in payment processing to undergo specialized training focused on recognizing fraud schemes and adhering to secure payment protocols.

Incident response is another critical area where clearly defined roles are essential for minimizing damage during breaches. Establishing an incident response team comprised of individuals from various departments brings diverse expertise into play when an incident occurs. For example, combining IT staff with legal representatives creates a well-rounded approach to addressing regulatory implications after a breach.

Clearly mapping out specific responsibilities—such as who communicates with stakeholders or how technical teams isolate affected systems—helps eliminate confusion during crises.

Effective communication channels must support these defined roles. Employees should have immediate access to guidelines outlining whom to notify about various incidents or concerns they might encounter—be it suspicious emails or unauthorized system access attempts. Implementing tools like internal chat platforms can facilitate swift reporting mechanisms while fostering a culture of transparency regarding cybersecurity challenges.

Regular training sessions should reinforce these definitions of responsibility across the organization. Hosting quarterly workshops allows team members at different levels to review their obligations and address questions about emerging threats and evolving cybersecurity practices. These sessions not only refresh knowledge but also promote camaraderie among teams united in the goal of protecting shared interests.

Leadership plays a vital role in endorsing this structure by consistently discussing roles during meetings or company-wide announcements. This not only reinforces the importance of these roles but also promotes accountability at every level of the organization.

Establishing feedback loops is equally important in refining these definitions over time. As employees engage with their responsibilities in real-world scenarios, they can identify gaps in understanding or areas needing clarification. Encouraging open dialogue enhances overall effectiveness while reinforcing individual ownership of cybersecurity measures throughout the organization.

defining roles and responsibilities lays a strong foundation upon which your entire security framework operates efficiently. When everyone—from executives to entry-level employees—is aligned with clear expectations regarding their involvement in safeguarding organizational assets against cyber threats, you cultivate an environment where proactive behaviors flourish.

Every member becomes not just a participant but an integral part of your organization's cybersecurity strategy—prepared to respond decisively when risks arise and contribute positively to fostering a lasting culture centered around safety and vigilance in today's ever-changing landscape.

Aligning Strategy with Business Objectives

Integrating your cybersecurity strategy with your overarching business objectives is more than just a compliance requirement; it's a strategic necessity. When cybersecurity becomes an integral part of your organization's goals, it creates an environment where security and growth work hand in hand. This alignment ensures that protective measures support, rather than impede, business processes, allowing both security and innovation to flourish.

Begin by clearly identifying your core business objectives, which often focus on areas like growth, customer satisfaction, operational efficiency, and market expansion. For example, if your primary aim is to enhance customer trust through superior service delivery, your cybersecurity initiatives should reflect that ambition. Implementing robust data protection practices not only safeguards sensitive customer information but also strengthens your brand's credibility. Consider a small financial advisory firm aiming for growth: by introducing two-factor authentication for client accounts, the firm secures access while demonstrating its commitment to client safety.

Once you've clarified your business objectives, map out how each cybersecurity initiative aligns with them. A helpful approach is to create a matrix that outlines specific security projects alongside relevant business goals. Take this example, if your organization intends to expand into e-commerce, investing in secure payment processing systems should be a top priority. This investment serves a dual purpose: it mitigates the risk of data breaches while facilitating smooth customer transactions—an essential aspect of success in online retail.

Involving key stakeholders from various departments during the strategy alignment process is also crucial. Engaging team members from IT, marketing, sales, and finance fosters a comprehensive understanding of how cybersecurity impacts different functions within the organization. While the IT department focuses on technical safeguards, the marketing team can provide insights on maintaining customer engagement without compromising data privacy. A collaborative approach enriches the strategy and cultivates a sense of ownership across departments.

Regular check-ins are vital to ensure that your cybersecurity measures evolve alongside shifting business priorities. The dynamic nature of technology and market demands requires ongoing reassessment of strategies. Organizing quarterly review meetings with representatives from different departments facilitates discussions about emerging threats or new regulations affecting business objectives. This iterative process allows for timely adjustments that keep cybersecurity aligned with broader goals.

Consistent communication about the importance of this alignment is essential for all employees. Crafting internal messaging that highlights how security measures contribute to overall organizational success can motivate staff to actively engage in these initiatives. Take this example, sharing success stories about thwarted attacks or increased customer satisfaction due to robust security practices can reinforce positive behaviors throughout the organization.

Metrics are critical for assessing how effectively your cybersecurity strategy supports business objectives. Establish key performance indicators (KPIs) that relate to both security outcomes and organizational goals. If enhancing customer satisfaction is a priority, track metrics like incident response times or the frequency of successful fraud attempts against baseline data prior to implementing new security measures. By correlating these metrics with business performance indicators such as customer retention rates or sales figures, you create a compelling narrative that illustrates the value of investing in cybersecurity.

A mid-sized software company provides a clear example: after integrating comprehensive training programs on secure coding practices into their development workflow—directly linked to their goal of releasing high-quality products—they experienced a measurable decrease in vulnerabilities reported post-launch and higher user satisfaction ratings.

Additionally, it's important to consider budget constraints when aligning your strategies; allocate resources based on risk assessments that prioritize safeguarding high-value assets tied directly to business objectives. If an organization plans significant investments in technology upgrades or new product launches, ensuring adequate funding for corresponding cybersecurity measures is essential.

Fostering cross-department collaboration creates synergy that can enhance your organization's overall resilience against threats while advancing shared goals. In this way, cybersecurity shifts from being viewed as an obstacle to becoming a facilitator of innovative solutions—one that protects digital assets while enhancing competitive advantage in an increasingly challenging landscape.

intertwining cybersecurity with business objectives cultivates a culture where vigilance becomes second nature for employees at every level—from entry-level staff recognizing phishing attempts in emails to executives advocating comprehensive risk management strategies at board meetings.

By successfully aligning cybersecurity initiatives with broader business aspirations, you not only protect against threats but also empower your organization toward sustainable growth in today's digital age.

Flexibility and Scalability in Strategy

A successful cybersecurity strategy must be tailored to the unique needs of your business; one size does not fit all. Flexibility and scalability are crucial components that enable your security measures to evolve alongside your organization. Small businesses, in particular, often undergo rapid growth and experience changes in product offerings and target markets, making it essential for their cybersecurity approach to be equally adaptable.

Consider a small e-commerce company that starts with a limited selection of products but quickly expands to offer hundreds. Initially, the focus may have been on securing customer data during the checkout process. However, as the product range grows and new payment methods are introduced, the cybersecurity strategy must evolve. This could involve enhancing protection through more robust encryption protocols for transactions and integrating multi-factor authentication for both customers and employees accessing sensitive information.

To create a flexible cybersecurity framework, it is important to establish baseline protections while remaining open to enhancements in response to new risks and technological advancements. For many small businesses, this means investing in modular solutions—like cloud-based services— that can be easily scaled up or down without requiring significant infrastructure changes. Such solutions offer both cost-effectiveness and adaptability. For example, if you start with a basic firewall but later realize you need intrusion detection capabilities as your operations grow, selecting a provider that can seamlessly integrate these features is essential.

And, flexibility should extend beyond technology to include policies and procedures as well. Conducting regular reviews of your security policies allows you to adapt as needed— whether in response to new regulations or emerging threats like ransomware attacks, which have become increasingly prevalent in recent years. Involving your team in these reviews ensures that everyone understands their role in maintaining security standards and can contribute ideas for improvement.

Employee training is also critical for fostering flexibility within your cybersecurity strategy. By equipping your team with knowledge about current threats and best practices, you empower them to respond effectively to changing circumstances. Workshops and simulations can enhance readiness; for instance, phishing simulations can help employees recognize malicious attempts more effectively than traditional lectures.

Building a scalable security strategy requires careful planning. Conducting a comprehensive risk assessment is vital; identifying potential vulnerabilities early allows you to prioritize adjustments as you scale operations or technology resources. Utilizing tools like vulnerability scanners can help you proactively address gaps in your current setup rather than waiting until issues arise.

A compelling example comes from a small financial services firm that faced compliance challenges due to rapid growth after an acquisition. By adopting flexible solutions—such as cloud storage with built-in compliance measures—they managed to scale their operations efficiently while adhering to industry regulations. This adaptability not only protected them from legal penalties but also positioned them favorably against competitors who were slower to adjust.

In summary, integrating flexibility and scalability into your cybersecurity strategy goes beyond implementing the right technology; it involves cultivating a culture that embraces ongoing change and innovation within your organization. As threats evolve and business landscapes shift, your approach to safeguarding assets and data integrity must evolve as well. Encouraging a proactive mindset among all team members fosters an environment where security becomes a collective responsibility—not just that of the IT department. This collaborative approach enhances defenses and positions your organization for sustained growth in an unpredictable digital landscape.

Budgeting for Cybersecurity

Creating a robust budget for cybersecurity is a crucial yet often overlooked step for small business owners. This process is vital for safeguarding valuable assets and ensuring long-term operational stability. Understanding budgeting for cybersecurity as an investment rather than merely an expense can yield significant returns, such as risk mitigation and enhanced customer trust. A well-structured budget serves as the foundation for your security strategy, aligning with both your current needs and future growth.

To begin, conduct a thorough assessment of your business's existing cybersecurity posture. Identify your current tools and practices, and pinpoint any potential vulnerabilities that may have been overlooked. Take this example, if you have antivirus software but lack endpoint detection solutions or regular security audits, recognizing these gaps will inform your budget allocation. Engaging your IT team in this analysis is essential, as their firsthand experience can help clarify which resources are critical versus optional, highlighting specific areas that require immediate attention or enhancement.

Once you understand your security needs, prioritize your spending based on risk levels and potential impact. A tiered approach can be beneficial: categorize expenses into essential, important, and optional expenditures. Essential items may include advanced threat protection and employee training programs, while optional enhancements could feature advanced analytics tools that provide deeper insights into security events. This prioritization ensures that your most critical assets receive protection first and that funds are allocated effectively to address the highest risks.

For example, if your business handles sensitive customer information like payment details, investing in data encryption should be a top priority. Conversely, if funds are tight, you might consider postponing less critical purchases. Establishing this hierarchy allows you to manage costs while still addressing your organization's most pressing vulnerabilities.

Budgeting also requires a forward-looking perspective as your business grows. Consider the costs associated with scaling security measures from the outset. If you anticipate entering new markets or expanding your workforce, think about what additional investments will be necessary to maintain effective cybersecurity during these transitions. While a cloud-based solution may seem costly initially, its scalability can ultimately save money by reducing the need for extensive hardware upgrades.

And, ongoing employee education must be a key component of your budget. The cyber threat landscape evolves rapidly, making continuous training essential for maintaining a strong defense posture. Allocate funds for regular workshops focused on emerging threats—such as ransomware or social engineering tactics—to equip staff with current knowledge on best practices. Take this example, investing in simulated phishing attacks can reinforce employee vigilance while providing real-time feedback on areas needing improvement.

Collaboration with third-party vendors should also be integrated into your budgeting strategy. Managed Security

Service Providers (MSSPs) can offer robust security solutions at a fraction of the cost of building an internal team. When evaluating vendors, ensure their offerings align with your unique requirements and budget constraints while allowing for flexibility as conditions change.

Regular reviews of expenses against this budget are necessary to gauge effectiveness and return on investment (ROI). Monitoring key performance indicators (KPIs)—such as incident response times or the number of thwarted phishing attempts—can provide valuable insights into how well your spending translates into improved security outcomes.

To illustrate the impact of thoughtful budgeting decisions, consider a small healthcare practice that opted for basic antivirus software to cut costs but later faced significant fines due to data breaches stemming from inadequate protection measures. In contrast, another firm that invested upfront in comprehensive cybersecurity insurance not only shielded itself from catastrophic losses after a breach but also earned trust among its clientele by demonstrating a commitment to safeguarding sensitive information.

To wrap things up, strategic budgeting for cybersecurity fosters resilience within an organization by promoting proactive defenses over reactive fixes. Approaching budgets with flexibility enables small businesses to adapt to evolving threats while maintaining adequate defenses against potential risks without incurring overwhelming financial strain. By emphasizing careful planning and prioritization alongside ongoing employee education and vendor collaboration, small business owners can cultivate an enduring culture of cybersecurity awareness that protects assets and builds trust —a cornerstone of sustainable success in today's digital landscape.

Integrating Cybersecurity into Business Processes

Integrating cybersecurity into your business processes

is essential for building a resilient organization. When cybersecurity practices are embedded in daily operations, they shift from being reactive measures to proactive elements that enhance overall performance. This seamless integration not only strengthens your defenses but also aligns security with your business objectives.

Begin by mapping your existing business processes to identify where cybersecurity can play a pivotal role. Focus on critical functions such as customer relationship management (CRM), supply chain logistics, and employee onboarding. Each of these areas presents unique security challenges and opportunities. For example, when managing customer data in a CRM system, implementing robust data protection measures like encryption and access controls is vital to safeguarding sensitive information.

As you evaluate your workflows, engage key stakeholders from various departments. This collaboration fosters a comprehensive understanding of how different functions intersect with cybersecurity. The marketing team may need insight into the risks associated with third-party vendors for email campaigns, while HR should prioritize secure onboarding practices for new employees accessing company resources. By forming cross-functional teams that include IT and security professionals, you cultivate a culture of shared responsibility for security throughout the organization.

Streamlining processes is another crucial aspect of effective cybersecurity integration. Automation can significantly reduce manual errors that often lead to vulnerabilities. Take this example, implementing automated patch management systems ensures that software updates are applied promptly across all devices, freeing employees from the burden of remembering these critical tasks. This not only enhances security but also allows IT resources to focus on more strategic initiatives.

Training is vital in this integration process. As you embed cybersecurity practices into everyday operations, ensure all employees receive targeted training relevant to their roles. Tailor programs to address specific threats associated with their tasks—sales teams should prioritize phishing awareness when using email for client outreach, while finance departments may need training on secure transaction processing methods. Engaging formats like interactive workshops or online simulations can enhance knowledge retention and application.

Regular assessments are essential for maintaining the effectiveness of integrated cybersecurity measures. Conduct periodic audits of business processes to evaluate compliance with established security protocols and identify areas needing improvement. Utilize metrics such as incident response times and the frequency of security incidents to measure the success of your integration strategies over time.

Take this example, consider a retail business that has integrated point-of-sale (POS) systems with strong security protocols. By routinely reviewing transaction logs for anomalies and conducting vulnerability scans on the POS network, they not only detect potential breaches early but also refine their operational procedures based on real-world insights.

Incorporating feedback mechanisms further strengthens your integration efforts. Encourage employees to report potential threats or weaknesses they encounter during their daily activities without fear of retribution. Establishing an open line of communication fosters a culture where everyone feels accountable for upholding security standards.

Finally, keep an eye on emerging technologies and evolving threats that could impact your industry. Continuous adaptation ensures that your integrated cybersecurity measures remain relevant amidst changing conditions. By staying informed about advancements such as artificial intelligence in threat detection or innovative encryption methods, you can adjust your strategies accordingly.

 integrating cybersecurity into business processes fosters a holistic approach that not only protects valuable assets but also drives operational efficiency and innovation. By aligning these practices with broader business goals, organizations build resilience against cyber threats while maximizing trust among clients and partners alike. The result is a fortified framework that empowers your small business to thrive in an increasingly complex digital landscape while remaining agile enough to adapt swiftly to new challenges.

Communicating the Strategy

Communicating your cybersecurity strategy goes beyond simply sharing information; it aims to foster understanding and engagement throughout your organization. When team members grasp not only the "what" but also the "why" behind your cybersecurity initiatives, they become active participants in safeguarding the business. This effective communication transforms your strategy from a collection of policies into a shared commitment.

To begin, clearly articulate the objectives of your cybersecurity strategy, ensuring they align with the broader goals of your organization. For example, if enhancing customer trust is a primary aim, explain how robust cybersecurity measures protect sensitive customer data and reinforce your brand's reliability. This connection helps employees understand the significance of their roles in supporting security efforts.

Utilize a variety of channels to share information about your cybersecurity strategy. Regular meetings, newsletters, and digital platforms can serve as effective conduits for updates and insights. Tailor each communication to its audience— executives may need high-level overviews, while technical teams might require detailed operational guidelines. Visual aids like infographics or charts can simplify complex concepts, making them more accessible.

Storytelling is another powerful tool in effective communication. Share real-world examples that illustrate potential threats and their impact on the business. Take this example, discussing a case study of an organization that experienced a data breach can serve as a wake-up call, underscoring the importance of vigilance. When employees see cyber threats as tangible risks rather than theoretical scenarios, they are more likely to take proactive measures.

Encouraging feedback on communicated strategies is essential for gauging understanding and addressing concerns. An open-door policy fosters dialogue, allowing employees to voice questions or suggestions regarding security practices. This interaction not only enhances comprehension but also cultivates an environment where security is perceived as a collaborative effort rather than an imposition.

Training sessions present another excellent opportunity to reinforce your message. Integrate cybersecurity topics into regular training programs, emphasizing their relevance across various roles within the organization. For example, when discussing secure password practices, demonstrate how easily attackers can exploit weak passwords through real-life simulations. The goal is to make cybersecurity training engaging and relevant so that employees retain and apply what they've learned.

Recognizing and celebrating employee contributions to maintaining security standards is equally important. Highlighting positive examples reinforces desirable behaviors and motivates others to actively participate in cybersecurity initiatives. Implementing recognition programs for teams or individuals who excel in adhering to security protocols fosters a culture of accountability.

Consistency is crucial as you communicate your strategy.

Regularly revisit key messages through multiple channels—reminders about phishing tactics or updates on policy changes should be woven into ongoing communications rather than treated as one-time announcements. By embedding these messages into everyday operations, you ensure that cybersecurity remains top-of-mind for everyone in the organization.

In addition to addressing current threats, your communication should include updates on new challenges and emerging technologies affecting your cybersecurity landscape. Consider creating a dedicated space for sharing insights from industry developments or lessons learned from recent incidents within the sector.

In summary, effectively communicating your cybersecurity strategy transforms passive compliance into active engagement at all levels of your organization. By aligning security objectives with business goals, utilizing diverse communication methods, and fostering an open culture for feedback and dialogue, you empower employees to play an integral role in protecting the organization's assets against cyber threats. This holistic approach not only strengthens defenses but also builds a resilient workforce committed to maintaining security excellence in an ever-evolving digital landscape.

Iterating and Adapting the Strategy

With your cybersecurity strategy firmly established and effectively communicated across the organization, it's essential to acknowledge that the landscape of threats and vulnerabilities is constantly evolving. As new challenges arise, your strategy must not only remain resilient but also adapt in response to these changes. This ongoing process of adaptation ensures that your cybersecurity measures remain effective and relevant, safeguarding your business against unforeseen risks.

The first step in this iterative process is to regularly assess the effectiveness of your current strategy. Establish a routine for evaluating how well your cybersecurity measures align with your organization's goals and the shifting threat landscape. Take this example, after a significant cybersecurity incident—whether it occurs within your organization or is reported in the news—conduct a comprehensive analysis of your existing protocols. Ask critical questions: Did our defenses hold up? What vulnerabilities were exposed? By scrutinizing these elements, you can pinpoint areas that require strengthening.

Next, leverage metrics to guide your adaptations. Tracking data such as incident response times, the number of thwarted breach attempts, and employee compliance rates with security protocols can provide valuable insights into your current posture. For example, if data indicates an increase in successful phishing attempts despite training efforts, it may signal a need to refine educational content or enhance awareness through more frequent reminders. Utilizing dashboards that visually represent these metrics can facilitate communication across teams, ensuring that everyone understands the rationale behind any changes.

Engaging with industry trends is equally important. Cybersecurity is dynamic, influenced by technological advancements and emerging threats. Stay informed about new tools and practices through industry publications, webinars, and conferences. A recent case where a company implemented machine learning to detect anomalies in network traffic could inspire similar innovations within your own strategy. Adopting such cutting-edge technologies can significantly enhance your ability to anticipate and mitigate risks.

Collaboration with internal stakeholders further strengthens this iterative approach. Regularly convene cross-functional teams—including IT, operations, legal, and management—to discuss cybersecurity strategies. These discussions should not only reflect on past incidents but also forecast potential threats based on current industry developments. Take this example, if regulatory requirements shift due to changes in data protection laws, ensure that all departments understand how these alterations impact their roles in maintaining compliance.

Feedback from employees is another cornerstone of effective adaptation. Encourage frontline staff to share their experiences regarding security protocols—what works well for them and what doesn't. This grassroots insight can lead to practical adjustments in training programs or communication styles that resonate more effectively with various teams. For example, if employees express difficulties understanding complex security policies, simplifying language or using relatable scenarios may enhance comprehension.

As you adapt your strategy, prioritize flexibility over rigidity. The ability to pivot quickly in response to new information will be critical in an environment characterized by rapid technological change and evolving cyber threats. Develop a framework for agility within your cybersecurity operations— this might include designated response teams ready to test new technologies or processes as they become available.

Another essential aspect of this continuous improvement cycle involves revisiting and updating documentation related to security policies and procedures. As roles evolve and new technologies are introduced, ensuring that all materials reflect current practices is vital for maintaining clarity and compliance across the organization. Regular audits can help ensure that documentation aligns with real-world applications, preventing discrepancies that could expose vulnerabilities.

Integrating lessons learned from past incidents also plays a crucial role in refining your strategy. After each significant event—be it a breach or a close call—conduct post-mortem reviews involving all relevant stakeholders. These reviews should go beyond merely identifying what went wrong; they should focus on actionable steps for improvement moving forward.

iterating and adapting your cybersecurity strategy isn't just about addressing weaknesses; it's about fostering a culture of resilience throughout the organization. Empowering team members at all levels to engage with cybersecurity principles ensures that everyone feels invested in protecting the company's digital assets.

By consistently reviewing metrics, embracing feedback loops, encouraging collaboration among departments, remaining flexible in implementation, updating documentation proactively, and learning from past experiences, you create an adaptive framework capable of weathering both present challenges and future uncertainties. This proactive stance not only fortifies defenses but also cultivates an organizational ethos rooted in security awareness—a vital ingredient for success in today's digital-first world where adaptability is key.

CHAPTER 4: IMPLEMENTING NETWORK SECURITY FOR SMALL BUSINESSES

Understanding Network Basics

To effectively grasp network basics, it helps to consider the architecture that supports your operations. Most commonly, businesses utilize a Local Area Network (LAN), which connects computers and devices within a confined area, such as an office or building. Within this network, routers and switches play crucial roles by managing data traffic and ensuring efficient data flow. Familiarity with how these components interact is vital for implementing effective security measures.

Take this example, imagine your office has several workstations accessing shared files stored on a central server. The server is pivotal because it centralizes data storage while allowing authorized users to access necessary files. If this server were compromised due to inadequate security protocols, sensitive information could be leaked or destroyed. Thus, securing this central node is a priority; you might begin by installing firewalls and regularly updating server software.

Next, let's explore the concept of IP addresses, which are crucial for identifying devices on your network. Each device requires an Internet Protocol (IP) address—think of it as a unique identifier similar to a phone number. Understanding both IPv4 and IPv6 formats equips you with the knowledge needed to manage and configure networks more effectively. For example, an IPv4 address appears as 192.168.1.1, while an IPv6 address is represented as a longer hexadecimal string, such as 2001:0db8:85a3:0000:0000:8a2e:0370:7334.

It's also important to distinguish between static and dynamic IP addresses. A static IP address remains constant over time, making it easier to host services like web servers or email servers but increasing vulnerability if not secured properly. In contrast, dynamic IP addresses change frequently through DHCP (Dynamic Host Configuration Protocol), reducing risk but complicating certain networking setups. Balancing these options according to your business needs is key for optimal functionality and security.

Understanding network protocols is equally crucial—the rules governing how data travels across your network. TCP/IP (Transmission Control Protocol/Internet Protocol) underpins nearly all communications in today's digital landscape, ensuring reliable transmission between devices. Familiarity with additional protocols such as HTTPS (for secure web browsing) and FTP (File Transfer Protocol) can further enhance your ability to protect sensitive information during transmission.

Wireless networks, which are increasingly prevalent in modern businesses due to their flexibility and ease of access, also require careful consideration. Securing these networks demands vigilance; implementing WPA3 encryption can help prevent unauthorized individuals from intercepting your signals or accessing connected devices.

Another strategy worth considering is network segmentation, which involves dividing a larger network into smaller sub-networks for improved security and performance monitoring. For example, separating guest Wi-Fi from your primary business network can thwart unauthorized access to sensitive systems while still providing connectivity for visitors.

As technology continues to evolve rapidly, so do the threats targeting networks. Staying informed about best practices can help mitigate risks associated with cyber intrusions. Regularly updating passwords for your routers and other networking equipment serves as an effective first line of defense against unauthorized access attempts.

It's also important to recognize that human behavior significantly impacts network security. Conducting regular training sessions on recognizing phishing attempts and other suspicious activities can empower employees to act defensively when faced with potential threats.

By solidifying your understanding of basic networking concepts—including architectures, protocols, IP configurations, wireless security measures, and human factors—you can better position your business against the cyber threats that many small enterprises face today. This foundational knowledge will inform every decision you make regarding cybersecurity investments and practices moving forward, reinforcing the notion that robust cybersecurity begins with informed strategic choices grounded in an understanding of underlying technologies.

Securing Wireless Networks

Wireless networks present both opportunities and challenges for small businesses. They offer unparalleled flexibility and convenience, enabling employees to connect devices without the hassle of cables. However, this convenience comes with vulnerabilities that could expose your organization to significant risks if not properly managed. By understanding these risks, you can take proactive steps to enhance the security of your wireless network.

The first step in securing your wireless network is selecting the right encryption protocol. WPA3 is the most advanced standard available today, providing enhanced protection against brute-force attacks and employing improved encryption methods to safeguard sensitive information. If your current router does not support WPA3, consider upgrading or replacing it to take advantage of this robust technology.

Once you've established a strong encryption standard, it's essential to change the default settings on your wireless router. Default usernames and passwords are often easy targets for attackers; modifying them can greatly reduce the risk of unauthorized access. Creating complex passwords that include a mix of letters, numbers, and symbols is a best practice. If keeping track of these credentials proves challenging, using a password manager can help ensure they remain secure.

Another important aspect of network security is visibility management. Disabling SSID broadcasting makes your network less detectable to casual users scanning for connections. While determined attackers may still find it through other means, reducing visibility can deter opportunistic intruders who lack advanced skills or motivation.

You might also consider implementing MAC address filtering as an additional layer of protection. Each device has a unique Media Access Control (MAC) address that identifies it within the network. By configuring your router to allow only specific MAC addresses access, you can limit connections to trusted devices. However, keep in mind that this method isn't foolproof, as MAC addresses can be spoofed.

Segmenting your wireless network into distinct zones is another effective strategy. Take this example, creating separate networks for employees and guests not only enhances security but also improves performance by managing bandwidth allocation more effectively. This approach allows guests internet access without compromising access to internal systems or sensitive data.

Regular updates are crucial for maintaining network security as well. Keeping your router's firmware up-to-date protects against vulnerabilities that cybercriminals might exploit to gain entry into your business systems. Manufacturers frequently release patches when new vulnerabilities are discovered; staying current with these updates ensures protection against known threats.

Incorporating a guest Wi-Fi network provides visitors with internet access while safeguarding sensitive company data and resources. This approach maintains the security of your primary business network while accommodating guests—an essential balance in today's interconnected work environment.

Monitoring traffic within your wireless network is another key opportunity for risk mitigation. Utilizing tools such as Intrusion Detection Systems (IDS) can help identify unusual activity and alert you before potential breaches occur. By understanding baseline traffic patterns, you can quickly recognize anomalies and respond effectively, thereby enhancing your overall security posture.

Human behavior plays a significant role in maintaining wireless security as well. Educating staff on recognizing phishing attempts and suspicious activity is vital; regular training sessions will equip employees with the knowledge needed to combat cybercriminal tactics aimed at breaching security defenses.

Securing your wireless network requires strategic planning and ongoing effort across multiple fronts—from choosing appropriate encryption standards and modifying default settings to implementing MAC filtering and establishing guest networks designed for visitor access without compromising sensitive data integrity.

With each layer of security added, you not only make it more difficult for potential intruders but also foster confidence within your organization—a commitment to prioritizing cybersecurity that resonates throughout all areas of operation as technology continues to evolve at an unprecedented pace.

By actively addressing these elements, small business owners can create robust defenses around their wireless networks—ultimately ensuring that connectivity does not come at the expense of security but rather supports resilience against emerging threats in today's digital landscape.

Firewalls and Their Importance

Firewalls play a vital role in the cybersecurity landscape, serving as essential barriers between your internal network and external threats. For small businesses, where resources are often limited but the stakes remain high, understanding and implementing effective firewall solutions can mean the difference between safe operations and catastrophic data breaches.

At their core, firewalls monitor and control both incoming and outgoing network traffic based on predetermined security rules. They filter data packets much like a security guard assessing who gains access to a secure building. Firewalls fall into two primary categories: hardware firewalls, which are physical devices positioned between your network and the internet, and software firewalls, which are applications installed on individual devices or servers. Both types play important roles in a comprehensive cybersecurity strategy.

When you think about hardware firewalls, consider them the first line of defense for your entire network. They provide strong protection against external threats while effectively managing traffic loads. Many small business routers include built-in firewall capabilities; however, these may lack advanced security features. Investing in dedicated firewall appliances can significantly enhance your security posture by offering additional functionalities, such as intrusion prevention systems (IPS) that actively block suspicious activities.

Software firewalls are equally crucial, as they protect individual devices within your network. These applications can be tailored to specific needs based on user behavior and device vulnerabilities. For example, in today's remote working environment, where employees often use personal laptops for work tasks, installing reliable software firewalls on those devices is essential to safeguard sensitive company information.

Configuring firewall rules strikes a balance between accessibility and security. Default settings typically prioritize convenience over stringent protection, leaving vulnerabilities that cybercriminals can exploit. Customizing these rules to align with the unique needs of your business operations is crucial. Take this example, allow access only to necessary ports while blocking unused ones that could serve as entry points for attacks.

The importance of regularly monitoring firewall activity cannot be overstated. By consistently reviewing logs and alerts generated by your firewall system, you gain insights into attempted breaches or suspicious activities that require immediate attention. This proactive approach enables you to respond swiftly to potential threats rather than waiting for a breach to occur.

Additionally, consider integrating next-generation firewalls

(NGFWs), which incorporate advanced technologies such as application awareness and deep packet inspection. Unlike traditional firewalls that filter traffic based solely on established rules, NGFWs analyze traffic patterns and behaviors to detect sophisticated threats like malware hidden within legitimate traffic. For example, if an employee inadvertently downloads malicious software disguised as a legitimate application from an unverified source, a traditional firewall might allow this download through because it appears harmless at first glance; however, an NGFW could recognize unusual behavior linked to that download and block it before any damage occurs.

Firewalls also facilitate secure remote access for employees who work from home or travel for business. By implementing virtual private networks (VPNs) alongside your firewall, you create encrypted connections that protect data transmitted over less secure public networks. This dual-layered approach is especially crucial as more businesses adopt flexible working arrangements without compromising their security integrity.

And, educating staff about the importance of firewalls is paramount; they must understand how these tools fit into the broader context of your cybersecurity strategy. Regular training sessions can help demystify technical jargon while empowering employees to take ownership of their role in maintaining cybersecurity standards.

As you develop your cybersecurity strategy, remember that firewalls are not standalone solutions—they should work in harmony with other security measures such as intrusion detection systems (IDS) and antivirus software for comprehensive protection against evolving cyber threats.

Investing time to understand how firewalls operate ensures you leverage their full potential while reinforcing your commitment to safeguarding sensitive information within your organization's ecosystem. In today's rapidly changing digital landscape, taking proactive steps to implement robust firewall measures not only protects your assets but also builds trust among clients and stakeholders alike—creating a resilient foundation for ongoing success in an increasingly interconnected world.

Virtual Private Networks (VPNs)

Virtual Private Networks (VPNs) have become essential tools for small businesses, particularly as remote work gains traction. By establishing secure, encrypted connections over potentially insecure networks, VPNs shield sensitive data from unauthorized access. They function as a protective tunnel between your device and the internet, masking your IP address and safeguarding your online activities.

The mechanics of a VPN involve routing your internet connection through a server managed by the VPN provider. This process encrypts your data and conceals your digital footprint, which is crucial for small businesses whose employees frequently access company resources from public Wi-Fi or other unsecured networks. Given the heightened risk of data interception in these scenarios, using a VPN can significantly reduce vulnerability.

Imagine an employee working from a coffee shop. Without a VPN, all online activities—ranging from accessing company emails to handling sensitive documents—are exposed to anyone sharing the same network. A cybercriminal could easily intercept this information using readily available tools. However, when that employee connects to a VPN, their internet traffic becomes encrypted, rendering it nearly impossible for anyone else on the network to interpret their actions.

When selecting a VPN service for your business, there are several key factors to consider. First and foremost is the level of encryption offered; opt for VPNs that utilize strong protocols such as OpenVPN or IKEv2/IPsec for robust data protection. Additionally, the jurisdiction of the VPN provider plays a critical role—choosing a service based in a privacy-friendly region can enhance protection against unwarranted data requests from law enforcement.

Another significant consideration is bandwidth and connection speed. Some VPNs may slow down internet performance due to encryption processes or server congestion. Evaluating various services and reading user reviews can help you identify reliable options that balance security with performance.

For organizations with larger teams, investing in a dedicated business VPN solution may be more effective than relying on consumer-grade options. Business-oriented services often come with features tailored to corporate environments, such as centralized management tools that empower administrators to oversee access permissions and monitor usage across teams. This level of control ensures that only authorized personnel can access sensitive company resources.

VPNs also play a vital role in securely facilitating remote work arrangements. As businesses adopt hybrid models where employees divide their time between home and office settings, ensuring safe access to internal networks becomes essential. A well-configured VPN allows employees to connect seamlessly to the corporate network from anywhere while upholding high security standards.

To further bolster security, consider implementing multi-factor authentication (MFA) alongside your VPN. By combining strong password policies with MFA, even if an unauthorized user acquires credentials through phishing or other methods, they will still need an additional authentication method—like a code sent to their mobile device —to complete the login process.

It's equally important to educate employees on how to use the VPN effectively. Conduct training sessions that clarify how the VPN protects their data and why it is crucial for maintaining corporate security policies. Highlight potential risks associated with not using the VPN and illustrate best practices for connecting and disconnecting safely.

Monitoring VPN usage can also reveal irregularities or suspicious behavior within your network. By maintaining logs of connection times and accessed resources, you can identify patterns that may signal potential security incidents.

Integrating VPN technology into your broader cybersecurity strategy reinforces your commitment to protecting sensitive information while ensuring business continuity in various work environments. With cyber threats evolving in complexity, investing in robust VPN solutions not only safeguards valuable assets but also builds trust with clients who rely on your organization's ability to protect their data.

To wrap things up, implementing Virtual Private Networks goes beyond enhancing security; it cultivates a culture of responsibility within your organization that prioritizes data protection at every level. This proactive approach ensures that as you navigate an ever-evolving digital landscape, your small business remains resilient against emerging cybersecurity challenges while confidently embracing modern work practices.

Utilizing Intrusion Detection Systems (IDS)

Intrusion Detection Systems (IDS) are vital components of the cybersecurity framework for small businesses. These systems monitor network traffic continuously, identifying suspicious activities and potential threats, effectively acting as an early warning system against intrusions. By detecting and analyzing anomalies in real-time, IDS can alert administrators to possible breaches before they escalate into serious incidents.

At the heart of an IDS is its ability to collect and examine data packets traveling through the network. It employs various detection methods, including signature-based detection, which identifies known threat patterns, and anomaly-based detection, which looks for deviations from typical traffic behavior. Take this example, if an employee who usually accesses specific files during business hours suddenly tries to access a large volume of data late at night, the IDS can flag this unusual activity for further investigation.

Implementing an IDS involves a strategic approach. The first step is to determine the type of system that best meets your business needs. For many small businesses, a network-based IDS (NIDS) is ideal since it monitors traffic at critical points in the network without requiring extensive modifications to existing infrastructure. Conversely, host-based IDS (HIDS) focuses on individual devices, monitoring files and system calls for signs of tampering or unauthorized access.

Once you've selected an appropriate IDS, effective configuration becomes crucial. This process entails defining what constitutes normal behavior within your network environment and establishing thresholds for alerts. It's important to minimize false positives, as excessive alerts can lead to alert fatigue among IT staff and result in genuine threats being overlooked. A practical strategy involves conducting a baseline analysis during peak operational hours to better understand typical traffic patterns.

Regular updates are essential for maintaining the relevance of your IDS against emerging threats. Cybercriminals continually evolve their techniques, so it's vital that signature databases are updated frequently to reflect new vulnerabilities and attack vectors. While many modern IDS solutions offer automated updates, periodic manual checks are still recommended to ensure comprehensive coverage.

Enhancing your IDS's effectiveness can also be achieved through integration with other security measures. For example, pairing it with a Security Information and Event Management (SIEM) system allows for centralized logging and analysis of security events across your organization. This integration provides deeper insights into potential threats by correlating data from various sources and enabling quicker responses.

Beyond technical measures, fostering a culture of cybersecurity awareness within your organization is equally important. Employees need to understand the significance of cybersecurity and how their actions impact overall security posture. Regular training sessions that focus on common threats—such as phishing attacks—empower employees to recognize potential risks before they escalate into incidents that could compromise sensitive data.

When an intrusion is detected, having a response plan is crucial. Establish clear protocols outlining the steps to take when alerts are triggered by the IDS. This plan should include strategies for quickly isolating affected systems and guidelines for communicating with stakeholders about potential breaches.

Testing your incident response plan through simulated exercises not only prepares your team but also helps identify areas needing improvement. Conducting tabletop exercises that mimic real-world scenarios enhances readiness and ensures everyone understands their role during an actual incident.

The benefits of utilizing an Intrusion Detection System extend beyond immediate threat detection; they play a significant role in building long-term resilience against cyber threats. By continuously monitoring network activity and fostering overall security awareness within the organization, small businesses can establish a proactive defense strategy that adapts to evolving challenges.

Incorporating an IDS into your cybersecurity infrastructure not only strengthens your defenses but also instills confidence among clients and stakeholders regarding your commitment to protecting their information. As you adopt these advanced protective measures, remember that cybersecurity is an ongoing journey—one that demands vigilance, adaptability, and collaboration at every level of your organization.

Network Segmentation Best Practices

Network segmentation is a crucial yet often underestimated component of cybersecurity for small businesses. By breaking a network into smaller, more manageable segments, organizations can significantly enhance their security, improve performance, and effectively contain potential threats. This strategy ensures that if one segment is compromised, the intruder's access to the remainder of the network remains limited.

At the heart of network segmentation lies the principle of least privilege. By restricting access to only those who need it for specific tasks, businesses can drastically reduce their attack surface. For example, consider a company that separates its customer database from its financial system. If an attacker gains entry through phishing into the customer database but cannot penetrate the financial segment, sensitive financial data remains protected.

To implement network segmentation effectively, begin by mapping out your current network architecture. Identify all devices, users, and data flows within your organization. This comprehensive inventory will help you pinpoint potential vulnerabilities and understand how different systems interact. Once you have a clear overview, categorize your assets based on sensitivity and function. Take this example, critical servers containing sensitive information should be segmented separately from less critical operational systems.

One common method for achieving network segmentation is through Virtual Local Area Networks (VLANs). VLANs enable the creation of distinct broadcast domains within your existing physical infrastructure without requiring additional hardware. By utilizing VLAN tags in Ethernet frames, devices across different VLANs can communicate while remaining logically separated. For example, a retail company could connect point-of-sale terminals to a VLAN distinct from employee workstations to better safeguard transaction data against breaches.

Another effective approach involves using firewalls or routers with advanced configuration options that allow you to establish rules governing traffic between segments. These devices can enforce policies regarding permissible communications across segments. Take this example, you might configure firewall rules that permit only specific applications or ports for communication between the administrative segment and the guest Wi-Fi segment— thereby minimizing unnecessary exposure.

In addition to segmentation measures, implementing robust monitoring and logging practices within each area is vital. By tracking traffic flow and logging events related to access attempts across segments, you gain valuable visibility into potentially suspicious activities. Tools such as Network Monitoring Systems (NMS) can automate this process, alerting administrators to unusual patterns that may indicate an attempted breach or misconfiguration.

As your business grows and evolves technologically, it's essential to regularly review your segmentation strategy. Changes in staff roles or technology deployments can alter data flows within your network. Conducting audits ensures that your segmentation remains effective and compliant with evolving regulatory standards or best practices in your industry.

Fostering a culture of awareness around network segmentation among employees further enhances security. Training staff on the importance of segmentation helps them understand their role in maintaining security protocols—

whether they are accessing sensitive files or connecting new devices to the network.

In cases where a breach does occur despite preventive measures, effective segmentation aids containment efforts. By restricting an intruder's movement within isolated sections of the network, incident response teams can quickly isolate affected areas without disrupting overall operations.

embracing network segmentation not only strengthens defenses but also cultivates a proactive approach to cybersecurity throughout your organization. As cyber threats grow increasingly sophisticated, establishing segmented networks positions your small business as resilient against attacks while simultaneously improving operational efficiency through targeted resource allocation and management.

By prioritizing these best practices in network segmentation today, you are laying down strong foundations for tomorrow's digital landscape—one where security becomes an integral part of your operations rather than a reactive measure.

Managing Network Access Control

Managing network access control is a fundamental aspect of an effective cybersecurity strategy. It goes beyond merely erecting barriers; it involves ensuring that every user, device, and application has appropriate access to the resources they need while simultaneously mitigating potential threats. By implementing robust access control mechanisms, businesses can significantly lower the risk of data breaches and unauthorized access, thereby protecting sensitive information.

At the heart of network access control are three critical principles: authentication, authorization, and accountability. These components work together to confirm users' identities (authentication), ensure they can only perform actions within their designated permissions (authorization), and maintain logs of their activities for future reference (accountability). This triad creates a secure environment in which employees can work without exposing the network to unnecessary risks.

To establish effective network access control, start by evaluating your current access policies. Determine which employees require access to specific resources based on their roles and responsibilities. For example, a small marketing team may need access to certain customer data for targeted campaigns. Their access should be limited to files relevant to their projects, ensuring that sensitive financial or HR data remains protected.

One practical approach to managing access is through Role-Based Access Control (RBAC). This method allows you to assign permissions based on predefined organizational roles. Take this example, a finance manager might have access to financial records and reporting tools, while a customer service representative could be granted limited visibility into customer support databases. This structure not only minimizes the risk of accidental data exposure but also enhances workflow efficiency.

In addition to RBAC, consider incorporating Multi-Factor Authentication (MFA) as an extra layer of security. MFA requires users to provide two or more verification factors when logging in—such as something they know (a password), something they have (a smartphone app for generating codes), or something they are (biometric verification). This additional step can deter potential intruders who may have obtained passwords but lack physical access to the required authentication factors.

Monitoring user activity is crucial for maintaining secure network access control. Regularly reviewing logs that track who accessed what information and when helps identify potentially malicious activity while fostering accountability among employees. Many organizations utilize automated monitoring solutions that alert administrators to suspicious behavior, such as multiple failed login attempts or unusual access times, which could signal an attempted breach.

To strengthen your network's defenses further, establish stringent policies around device management and Bring Your Own Device (BYOD) protocols. While many small businesses allow employees to use personal devices for work, this practice can introduce vulnerabilities if those devices aren't adequately secured. Create clear guidelines regarding the types of devices permitted to connect to the corporate network and ensure that all devices meet specific security standards—such as updated antivirus software or encryption protocols.

Regular audits should also be part of your ongoing management of network access controls. As your business evolves, so will its security needs. Conducting audits allows you to verify whether current access levels align with employee responsibilities and identify any potential gaps in security policies. If an employee changes roles or leaves the company, promptly revoking their access rights is essential to preventing unauthorized entry into sensitive areas of your network.

Cultivating a culture of security awareness around network access control empowers employees to be vigilant in safeguarding sensitive information. Regular training sessions on cybersecurity protocols—including how to recognize phishing attempts—can help instill a security-first mindset throughout your organization.

When incidents do occur—despite even the best-laid plans —effective management of network access control aids in containment efforts. By limiting an intruder's ability to move laterally across networks, incident response teams can quickly isolate affected systems and mitigate damage without disrupting overall operations.

Integrating these strategies into your cybersecurity

framework is not just a defensive measure; it represents a proactive approach against evolving threats. By managing network access with precision and care, you're not only protecting data but also fostering an environment where security is prioritized in daily operations.

investing time and resources into robust network access control practices will equip your small business with resilience against cyber threats while enhancing operational efficiency through clear protocols and streamlined resource allocation. In today's digital landscape—where risks are ever-present—this approach ensures you remain a step ahead, creating a fortress that safeguards both your assets and your peace of mind.

Regular Network Security Audits

Regular network security audits are essential for enhancing your small business's cybersecurity posture. These audits help identify vulnerabilities and ensure that existing security measures are functioning effectively. Much like maintaining a vehicle, routine checks on your network can prevent breakdowns and keep operations running smoothly.

Begin by defining the scope of your audit. Identify which systems, applications, and data will be included in the review. Take this example, if your business relies heavily on cloud services, be sure to include those in your assessment. Don't overlook any endpoints, including employee devices and IoT gadgets connected to your network. A thorough audit examines the entire ecosystem that supports your operations, going beyond the obvious.

Next, decide on the method for conducting the audit. You can choose between an internal review or hiring an external cybersecurity firm. Each option has its benefits: internal audits can cultivate a culture of security awareness within your team, while external audits offer fresh perspectives and specialized expertise. For example, one small business discovered vulnerabilities overlooked by their internal team when they brought in an outside consultant—specifically, outdated software versions that were susceptible to exploits.

Once you've defined the scope and chosen a method, create an audit checklist tailored to your specific needs. This checklist should cover key areas such as:

- Network configurations
- Firewall settings
- User access controls
- Software updates and patch management
- Intrusion detection systems

You might organize this information in a simple spreadsheet that lists each element to be audited alongside its compliance status. This approach makes tracking progress straightforward and highlights areas requiring attention.

After completing the audit, compile your findings into a report that identifies vulnerabilities and offers actionable recommendations for improvement. Prioritize these findings based on their risk levels—determine which issues pose the most significant threats to your business. Perhaps it's an unpatched system or excessive user permissions granting too much access to sensitive data. Your report should not only highlight weaknesses but also suggest immediate actions to mitigate these risks.

Implementing changes based on the audit findings is critical. Assign specific responsibilities to team members for addressing each issue identified in the report. For example, if a vulnerability exists in a particular software application, designate someone to oversee its update or replacement. This accountability ensures that everyone understands their role in maintaining network security.

Establish a timeline for re-evaluating the changes made.

Regular follow-ups will help confirm that improvements are effective and sustained over time. Consider scheduling quarterly audits or at least annual reviews based on your business's risk profile and industry requirements.

Fostering a culture of continuous improvement around security practices will enhance the effectiveness of these audits over time. Encourage staff to report any anomalies they notice during their daily work; this proactive approach can lead to early detection of potential threats before they escalate into significant issues.

By incorporating regular network security audits into your business processes, you create an environment of vigilance and resilience against cyber threats. Staying ahead of potential vulnerabilities through systematic reviews allows you not just to react to issues as they arise but also to build a robust foundation for long-term security success.

Leveraging the Cloud for Network Security

Cloud technology has revolutionized the operations of small businesses, providing flexibility and scalability that were previously unattainable. However, these benefits also introduce unique security challenges that require careful attention and proactive strategies. To enhance your overall cybersecurity posture through cloud solutions, it's essential to understand both the opportunities and risks involved.

One of the primary advantages of utilizing cloud services for network security is access to advanced security technologies without the hefty upfront costs typical of traditional hardware-based systems. Many cloud service providers incorporate built-in security features—such as encryption, firewalls, and intrusion detection systems—into their service offerings. Take this example, a small e-commerce business can take advantage of a cloud provider's DDoS protection to safeguard its online store from malicious attacks during peak shopping seasons, ensuring uninterrupted operations.

When integrating cloud solutions into your network security strategy, it's vital to assess the security measures implemented by your provider. Look for certifications like ISO 27001 or compliance with frameworks such as NIST, which indicate adherence to high-security standards. Additionally, inquire about how data is managed, specifically regarding encryption both at rest and in transit. If you're using services like AWS or Azure, their documentation can offer detailed insights into their data protection policies, helping you ensure that your data remains secure throughout its lifecycle.

Understanding the shared responsibility model is another critical aspect of leveraging the cloud for security. While your cloud provider is accountable for securing the underlying infrastructure, you are responsible for protecting your applications and data within that environment. This responsibility often includes implementing access controls, diligently managing user permissions, and maintaining compliance with relevant regulations. For example, a small financial firm utilizing a cloud accounting solution must ensure that sensitive customer information is accessible only to authorized personnel and conduct regular audits of permissions to prevent unauthorized access.

Integrating multi-factor authentication (MFA) across all applications linked to your cloud services is also essential. MFA adds an extra layer of protection by requiring users to verify their identity through multiple methods before accessing sensitive information. This simple yet effective measure can significantly mitigate the risk of unauthorized access stemming from compromised credentials—a prevalent vulnerability in many organizations today.

In addition to these preventive measures, establishing a robust incident response plan tailored specifically for your cloud environment is crucial. Create clear protocols outlining how your team should respond in the event of a breach involving any of your cloud services. This plan should detail communication strategies for both internal staff and external customers or stakeholders impacted by the incident. Take this example, if a data breach occurs on a third-party platform housing customer information, timely communication about potential impacts fosters trust and maintains transparency.

Regularly reviewing configurations and settings within your cloud environment is vital for ongoing protection against emerging threats. Utilize tools provided by your cloud service provider to monitor activity logs for unusual behavior or unauthorized changes; this proactive approach enables early detection of anomalies before they escalate into larger issues.

Lastly, employee training on best practices for accessing company resources via the cloud cannot be overstated. Conducting workshops focused on recognizing phishing attempts and practicing secure password management cultivates a culture of vigilance within your organization. Engaged employees become your first line of defense against cyber threats; after all, human error accounts for a significant portion of successful cyber-attacks.

By strategically harnessing the capabilities offered by cloud technology while implementing rigorous security protocols tailored to this new landscape, small businesses can effectively strengthen their defenses against cyber threats. Embracing these principles not only enhances operational efficiency but also positions organizations favorably in an increasingly complex digital world where resilience is key to maintaining trust and credibility with customers and stakeholders alike.

CHAPTER 5: DATA PROTECTION AND ENCRYPTION

Identifying Sensitive Data

I dentifying sensitive data is the cornerstone of an effective cybersecurity strategy. As a small business owner, it's crucial to understand what sensitive data encompasses within your organization. This goes beyond personal information to include proprietary business data, financial records, intellectual property, and customer interactions. Each piece of data poses potential risks if mishandled or exposed, making it essential to categorize and protect it accordingly.

Begin by conducting a thorough inventory of all data assets. This process involves mapping out where sensitive data is stored, whether on local servers, in cloud services, or on employee devices. Take this example, a marketing firm may house client information in a customer relationship management (CRM) system, while financial records could be stored in accounting software. Documenting these locations clarifies your data landscape and helps you identify vulnerabilities.

Next, assess the types of data you manage. Personally identifiable information (PII), such as names, addresses, Social Security numbers, and payment card details, are prime targets for cybercriminals. A breach involving this type of information can lead to financial loss and damage to your reputation. For example, if a local restaurant suffers a data breach that exposes customer credit card information, the fallout could result in lost business as customers lose trust in the restaurant's ability to protect their data.

In addition to PII, evaluate proprietary and intellectual property unique to your business. This could include trade secrets, design files, or marketing strategies—essentially any information that gives you a competitive advantage. Implementing stringent controls around this data is vital; unauthorized access could result in significant financial losses or harm your market position.

Once you've identified your sensitive data and its storage locations, classify it based on its sensitivity and criticality. You might categorize your data into three tiers: public information (which can be shared freely), internal use (important but less sensitive), and confidential (requiring strict protection). This classification helps prioritize security measures—deploying advanced encryption for confidential data while applying basic access controls for internal use information.

Understanding the legal requirements surrounding sensitive data management is also crucial. Different industries face various regulations regarding the protection of certain types of information. For example, businesses in the healthcare sector must comply with HIPAA regulations that mandate specific safeguards for patient health information. Non-compliance can lead to hefty fines and legal repercussions.

After mapping out and classifying your sensitive data while considering relevant regulations, establishing robust access controls becomes paramount. Limit access to sensitive information strictly on a need-to-know basis; only employees who require specific data for their roles should have access. Regularly review these permissions as staff roles change or when employees leave the company.

Implementing technical safeguards is equally essential. Encryption is one of the most effective methods for protecting sensitive data both at rest (stored) and in transit (being transmitted). Tools like AES (Advanced Encryption Standard) ensure that even if cybercriminals gain access to your systems, they cannot decipher the encrypted information without the proper keys.

Additionally, develop clear policies outlining how employees should handle sensitive data. These policies should include guidelines for secure storage practices—such as avoiding unprotected files for storing passwords—and safe communication channels for sharing sensitive information.

Training employees on how to identify and handle sensitive data is vital for building a strong defense against potential breaches. Conduct workshops that explain the significance of various types of sensitive data and common threats like phishing attacks targeting this information. Engaged employees who understand their role in safeguarding company assets become invaluable allies in your cybersecurity strategy.

The identification of sensitive data doesn't end with implementation; it requires ongoing vigilance and regular audits to ensure compliance with established policies. Establish a routine schedule for reviewing access logs and permissions and conducting penetration tests to identify potential vulnerabilities before they can be exploited.

In summary, identifying sensitive data forms the foundation of a comprehensive cybersecurity framework that aligns with your overall business strategy. By prioritizing what matters most within your organization and implementing rigorous protection measures around it, you not only safeguard your operations but also instill confidence among stakeholders that their interests are secure under your care. This proactive approach will ultimately pave the way for sustained growth amidst evolving digital threats.

Data Encryption Basics

Data encryption is a vital component in protecting sensitive information. As threats to data integrity and confidentiality become increasingly prevalent, it's essential for small business owners to understand the fundamentals of encryption. This knowledge equips you to implement effective measures that safeguard your business's most valuable assets.

To understand encryption, it's important to familiarize yourself with its two primary forms: symmetric and asymmetric encryption. Symmetric encryption uses a single key for both the encryption and decryption processes, making it efficient for quickly encrypting large volumes of data. Algorithms like AES (Advanced Encryption Standard) are popular choices in this category and are widely considered secure. However, the challenge arises in securely sharing this key among authorized users without exposing it to potential attackers.

On the other hand, asymmetric encryption employs a pair of keys: a public key accessible to anyone and a private key kept confidential by the owner. This dual-key system allows for secure communication; for instance, when a sender encrypts data with the recipient's public key, only the recipient can decrypt it with their private key. While this method enhances security—particularly for communications such as emails or file transfers—it tends to be slower than symmetric encryption due to its complexity.

When deciding on encryption solutions, it's crucial to consider the type of data you need to protect. For example, customer payment information should be encrypted both at rest—when stored on servers—and in transit—when transmitted over networks. Utilizing protocols such as TLS (Transport Layer Security) can help ensure that sensitive information like credit card numbers remains secure during online transactions.

An effective key management strategy is also essential. Protecting your encryption keys is just as critical as encrypting your data. Establish procedures for generating strong keys and storing them securely using hardware security modules (HSMs) or dedicated key management systems (KMS). Regularly rotating keys can further reduce risks associated with long-term exposure.

To illustrate practical encryption implementation, consider an online retailer looking to protect customer orders. The retailer might use AES to encrypt stored order details in its database while employing TLS for securing order information during transmission between the user's browser and the server. This dual-layered approach not only safeguards sensitive customer information but also fosters trust among consumers who prioritize their privacy.

Training employees on data encryption principles significantly enhances your organization's overall security posture. It's important that staff members understand which data requires encryption and how to handle sensitive information throughout its lifecycle—from creation and storage to sharing and destruction. Providing real-world examples of phishing attempts that target unencrypted data can make these lessons more relatable and impactful.

Compliance with industry regulations often requires adherence to specific encryption standards. Take this example, organizations that handle credit card transactions must meet PCI DSS requirements mandating strong encryption practices for payment data. Failing to comply can lead to severe financial penalties and damage your business's reputation.

Regular audits of your encryption strategies are vital for

maintaining an effective security posture. Periodically assess which data needs encryption based on evolving threats or changes within your business operations. Additionally, having an incident response plan that outlines steps to take if encrypted data is compromised ensures swift action while minimizing damage.

adopting robust data encryption practices not only protects your organization from unauthorized access but also helps ensure compliance with industry regulations. By integrating these principles into your cybersecurity framework, you create a fortified environment where sensitive information remains secure, instilling confidence among clients and stakeholders alike. This proactive approach will fortify your business against an ever-evolving array of digital threats while reinforcing trust in your brand's commitment to security excellence.

Encryption Protocols and Standards

Encryption protocols and standards are fundamental to modern data security, serving as protective barriers that safeguard sensitive information from unauthorized access. These protocols define the processes for encrypting, transmitting, and decrypting data, ensuring that only authorized users can access it. For small business owners, grasping these protocols is crucial for establishing effective security measures.

One of the most recognized encryption standards is the Advanced Encryption Standard (AES). This symmetric key encryption algorithm uses the same key for both encryption and decryption, making it efficient and robust. AES offers key lengths of 128, 192, or 256 bits, each providing different levels of security. Take this example, a small business handling customer payment information might opt for AES-256 to encrypt transaction data stored in its database. This strong level of encryption significantly lowers the risk of data breaches.

In addition to encryption at rest, securing data in transit is equally vital. Transport Layer Security (TLS) is a widely used protocol that protects communications over computer networks by enabling end-to-end encryption between clients and servers. When users enter their credit card information on an e-commerce site, TLS ensures that this sensitive data remains encrypted during transmission, thwarting potential interception by malicious actors. Adhering to such standards not only safeguards sensitive information but also signals a commitment to protecting client data.

For businesses handling personal health information (PHI), compliance with the Health Insurance Portability and Accountability Act (HIPAA) mandates strict adherence to specific encryption standards. HIPAA requires all electronic PHI to be encrypted during storage and transmission, offering guidelines on acceptable methods to ensure patient confidentiality. Non-compliance risks patient privacy and could result in significant fines and damage to reputation.

Beyond AES and TLS, organizations may also consider more sophisticated encryption protocols like Pretty Good Privacy (PGP) or Secure/Multipurpose Internet Mail Extensions (S/MIME) for securing email communications. These methods utilize asymmetric encryption techniques involving both public and private keys, providing a secure means of sending confidential messages over less secure channels like email.

Effective key management practices are critical for maintaining the integrity of encryption protocols. Businesses should implement secure systems for generating, storing, and managing encryption keys. Using hardware security modules (HSMs) enhances security by keeping cryptographic keys within dedicated hardware devices. Regularly rotating these keys further minimizes the risk of unauthorized access due to long-term exposure or compromised keys.

Real-world applications illustrate these principles well. Take a financial advisory firm that processes sensitive client investment data; by employing AES for data at rest and using TLS for online communications, the firm establishes a multi-layered defense against potential breaches. Additionally, training staff on proper key management ensures that employees know how to handle encryption keys safely.

Conducting regular audits of your encryption protocols is also essential; these assessments help identify vulnerabilities or areas for improvement in your security strategy. Evaluating compliance with relevant standards ensures adherence to regulations while enhancing overall security effectiveness.

Finally, as cybersecurity threats continually evolve, staying informed about emerging standards and best practices is crucial. Engaging with industry forums or consulting cybersecurity professionals can provide valuable insights into the latest advancements in encryption technology.

By understanding and effectively implementing these encryption protocols and standards, small business owners can build a robust framework that protects sensitive data while fostering client confidence. Investing in solid encryption measures not only secures business assets but also positions your organization as a trustworthy entity committed to high levels of data security in today's digital landscape.

Secure Data Storage Solutions

To effectively safeguard sensitive information, small businesses must prioritize secure data storage solutions that enhance their encryption strategies. In today's digital landscape, merely encrypting data is not enough; the methods of storing this data are equally crucial to its overall security.

Cloud storage has gained popularity among small businesses for its scalability and accessibility. However, the security of data stored in the cloud depends significantly on selecting reputable providers with strong security measures. When choosing a cloud service, businesses should seek options that offer end-to-end encryption, ensuring that data is encrypted before it leaves their premises and remains secure during transit and while stored on the provider's servers. For example, a small legal firm might opt for cloud services like Box or Dropbox Business, which feature built-in encryption and comply with regulations such as GDPR and HIPAA, effectively protecting sensitive client information throughout its lifecycle.

Beyond selecting the right provider, implementing strong access controls is essential. Role-based access control (RBAC) can limit data access to authorized personnel only, thereby reducing the risk of breaches. Within an organization, employees should have access only to the data necessary for their specific roles; for instance, members of a marketing team may need customer contact information but should not have access to sensitive financial records.

On-premises storage solutions also warrant consideration, especially for businesses handling highly sensitive data. Utilizing secure servers equipped with firewalls and intrusion detection systems can provide a robust defense against unauthorized access. These servers should be housed in physically secure locations—such as locked server rooms with restricted access—to further mitigate risks. A small healthcare practice might establish an internal server with stringent physical security measures alongside comprehensive cybersecurity protocols to protect patient records from both external and internal threats.

Data redundancy is another vital aspect of secure data storage. Regular backups ensure that information can be restored in the event of hardware failures or cyber incidents like ransomware attacks. A recommended approach is the 3-2-1 backup strategy: maintaining three copies of data across two different media types, with one copy stored off-site. This strategy ensures that even if primary storage fails or is compromised, multiple safe copies of critical data remain intact.

Compliance with relevant regulations is also essential in shaping data storage practices. Regulations such as the General Data Protection Regulation (GDPR) impose specific requirements on how personal data is stored and processed. By adhering to these regulations through secure storage solutions, businesses protect their clients and avoid potential fines for violations.

Regular security assessments can help identify vulnerabilities in existing storage solutions and ensure alignment with industry best practices. Take this example, conducting semi-annual audits can evaluate both physical and digital security measures surrounding stored data.

Finally, investing in employee training is crucial for maintaining data security within the organization. Staff should be educated on proper protocols for handling sensitive information and made aware of the risks associated with inadequate storage practices. A clear understanding of these policies fosters a culture of security awareness and accountability.

Establishing a robust framework for secure data storage not only protects sensitive information but also reinforces customer trust in your business. By prioritizing best practices —from selecting reliable cloud providers to implementing stringent access controls—small business owners can create an environment where valuable data remains protected against evolving cyber threats. This commitment positions your organization not only as compliant but also as a leader in responsible data stewardship within your industry.

Data Backup and Recovery Strategies

Creating effective data backup and recovery strategies is

vital for small businesses aiming to safeguard their critical information against unexpected disruptions. A well-designed backup plan ensures that operations can swiftly resume with minimal impact in the event of data loss—whether caused by hardware failures, cyberattacks, or natural disasters.

The first step in developing a solid backup strategy is to identify the data essential for business continuity. This encompasses not only customer records and financial documents but also operational data, such as emails, project files, and proprietary information unique to the business. Take this example, a small accounting firm might prioritize clients' financial statements and tax documents, warranting more frequent backups than less critical information.

Once essential data is identified, businesses should adopt a systematic approach to backups, such as the 3-2-1 strategy: maintain three copies of your data on two different types of storage media, with one copy stored off-site. This method minimizes the risk of total data loss. For example, a company might keep one backup on an external hard drive at the office, another in the cloud, and a third on a local server located elsewhere.

Cloud solutions have revolutionized how businesses manage data storage and backups. Many providers offer automatic backup features that can significantly simplify this process. Services like Google Drive or Microsoft OneDrive are excellent for scheduling daily backups of important files. However, it's crucial to choose cloud providers with robust security protocols and reliable uptime records, as this reliance necessitates careful selection. Understanding service-level agreements (SLAs) is essential for clarity regarding recovery times and responsibilities in case of data loss.

While cloud solutions are effective, having an on-premises backup adds an extra layer of security. Local storage options, such as Network Attached Storage (NAS), allow for quick recovery times when minimizing downtime is critical. For example, a local retailer might keep vital sales data backed up on NAS while also leveraging cloud storage for comprehensive disaster recovery.

Regularly testing backup systems is just as important as creating them. Routine restore tests confirm that backups function correctly and that all necessary data can be quickly retrieved when needed. Take this example, an IT manager at a small business could conduct a test restore of the most recent backup once every quarter to ensure there are no discrepancies or corrupt files that might complicate recovery efforts during an actual incident.

In addition to technical measures, establishing clear protocols for employees regarding data management is essential for minimizing human error—the leading cause of data loss. Providing training sessions on proper file-saving practices and emphasizing adherence to established protocols fosters a culture of accountability around data management.

Even with preventive measures in place, having a well-defined incident response plan is crucial should disaster strike. This plan should detail steps for swiftly restoring lost or compromised data while maintaining communication with stakeholders throughout the process. For example, if a retail business falls victim to ransomware, its incident response team should follow predefined procedures: isolate affected systems, notify customers about potential breaches if necessary, and begin executing the recovery plan.

establishing comprehensive backup and recovery strategies does more than protect against data loss; it cultivates resilience within the organization. By proactively implementing these strategies, small businesses not only mitigate risks but also enhance their reputation among clients who value reliability and professionalism in handling sensitive information. Investing time and resources into these processes empowers businesses to navigate unforeseen challenges confidently while ensuring continuity in their operations.

Data Loss Prevention (DLP) Tools

Data Loss Prevention (DLP) tools are a vital component of cybersecurity strategies for small businesses. Their primary purpose is to safeguard sensitive information from unauthorized access, leaks, or loss. As organizations increasingly rely on digital data, the risks associated with mishandling this information have escalated significantly. Small businesses, which often lack the extensive resources available to larger corporations, face unique challenges but can effectively leverage DLP solutions to bolster their security measures.

To begin with, it's crucial for businesses to identify what constitutes sensitive data. This can encompass customer information, payment details, proprietary business strategies, and employee records. Take this example, a small e-commerce operation must ensure that customers' credit card numbers and personal details are securely handled and stored. By pinpointing these critical data types, businesses can direct their DLP efforts where they are needed most.

Implementing DLP tools typically involves a combination of software and policies designed to monitor and control the flow of sensitive data both within and outside the organization. Many DLP solutions come equipped with real-time monitoring capabilities that can detect suspicious activities, such as unauthorized attempts to transfer sensitive files via email or cloud services. For example, if an employee tries to email a customer database without proper authorization, the DLP system can immediately alert IT personnel, preventing potential data breaches.

When selecting the right DLP solution, careful consideration of various factors is essential—such as ease of deployment, scalability, and compatibility with existing systems. Several popular DLP tools are available on the market, including Symantec Data Loss Prevention, McAfee Total Protection for Data Loss Prevention, and Digital Guardian. Each tool has its own strengths; for instance, Symantec offers robust endpoint protection while McAfee excels in comprehensive network monitoring options. Utilizing trial versions can help businesses assess which tool aligns best with their specific needs before making a commitment.

Effective policy implementation is equally important in ensuring that DLP tools function at peak efficiency. A well-defined policy should outline acceptable use of sensitive data and establish clear expectations regarding data handling among employees. Regular training sessions enhance understanding and adherence to these policies; consider scheduling quarterly workshops that review best practices for data handling along with updates on emerging cybersecurity threats.

Also, integrating DLP tools with other security measures helps create a multi-layered defense strategy. Take this example, combining DLP solutions with encryption technologies ensures that even if sensitive data is compromised, it remains unreadable without the correct decryption keys. This proactive approach minimizes potential damage from breaches by adding an additional layer of protection.

Regular audits are also critical in maintaining the effectiveness of DLP strategies. These audits assess whether policies are being followed and evaluate how well DLP tools are functioning in real-world scenarios. By analyzing logs generated by the DLP system, businesses can identify patterns indicating vulnerabilities or areas needing improvement. A case study involving a mid-sized healthcare provider demonstrated that consistent audits helped them uncover training gaps among employees that led to accidental data exposures.

Incorporating incident response protocols into your DLP strategy is another essential step in preparation for potential breaches. Should a breach occur despite preventive measures, having a response plan enables swift action to contain the situation and mitigate damages. For example, if an employee inadvertently sends sensitive data to an external party due to a phishing attempt, your incident response team should quickly notify all affected parties while investigating how the breach occurred.

adopting robust Data Loss Prevention tools not only fosters compliance with regulatory standards but also instills confidence among customers and stakeholders regarding their data's safety. Small businesses prioritizing DLP strategies demonstrate their commitment to safeguarding sensitive information—a stance that can significantly enhance their reputation in competitive markets.

Investing in effective DLP measures goes beyond merely checking off compliance boxes; it's about cultivating a culture where every employee understands their role in protecting valuable company assets. By equipping staff with knowledge and deploying advanced technology strategically, small business owners can navigate the complex landscape of cybersecurity more confidently—ensuring their operations remain resilient against emerging threats while safeguarding invaluable customer trust.

Protecting Data in Transit

Protecting data in transit is a critical component of an effective cybersecurity strategy for small businesses. Given that sensitive information often travels across both internal and external networks, it is particularly vulnerable to interception. Every time data is exchanged—whether through emails, cloud services, or online transactions—there's a risk of unauthorized access. Effectively addressing these vulnerabilities is essential for maintaining trust with customers and partners.

To begin with, implementing encryption protocols is fundamental. Encryption transforms readable data into an unreadable format, ensuring that only authorized parties can access it. One of the most widely used protocols for secure internet communications is Transport Layer Security (TLS). This technology encrypts data exchanged between web browsers and servers, making it nearly impossible for hackers to access sensitive information during transmission. For example, an online retailer that employs TLS can protect customer credit card details during checkout, safeguarding them from potential breaches.

Beyond encryption, utilizing Virtual Private Networks (VPNs) can further enhance data security in transit. A VPN creates a secure tunnel for data transmission, masking the IP address and encrypting the data packets being exchanged. That means even if someone intercepts data traffic on a public Wi-Fi network—a common target for cybercriminals—they would encounter only encrypted information rather than easily exploitable data. Small businesses with remote employees can particularly benefit from VPNs, ensuring safe access to company resources over unsecured networks.

Additionally, it's crucial to recognize the importance of secure file transfer protocols. Protocols such as Secure File Transfer Protocol (SFTP) and File Transfer Protocol Secure (FTPS) bolster the security of file sharing by encrypting both commands and data during transmission. Take this example, when a marketing team shares sensitive client files with external vendors, using SFTP ensures that even if those files are intercepted, they remain protected against unauthorized access.

Regular software updates and security patches are also vital in safeguarding data in transit. Vulnerabilities in outdated software can be exploited by cybercriminals to intercept unprotected data streams. For example, if a small business relies on outdated email software lacking the latest security features, attackers could exploit these weaknesses to gain access to sensitive communications. By keeping all systems updated—from email platforms to file-sharing applications—companies can minimize the risk of such exploits.

Establishing clear policies regarding data handling and sharing practices is essential for ensuring safe transit. Employees should receive training on what constitutes sensitive information and how to handle it appropriately in communication processes. Take this example, staff should be aware that sending confidential client information through unsecured channels like personal email accounts or unencrypted messaging apps poses significant risks.

Incorporating monitoring tools adds an additional layer of security for data in transit. These tools analyze traffic patterns and detect anomalies that may indicate breach attempts or unauthorized access. With real-time visibility into data flows, businesses can respond swiftly to potential threats before they escalate into serious incidents.

Conducting regular risk assessments helps identify vulnerabilities related to data transit within an organization's infrastructure. Small business owners should routinely evaluate their systems to ensure they adequately protect against interception risks and consider new technologies or methods that could enhance their current capabilities.

A real-world incident involving a small financial firm highlights the significance of these measures: after implementing robust encryption protocols and adopting SFTP for file transfers, they significantly reduced their exposure to potential breaches during sensitive transactions. Additionally, regular training sessions ensured that employees understood best practices for maintaining security throughout the communication process.

protecting data in transit goes beyond simply employing

technology; it requires fostering a culture of cybersecurity awareness within your organization. When every employee recognizes their role in safeguarding information as it traverses networks—through encryption techniques or responsible handling—the overall security posture strengthens significantly.

By prioritizing these strategies within your cybersecurity framework, small businesses can build confidence among clients and partners while safeguarding critical assets against increasingly sophisticated cyber threats. This commitment represents not just an investment in compliance but also in long-term trust and reputation within the marketplace.

Managing Encryption Keys

Managing encryption keys is a critical aspect of securing sensitive data within your organization. While encryption itself is vital for data protection, its effectiveness largely depends on the quality of key management. Inadequate practices can render even the strongest encryption vulnerable, undermining your security efforts.

Effective key management begins with a clear understanding of the encryption key lifecycle—from creation and storage to usage and eventual retirement. Keys must be generated using secure methods to ensure they cannot be easily predicted or reproduced by unauthorized users. Take this example, employing strong algorithms like AES (Advanced Encryption Standard) with key lengths of 256 bits or more adds complexity that makes brute-force attacks impractical.

Once generated, keys need to be stored securely to prevent unauthorized access. This often involves using hardware security modules (HSMs), which are dedicated devices designed for key management and cryptographic operations. HSMs protect private keys from software vulnerabilities. In contrast, storing encryption keys on a shared server can pose significant risks if that server is compromised. Investing in an

HSM can provide a much-needed layer of security.

Access controls are another essential element of effective key management. Implementing role-based access control (RBAC) ensures that only authorized personnel can access specific keys based on their roles within the organization. For example, a systems administrator might require access to certain keys for daily operations, while financial staff may need access to different keys for processing client transactions. This principle of least privilege minimizes exposure and helps reduce the risk of insider threats.

Regularly rotating encryption keys is also a best practice that enhances security. If a key were to be compromised, having a rotation policy in place would limit the potential damage by shortening the time an attacker has access. Take this example, if your business processes credit card transactions, implementing a key rotation policy every six months can mitigate risks associated with long-term key exposure.

In addition to rotation, maintaining detailed logs of all key management activities is crucial for auditing and compliance purposes. These logs provide insight into who accessed or modified encryption keys and when these actions took place. In the event of an incident, having comprehensive records enables you to quickly identify anomalies or unauthorized access attempts.

It's equally important to educate employees about the significance of encryption key management as part of your broader cybersecurity training programs. Staff should understand how mishandling or neglecting protocols can jeopardize data integrity. For example, if an employee shares an encrypted file without considering its sensitivity or the security measures surrounding the associated decryption key, it could lead to serious repercussions.

Consider a real-world scenario involving a healthcare provider that experienced data breaches due to poor key management practices. Although the organization had implemented strong encryption, it failed to enforce strict access controls around their decryption keys. When a disgruntled employee accessed these keys without proper oversight, they leaked sensitive patient data—an incident that could have been prevented with more stringent key management protocols.

effective encryption key management transcends technology; it requires integrating these practices into your organization's culture. When all team members recognize their responsibility in safeguarding keys—whether through secure storage methods or adherence to established policies—the overall security framework becomes significantly stronger.

By focusing on these strategies for managing encryption keys within your cybersecurity plan, small businesses can better protect their sensitive data while fostering trust among clients and partners. This proactive approach not only enhances data integrity but also positions your organization as a leader in cybersecurity best practices within your industry.

CHAPTER 6:
ENDPOINT SECURITY ESSENTIALS

Understanding Endpoint Security

U nderstanding endpoint security is essential for safeguarding your organization's overall cybersecurity posture. Individual devices—such as computers, smartphones, and tablets—serve as potential entry points for cyber threats. Therefore, protecting these endpoints is crucial for securing sensitive data and systems. As we explore this topic, it's important to realize that endpoint security goes beyond merely defending devices; it encompasses a comprehensive strategy that integrates seamlessly into your broader cybersecurity framework.

The foundation of effective endpoint security lies in recognizing the various types of endpoints within your organization. Laptops used by remote employees, smartphones containing company data, and even Internet of Things (IoT) devices like smart printers all contribute to this ecosystem. Each device presents unique vulnerabilities and requires tailored protection strategies. For example, a smartphone necessitates different security measures than a desktop computer due to its portability and usage patterns. An effective strategy acknowledges these differences while maintaining a cohesive approach to endpoint management.

Implementing robust antivirus and anti-malware solutions across all endpoints is a critical next step. These tools serve as the first line of defense against malicious software designed to exploit vulnerabilities. However, simply installing these solutions isn't sufficient; regular updates are essential for recognizing new threats. Consider the difference between antivirus software that updates its virus definitions weekly versus one that does so daily—the latter is far more likely to protect against emerging threats in real time.

Beyond software installation, securing endpoints requires clear policies around device usage. A thoughtfully executed Bring Your Own Device (BYOD) policy can be particularly effective. This policy allows employees to use personal devices for work while enforcing strict security guidelines, such as enabling device encryption and requiring password protection. This way, organizations not only secure business data but also empower employees with flexibility in their work arrangements.

Mobile Device Management (MDM) systems can play a pivotal role in enforcing these policies effectively. MDM enables organizations to monitor and manage employee devices remotely. Take this example, if an employee's phone is lost or stolen, an MDM solution allows the IT team to wipe all corporate data from the device instantly—mitigating the risk of sensitive information falling into the wrong hands.

Regular patching and software updates are another cornerstone of endpoint security that should never be overlooked. Cyber attackers often exploit known vulnerabilities in software applications to gain unauthorized access to networks. By establishing a routine schedule for applying patches—whether monthly or bi-weekly—you significantly reduce risks associated with unpatched vulnerabilities. Take a proactive approach by setting reminders or automating updates wherever possible.

Adding an extra layer of protection, Endpoint Detection and Response (EDR) solutions continuously monitor endpoints for suspicious activity. Unlike traditional antivirus software that relies primarily on signatures or known threats, EDR employs behavioral analysis to identify anomalies indicative of cyberattacks. For example, if an application on an endpoint suddenly begins accessing large amounts of sensitive data at odd hours—behavior typical of ransomware—the EDR system can alert your IT team before significant damage occurs.

Access controls further enhance endpoint security by ensuring only authorized users can access specific data or systems through their devices. Role-Based Access Control (RBAC) can limit access based on employee roles within the organization; for example, administrative personnel may have broader access compared to marketing staff who might only need access to relevant client databases.

When incidents occur, swift response is just as important as prevention strategies. Establishing clear protocols for addressing potential breaches ensures that when an endpoint is compromised, the organization can react efficiently and effectively. This could involve isolating affected devices from the network or executing incident response plans tailored for various scenarios—ranging from malware infections to unauthorized access attempts.

As you develop your endpoint security strategy, remember that employee education plays a crucial role in strengthening defenses against cyber threats at this level. Regular training sessions focused on identifying phishing attempts and understanding safe browsing practices empower team members to actively participate in protecting company assets rather than remaining passive observers.

To illustrate these concepts practically: imagine a mid-sized retail company where employees frequently use laptops both at home and on-site at stores across town. They faced significant risks due to varied usage environments—home networks might lack robust security measures compared to corporate networks. By implementing MDM solutions alongside strict access controls and ongoing employee training aimed at recognizing potential threats like phishing emails, this company significantly reduced instances of compromised accounts stemming from unsecured endpoints.

In summary, endpoint security embodies a multifaceted approach vital for any organization seeking effective protection of its digital assets—it requires ongoing attention and adaptation as new technologies emerge and threat landscapes evolve continuously. By implementing comprehensive protections tailored specifically for each type of endpoint while fostering a culture of security awareness among employees, organizations can build formidable defenses against cyber threats lurking just around every corner.

Antivirus and Anti-malware Solutions

Antivirus and anti-malware solutions are essential pillars of any effective cybersecurity strategy, especially when it comes to protecting endpoints. These tools act as the first line of defense against various forms of malicious software —including viruses, worms, spyware, and ransomware—that can jeopardize sensitive data and disrupt business operations. To effectively implement these solutions, organizations must have a nuanced understanding of their functions and how to integrate them seamlessly into their overall security architecture.

Choosing the right antivirus software is a critical step in this process. It goes beyond simply selecting a well-known brand; organizations must assess their specific needs. For example, a small graphic design firm will have different requirements than a healthcare provider managing sensitive patient information. A thorough evaluation of key features—such as real-time scanning, heuristic analysis for identifying unknown threats, and minimal impact on system performance—is vital. Additionally, opting for platforms with centralized management dashboards can significantly enhance oversight, allowing IT administrators to monitor security across all devices in real time and streamline response efforts.

Once antivirus solutions are in place, keeping them updated is equally important. Cyber threats are constantly evolving, and defenses must evolve alongside them. Take this example, consider the frequency with which malware signatures change; an antivirus that updates daily will be far more effective at detecting and neutralizing emerging threats than one that updates weekly. To ensure consistent protection, it's advisable to set regular updates to occur automatically, reducing reliance on manual intervention.

In addition to traditional antivirus tools, anti-malware solutions provide an added layer of security by addressing more complex forms of malware that standard antivirus may overlook. These programs often utilize behavioral analysis techniques to detect threats based on their actions rather than solely relying on known signatures. This capability is particularly beneficial for identifying zero-day vulnerabilities —exploits that can occur before developers have had the opportunity to release patches or updates.

To maximize protection, implementing a layered security strategy is essential. This approach involves deploying multiple complementary security measures rather than relying solely on antivirus software. Firewalls, intrusion detection systems (IDS), and intrusion prevention systems (IPS) work in tandem with antivirus and anti-malware tools to create a fortified network perimeter. Each layer addresses different aspects of potential threats, providing redundancy in case one measure fails.

Establishing clear guidelines for user behavior further enhances the effectiveness of these tools. Despite having advanced software in place, human error remains one of the most significant vulnerabilities in cybersecurity. Take this example, if employees frequently download unverified files or click on suspicious links without caution, even the best antivirus may struggle to keep pace with incoming threats. Providing training sessions focused on safe browsing habits can significantly mitigate risks associated with user behavior.

Consider a real-world scenario: a financial services company employs comprehensive antivirus solutions but lacks employee training on recognizing phishing attacks. An employee clicks a link in a fraudulent email and inadvertently downloads malware onto their device. In this case, ineffective user behavior combined with potentially insufficient anti-malware capabilities resulted in a breach that could have been prevented with proper training.

Regular audits of antivirus and anti-malware effectiveness are crucial for ensuring these systems remain robust against evolving threats. This may involve simulated attacks or penetration testing exercises designed to challenge current security measures and identify areas needing improvement. Engaging cybersecurity professionals for these evaluations can provide insights into emerging risks that may not be immediately visible from an internal perspective.

Incorporating threat intelligence into your security strategy enables organizations to stay ahead of emerging trends in malware development. By subscribing to threat intelligence feeds, businesses gain access to information about newly identified malware strains and prevalent attack vectors targeting similar organizations. This proactive approach enhances your ability to tailor antivirus configurations based on real-time data relevant to your industry.

To bolster defenses against sophisticated attacks, consider adopting advanced endpoint protection platforms (EPP) that combine traditional antivirus capabilities with modern features like machine learning-based threat detection and response automation. These platforms offer dynamic protection that adapts alongside new types of malware.

As you refine your strategy around antivirus and anti-malware solutions, it's essential to remember that technology alone cannot fully safeguard against cyber threats; fostering an organizational culture where cybersecurity is prioritized at every level—from the executive suite down to every employee —is equally important.

By taking these concerted steps—selecting appropriate software, maintaining updates, implementing layered defenses, educating employees, conducting regular audits, and leveraging threat intelligence—you create a resilient environment capable of defending against a wide array of cyber adversaries while ensuring continuity in operations amidst ever-evolving digital landscapes.

Securing BYOD (Bring Your Own Device) Policies

In today's business landscape, the Bring Your Own Device (BYOD) trend is gaining momentum. Employees often prefer using their personal devices for work due to the convenience and familiarity they offer. However, this trend also brings significant cybersecurity challenges that small business owners must address. Effectively securing BYOD policies is crucial for safeguarding sensitive data while promoting flexibility and productivity among staff.

To establish a robust BYOD policy, it is important to first understand the types of devices employees are likely to use. These can range from smartphones and tablets to laptops and even wearables, each presenting unique security challenges. Take this example, smartphones often lack the robust security features found in corporate devices, making them more vulnerable to malware and phishing attacks. Recognizing these risks is the essential first step in developing a comprehensive security strategy that mitigates potential vulnerabilities.

With a clear understanding of the devices in use, the next step is to define acceptable usage guidelines. This should cover aspects such as which applications can be downloaded, how company data may be accessed, and procedures for reporting lost or stolen devices. Implementing a mobile device management (MDM) solution can be particularly effective; it enables remote wiping of corporate data if an employee's device is compromised. Such measures not only protect sensitive information but also instill confidence among employees regarding data security.

Training is another critical component in the successful implementation of BYOD policies. Regularly educating employees about potential threats—such as phishing schemes or insecure Wi-Fi networks—can significantly reduce risks. Conducting workshops that simulate real-world scenarios helps employees recognize suspicious activity and respond appropriately, fostering a culture of vigilance within the organization.

Integrating multi-factor authentication (MFA) into your BYOD policy further enhances security. MFA requires users to provide two or more verification factors before accessing sensitive systems or information, greatly reducing the likelihood of unauthorized access, even if a password is compromised. This could involve sending a one-time code to an employee's phone each time they log in from an unfamiliar device.

Additionally, regular audits and updates are vital for maintaining an effective BYOD policy. Cyber threats evolve rapidly, making it essential to review and revise policies regularly. Establish specific intervals—perhaps quarterly or bi-annually—for comprehensive reviews of your BYOD protocols. Use these assessments to gauge compliance among employees, analyze incident reports, and refine training programs based on emerging threats.

Creating a feedback loop with employees regarding the BYOD policy is equally important. Encouraging staff to share their experiences and challenges when using personal devices for work-related tasks can provide valuable insights that may not have been considered during initial policy development. This input can help shape more practical guidelines that address real-world usage.

Securing BYOD policies goes beyond merely establishing rules; it involves fostering an environment where security is viewed as everyone's responsibility. By focusing on training, clear guidelines, technology integration, regular updates, and open communication, small businesses can effectively mitigate the risks associated with BYOD while enhancing employee satisfaction and productivity. Striking the right balance between flexibility and security is not only achievable but essential for thriving in today's digitally-driven world.

Mobile Device Management (MDM)

In today's workplace, where mobile devices are prevalent, establishing a comprehensive Mobile Device Management (MDM) strategy is essential. The integration of personal smartphones, tablets, and laptops into business operations has not only changed the way we work but has also introduced a range of security challenges. MDM offers a structured approach that enables small business owners to address these challenges effectively, ensuring sensitive data remains protected while allowing employees the flexibility to work from virtually anywhere.

At the heart of a successful MDM strategy is the ability to

manage and secure devices remotely. This involves deploying security policies and monitoring compliance with those guidelines. Take this example, an MDM solution empowers IT administrators to enforce encryption on devices accessing company data. Without encryption, lost or stolen devices could expose sensitive information to malicious actors. By mandating encryption for all devices, businesses can protect against unauthorized access, even in dire circumstances.

Application management is another crucial aspect of MDM. Employees frequently download various applications to enhance their productivity; however, not every app meets security standards or complies with corporate policies. A robust MDM system allows administrators to regulate which applications can be installed on work-related devices by whitelisting approved apps and blocking potentially harmful ones. For example, if your team uses a specific productivity app that aligns with security protocols, you can facilitate its installation while restricting access to less secure alternatives that could threaten your network.

Password management is another critical area where MDM plays an important role. Strong password policies form the backbone of access protection for company resources. MDM systems can enforce rules regarding password complexity and expiration, prompting employees to regularly update their passwords and thus reducing the risk of unauthorized access. Additionally, incorporating features like biometric authentication—such as fingerprint or facial recognition—can further bolster security without compromising convenience.

Maintaining device security over time requires regular updates and patch management, which are non-negotiable in today's fast-evolving cyber threat landscape. Keeping operating systems and applications up-to-date is essential for defending against vulnerabilities. An effective MDM solution allows businesses to automate software updates across all managed devices, ensuring that every employee's tools are equipped with the latest security patches.

Employee training is equally vital within an MDM framework. Despite having robust technology in place, human error remains one of the leading causes of data breaches. Comprehensive training programs should educate employees on best practices for mobile device use—including how to identify phishing attempts and recognize unsecured Wi-Fi networks during business travel. By fostering awareness around these threats, businesses empower their employees to serve as an additional layer of defense against potential breaches.

Finally, it's crucial to establish protocols for incident response when mobile devices are compromised. If an employee reports a lost or stolen device, swift action must be taken to prevent unauthorized access to sensitive information. Many MDM solutions offer remote wipe capabilities that enable IT teams to quickly and efficiently erase corporate data from lost devices—a vital step in mitigating risks associated with potential data leaks.

Implementing a successful Mobile Device Management strategy goes beyond simply installing software; it represents a holistic approach to securing organizational assets while embracing the flexibility that modern workplaces demand. By blending advanced technology with proactive employee education and robust policy enforcement measures, small business owners can confidently navigate the challenges posed by mobile device usage—an essential step toward fostering both security and productivity in today's dynamic environment.

Patching and Software Updates

A robust patch management strategy is essential for small businesses, particularly in an age of rapid technological advancement and increasingly sophisticated cyber threats. Neglecting software updates can leave systems vulnerable, making them easy targets for malicious actors. To safeguard their operations, small business owners must adopt a proactive approach, ensuring that their software remains secure and resilient against emerging threats.

To establish an effective patch management process, business owners should begin by inventorying all software and systems used within their organization. Creating a comprehensive list of installed applications and tracking their current versions is a crucial first step. For businesses operating across various platforms—from web servers to employee workstations—tools like Microsoft's System Center Configuration Manager (SCCM) or third-party solutions such as ManageEngine Patch Manager Plus can automate the inventory tracking and patch deployment processes.

Prioritizing updates based on the severity of vulnerabilities is vital for efficient resource allocation. Not all patches carry the same level of urgency; some address critical vulnerabilities that require immediate attention, while others might simply enhance features. Utilizing frameworks like the Common Vulnerability Scoring System (CVSS) can help businesses assess the risk associated with specific vulnerabilities and prioritize their patching efforts accordingly. Take this example, a small retail business facing an urgent security flaw in its payment processing system should prioritize that patch over routine updates for non-critical applications like employee productivity tools.

Establishing a regular schedule for applying patches is crucial for maintaining security without disrupting business operations. Implementing weekly or monthly patch cycles can help ensure consistent compliance. Effective communication about scheduled downtimes during updates can further minimize disruptions; notifying employees about system maintenance during off-hours allows them to plan accordingly, preserving productivity.

While timely application of patches is critical, testing them before widespread deployment is equally important. Incompatibilities or unforeseen issues can arise post-installation, potentially disrupting services or affecting system performance. Small businesses should create a testing environment where patches can be evaluated on non-critical systems before broad rollout. This practice reduces the likelihood of negative impacts on essential operations, particularly for organizations dependent on specific software functionalities.

User training also significantly enhances the effectiveness of patch management. Staff need to understand why updates are necessary and how they protect both individual and company data. Fostering a culture of awareness can drive compliance; consider hosting brief training sessions that highlight recent security incidents caused by outdated software, illustrating real-world consequences and underscoring the importance of timely updates.

Lastly, maintaining an audit trail of applied patches bolsters accountability and compliance reporting—critical factors for regulatory obligations in many industries. Automated systems often feature reporting capabilities that track which updates have been installed, when they were applied, and any exceptions made during the process.

To wrap things up, effective patch management demands diligence, structured processes, and ongoing communication across teams. By prioritizing updates, implementing thorough testing protocols, engaging employees through training initiatives, and keeping meticulous records, small businesses can significantly mitigate their risk exposure while fostering a culture of cybersecurity awareness. These integrated practices empower business owners to navigate an ever-evolving digital landscape with confidence, ensuring their systems remain secure against potential threats.

Endpoint Detection and Response (EDR)

Endpoint Detection and Response (EDR) is crucial for the cybersecurity strategies of small businesses, especially as cyber threats continue to evolve in sophistication. Traditional security measures alone are no longer adequate; EDR solutions provide a proactive framework that includes real-time monitoring, detection, and response specifically designed for endpoint devices such as computers, laptops, mobile devices, and servers.

Essentially of EDR systems is their ability to identify suspicious activities on endpoints. They continuously gather data from these devices and analyze patterns that may indicate malicious behavior. For example, if an employee inadvertently downloads a harmful attachment from an email, the EDR system can swiftly detect unusual activity related to that file and alert the IT team to intervene. This rapid identification of threats is essential, as early detection often enables quicker mitigation, potentially protecting the business from severe damage or data breaches.

To implement an effective EDR solution, the first step is selecting the right provider. Not all EDR tools offer the same level of protection; some provide more comprehensive features than others. Small business owners should carefully assess options based on factors like threat intelligence capabilities, ease of integration with existing systems, and vendor support. Popular tools such as CrowdStrike Falcon and SentinelOne stand out for their advanced analytics and user-friendly interfaces.

Once an appropriate EDR tool has been chosen, configuring it correctly is critical. This involves establishing security policies tailored to the specific needs of the organization. These policies dictate how alerts are generated and outline actions to be taken when potential threats are detected. Take this example, an e-commerce business that handles sensitive customer payment information might set a policy requiring immediate isolation of any device showing signs of compromise to safeguard critical data.

Another important aspect of EDR implementation is ensuring endpoint visibility. Effective EDR solutions provide detailed insights into endpoint health and activity logs. This level of visibility allows security teams to monitor not only current threats but also historical data that can highlight trends or repeated attacks targeting specific systems. If multiple alerts arise from a single device over time, it may signal an ongoing vulnerability that requires urgent attention before it escalates.

When responding to threats identified by an EDR system, it's essential to follow predefined protocols that are clearly communicated across teams. For example, if malware is detected on an endpoint, the response might include quarantining the affected device and conducting a forensic analysis to understand how the breach occurred. Additionally, documenting each step taken during incident response ensures thorough records for future reference and compliance purposes.

Training staff members is another vital component in maximizing the effectiveness of EDR technology. Employees should be made aware of how their actions can impact security measures. Regular training sessions can equip them to recognize phishing attempts and emphasize the importance of adhering to established security protocols—ultimately minimizing human error, which often contributes to breaches.

Also, fostering collaboration between IT teams and management is key to cultivating a culture of cybersecurity awareness throughout the organization. Sharing insights gained from incidents detected by EDR during company meetings or newsletters reinforces security principles among all staff members.

Finally, regularly testing and adjusting your EDR deployment is essential for maintaining its effectiveness over time. As cyber threats rapidly evolve, consistently evaluating your EDR's performance against emerging risks helps ensure robust defenses. Conducting simulations or tabletop exercises can offer valuable insights into how well your systems respond in various scenarios.

In summary, integrating Endpoint Detection and Response into a small business's cybersecurity strategy significantly enhances its ability to detect and respond to threats in real time. By carefully selecting appropriate tools, configuring them effectively, training employees thoroughly, and promoting collaboration within teams, small businesses can build a formidable defense against increasingly complex cyber threats. Embracing these practices not only secures assets but also nurtures a proactive cybersecurity culture that remains resilient against future challenges in the digital landscape.

Device Access Controls

Device access controls are a cornerstone of any cybersecurity strategy, especially for small businesses that may not have extensive IT resources. These controls act as the first line of defense against unauthorized access to sensitive data and critical systems. As cyber threats become increasingly sophisticated, establishing strong device access protocols is essential.

To begin implementing effective device access controls, it's crucial to identify what needs protection. This process starts with mapping all devices connected to your network, including computers, smartphones, tablets, and even IoT devices like printers and smart thermostats. Each of these devices can serve as a potential entry point for attackers if they are not properly monitored or secured. Conducting a thorough inventory will help you understand your attack surface and facilitate the implementation of necessary access restrictions.

After identifying your devices, it's important to apply the

principle of least privilege. This security concept ensures that users only have the minimum level of access required to perform their job functions. For example, a marketing employee should not have administrative access to financial records or sensitive customer databases. By implementing role-based access control (RBAC), you can tailor permissions based on user roles within the organization, significantly reducing the risk of data breaches.

The configuration of device settings also plays a vital role in securing access. Disabling USB ports on employee computers can prevent unauthorized data transfers and block malware that may come from infected external drives. Additionally, enforcing strong password policies across all devices helps mitigate risks associated with compromised credentials. Passwords should be complex and changed regularly; consider using password managers to streamline this process.

Multi-factor authentication (MFA) adds another layer of security by requiring users to verify their identity through multiple methods before accessing systems. This could include a combination of something they know (like a password), something they have (like a smartphone app), or something they are (such as biometric recognition). Even if passwords are stolen, MFA serves as an additional barrier against unauthorized access.

Regular monitoring and logging of device activity are essential for identifying potential security incidents early. By tracking who accesses which devices and when, you can detect unusual patterns that may indicate an attack or policy violation. Take this example, if an employee accesses sensitive data outside regular hours or from an unrecognized location, this behavior should trigger alerts for further investigation.

To enhance monitoring capabilities, consider employing endpoint management solutions that provide real-time visibility into device statuses and user activities across the network. These tools enable IT teams to verify compliance with security policies and take corrective actions when necessary—such as applying patches or restricting access until issues are resolved.

Training employees is another critical component in effectively enforcing device access controls. Often, employees inadvertently compromise security by neglecting protocols or falling victim to social engineering attacks like phishing scams. Regular training sessions should cover topics such as recognizing phishing emails and adhering to company policies regarding sensitive information management and device usage.

In addition to technical training, fostering a culture where cybersecurity is viewed as everyone's responsibility promotes vigilance among employees. Encouraging team members to report suspicious activities or security concerns helps create an environment where proactive measures become second nature.

Finally, conducting periodic reviews and updates of device access policies ensures that your organization remains responsive to evolving threats and changes in workforce dynamics—such as new hires or shifting roles within the company. Regular audits not only confirm compliance with established protocols but also provide opportunities for improvement based on recent developments in the cybersecurity landscape.

By implementing effective device access controls, you lay a solid foundation for your overall cybersecurity posture. Clearly defining what needs protection, applying robust configurations, utilizing MFA, maintaining comprehensive monitoring practices, thoroughly training staff, and regularly reviewing policies can significantly minimize vulnerability to cyberattacks while safeguarding critical assets against future threats in an ever-changing digital environment.

Securing Internet of Things (IoT) Devices

Securing Internet of Things (IoT) devices has become a critical priority for small businesses grappling with the complexities of cybersecurity. As smart devices proliferate—ranging from connected cameras and smart thermostats to industrial sensors—the potential attack surface has expanded dramatically. Each IoT device can introduce vulnerabilities that, if overlooked, may jeopardize the entire network.

The journey to securing IoT devices begins with a comprehensive inventory of all connected devices. This process involves not just identifying what devices are present, but also understanding their functions and the types of data they handle. An outdated or unmonitored device can serve as a weak link in your security chain. Take this example, a smart printer left with default manufacturer settings can become an easy target for attackers. By cataloging each device and assessing its role within your organization, you can prioritize which ones require more stringent security measures.

Once your inventory is complete, implementing network segmentation becomes essential. Dividing your network into distinct segments allows IoT devices to operate on separate channels from critical business systems. For example, placing IoT devices on a dedicated subnet limits their access to sensitive data and systems, thereby reducing the potential impact of a breach. If an IoT device were compromised, attackers would find it significantly more difficult to access core business applications and databases.

Updating firmware regularly is another critical step that cannot be overstated. Many IoT manufacturers release updates designed to patch known vulnerabilities. Neglecting to keep these devices up to date leaves them exposed to exploits that hackers can easily exploit. Establishing a routine for firmware checks ensures that your devices run on the latest security patches and features, making it harder for malicious actors to take advantage of weaknesses.

In addition to updates, incorporating strong authentication practices adds another layer of protection against unauthorized access. Many IoT devices come with default usernames and passwords that are widely known or easily guessable. Changing these credentials to unique, complex combinations significantly reduces the likelihood of unauthorized users gaining control over the device. Also, implementing multi-factor authentication (MFA) for accessing administrative settings enhances security even further.

Monitoring IoT network traffic is also crucial for early identification of potential threats. By deploying intrusion detection systems (IDS) or network monitoring tools, you can observe unusual patterns in data flow that may indicate malicious activity. Take this example, if a thermostat suddenly begins sending large amounts of data outside normal operating hours or at odd intervals, this could signal an intrusion attempt worthy of investigation.

Equally important is providing employee training on the secure use of IoT devices. Staff should be equipped with the knowledge to manage these devices effectively and recognize potential threats associated with them. Training sessions could cover best practices such as avoiding unsecured public Wi-Fi when accessing company IoT devices and reporting any suspicious activities they encounter.

Another often-overlooked aspect is establishing clear policies for personal IoT device usage within the workplace. Employees may bring their own smart devices under a Bring Your Own Device (BYOD) policy without adequate protections in place. Defining strict guidelines around what types of personal devices can connect to the business network—and ensuring they adhere to robust security measures—can significantly mitigate risks.

Finally, as technology continues to evolve, regularly reviewing and updating your IoT security strategy must remain a priority. Cyber threats are not static; they rapidly change as new vulnerabilities are discovered and exploited by attackers. Conducting periodic risk assessments will help identify emerging threats and enable your organization to adapt accordingly.

As you navigate the landscape of IoT security, remember that each device represents both convenience and risk. By committing to ongoing monitoring, timely updates, comprehensive training, and robust policy enforcement, you create a resilient environment where innovation can thrive without compromising security integrity. A proactive approach today ensures your small business is well-prepared for tomorrow's evolving cyber threats related to IoT technologies.

Responding to Endpoint Breaches

Responding to endpoint breaches is a critical aspect of an organization's cybersecurity framework. When an endpoint is compromised, swift action is essential to contain the threat and mitigate potential damage. Understanding how to respond effectively can significantly reduce the impact of such incidents on your small business.

Establishing an incident response plan is the first step in this process. This plan should outline specific procedures for identifying, investigating, and responding to breaches. A well-defined protocol enables your team to act quickly and decisively. It's beneficial to assign roles within your team; for instance, designating a lead investigator can streamline decision-making during a crisis. This individual serves as the primary contact for all communications related to the incident, ensuring that everyone remains aligned.

When a breach occurs, rapid identification of the issue becomes paramount. Implementing robust monitoring tools can help detect unusual behaviors or unauthorized access attempts at endpoints. For example, if an employee's laptop starts transmitting large amounts of data at odd hours—behavior that deviates from typical usage patterns—it may signal a security breach. Automated alerts can facilitate quicker detection, allowing your team to respond before significant damage occurs.

Once an anomaly is identified, the next crucial step is isolating the affected endpoint. Disconnecting the device from the network prevents further access by attackers and halts any ongoing data exfiltration. This isolation can involve physically unplugging the device as well as disabling its network connection through software controls. By quarantining the device, you protect sensitive data and limit potential spread across your network.

After isolation, conducting a thorough investigation into the breach is vital. This process involves analyzing logs and system activity to determine how the compromise occurred and which vulnerabilities were exploited. Documenting every finding during this phase is essential; it not only aids in understanding the attack vector but also prepares your organization for any legal or regulatory obligations that may arise post-incident.

Once you've assessed the extent of the breach, it's time to eradicate threats from your systems. Removing malware or unauthorized access points requires meticulous attention —simply deleting malicious files may not be sufficient if backdoors remain open or configurations are altered for future exploitation. Tools like antivirus software and endpoint detection response (EDR) solutions can be invaluable in this stage, as they often provide automated remediation options tailored to specific threats.

Recovery is another critical stage that requires careful planning. Restoring affected systems from secure backups ensures that you return to normal operations without reintroducing vulnerabilities exploited during the breach. It's wise to validate these backups before restoration—checking their integrity and confirming that they are free from compromise.

Communicating about a breach is often overlooked but plays a crucial role in maintaining trust with employees and customers alike. Transparency regarding what occurred —while safeguarding sensitive details—can foster confidence in your commitment to cybersecurity practices. Establish clear communication channels to inform stakeholders about actions taken in response to the incident and steps being implemented to prevent future occurrences.

Finally, once recovery efforts have concluded, conducting a post-incident review or retrospective analysis becomes essential. Gathering insights into what went wrong allows organizations not only to improve their security posture but also to strengthen their incident response plan for future scenarios. Discussing these findings with your team provides opportunities for training improvements; addressing knowledge gaps exposed by real-world incidents enhances readiness against future attacks.

In summary, responding effectively to endpoint breaches demands preparation rooted in proactive strategies combined with real-time reactions when incidents occur. Each step —from detection through investigation and recovery—is interconnected; enhancing one aspect invariably supports another within your overall cybersecurity framework. By committing resources toward developing comprehensive incident response capabilities today, you equip your small business with resilience against tomorrow's evolving cyber challenges.

CHAPTER 7: IDENTITY AND ACCESS MANAGEMENT (IAM)

The Basics of IAM

U nderstanding the fundamentals of Identity and Access Management (IAM) is crucial for any small business owner looking to enhance cybersecurity. IAM encompasses the policies, technologies, and processes that ensure the right individuals have appropriate access to technology resources. By implementing IAM effectively, you not only protect sensitive data but also streamline operations and improve compliance with regulations.

Access controls are another critical aspect of IAM, dictating who can access specific resources based on predefined permissions. One widely used approach is Role-Based Access Control (RBAC), where permissions are assigned according to roles rather than individual users. For example, a marketing employee may need access to customer data and marketing tools, while an IT technician requires administrative access to network configurations. By implementing RBAC, you minimize risks by ensuring employees only have access to the information necessary for their job functions.

Authentication methods also play a significant role in verifying user identities before granting access. Strong authentication mechanisms enhance security by requiring users to provide more than just a username and password. Multi-Factor Authentication (MFA) exemplifies this strategy; it adds layers of security by asking users for something they know (like a password) alongside something they possess (such as a mobile device). This combination makes it considerably more difficult for malicious actors to gain unauthorized access.

Establishing robust password policies is another best practice within IAM. Encourage employees to create complex passwords and implement guidelines for regular updates. For example, passwords should include a mix of uppercase letters, lowercase letters, numbers, and special characters while avoiding easily guessable information like birthdays or common words. Additionally, consider using password managers to help users generate and securely store complex passwords.

Beyond technology implementations, fostering a culture of security awareness within your organization is crucial for effective IAM practices. Regular training sessions can empower employees by educating them about phishing attacks or social engineering tactics aimed at compromising their credentials. Involving your team in discussions about IAM policies enhances buy-in and promotes responsible behavior regarding data handling.

Managing the user lifecycle—encompassing onboarding, role changes, and offboarding—is another vital aspect of IAM. New employees should be provisioned with appropriate access immediately upon their start date. Conversely, when someone leaves the company or changes roles within it, timely revocation of their access is essential to protect sensitive data from potential threats.

Monitoring access logs provides valuable insights into user activities within your systems. Implementing logging solutions helps detect unusual patterns or unauthorized attempts to access sensitive information. Regular audits of these logs can identify irregularities that may indicate security breaches or compliance issues.

Lastly, aligning IAM strategies with compliance requirements is imperative for small businesses operating in regulated industries such as healthcare or finance. Regulations like GDPR and HIPAA impose strict rules on data protection; integrating IAM solutions that ensure compliance mitigates legal risks while strengthening your overall cybersecurity posture.

In summary, mastering the fundamentals of Identity and Access Management equips small business owners with the tools necessary to safeguard their digital assets effectively. By understanding user identities, implementing robust access controls, enforcing strong authentication measures, fostering security awareness among employees, managing user lifecycles diligently, monitoring activities closely, and aligning strategies with regulatory demands—all these facets significantly contribute toward building a resilient organizational framework against cyber threats. The proactive steps you take today will yield lasting benefits as you navigate an increasingly complex digital landscape tomorrow.

Implementing Strong Password Policies

Implementing strong password policies is a crucial first step for small businesses looking to enhance their cybersecurity framework. Passwords are often the first line of defense against unauthorized access to sensitive information, and weak or compromised passwords can expose businesses to significant risks. Therefore, it is essential to establish comprehensive guidelines that prioritize both strength and security.

A robust password policy should require the use of complex passwords. Encouraging employees to create passwords that contain at least twelve characters, including a mix of uppercase and lowercase letters, numbers, and special symbols, is key. Take this example, "G@rden2023!" is much stronger than "password123." A strong password not only needs to be lengthy but also unpredictable; personal identifiers like names or birthdays can make it easier for attackers to guess passwords using social engineering tactics.

Regular updates to passwords are also vital. Implementing a schedule that requires employees to change their passwords every three to six months can help maintain security. To ease this process, consider recommending password managers. These tools generate complex passwords and securely store them, alleviating the burden of memorization. Employees can use options like LastPass or 1Password to create unique logins for every service while retaining easy access.

While complexity and periodic changes are important, they are just part of the solution. Multi-Factor Authentication (MFA) should be a key component of your security strategy. MFA adds an extra layer of security by requiring users to verify their identity through more than one method. For example, after entering a password, an employee might receive a text message with a verification code that must be entered for access. That means even if a password is compromised, gaining entry would still be challenging for an attacker without the secondary verification method.

Education is essential in enforcing strong password policies. Regular training sessions help employees understand the importance of these measures. Sharing real-world examples of companies that suffered breaches due to weak passwords can highlight the consequences of non-compliance. Incorporating phishing simulations into your training curriculum can further equip employees to recognize suspicious emails aimed at harvesting their credentials.

Managing user credentials also requires strict protocols for onboarding and offboarding employees. New hires should receive login credentials that meet company standards as soon as they start work. Conversely, when employees leave or change roles within the organization, prompt revocation of access rights is necessary. This practice not only protects sensitive data but also ensures compliance with industry regulations.

Monitoring user activity is another critical practice in maintaining effective password security. Tools that log access attempts and track failed login attempts can alert you to potential breaches before they escalate into serious issues. Regular audits of these logs provide insights into user behavior and help identify irregularities—such as repeated failed login attempts—that may indicate malicious intent.

For businesses operating under regulatory frameworks like GDPR or HIPAA, aligning password policies with compliance requirements is essential. Regulations often mandate specific security measures; failing to comply can lead to hefty fines and damage to your reputation. Ensure that your policies address these requirements while incorporating best practices in cybersecurity.

establishing strong password policies goes beyond merely setting rules; it involves fostering a culture of security awareness within your organization. By emphasizing the importance of secure passwords and providing ongoing education and support, you empower employees to take ownership of their digital safety. These proactive steps will not only create a solid foundation for your overall cybersecurity strategy but also significantly reduce vulnerabilities in today's ever-evolving threat landscape.

The commitment you make today toward rigorous password protocols will protect your organization against future cyber threats. As small business owners navigate this complex digital age, prioritizing strong password practices serves as both a shield against attacks and a step toward building a resilient enterprise capable of thriving amid uncertainty.

Multi-Factor Authentication (MFA)

Multi-Factor Authentication (MFA) serves as a vital security layer, significantly enhancing the protection of sensitive information for small businesses. While strong passwords provide a foundational level of security, MFA acts as a crucial barrier against unauthorized access. Its implementation not only strengthens defenses but also aligns with best practices in cybersecurity, underscoring a commitment to safeguarding assets from ever-evolving threats.

One effective way to implement MFA is through mobile authentication apps like Google Authenticator or Authy. These applications generate time-sensitive codes that are challenging for attackers to intercept. Alternatively, hardware tokens such as YubiKeys enhance security by requiring physical possession of the device for access. These methods not only bolster security but also foster confidence among employees and customers regarding the integrity of your systems.

Integrating MFA into existing systems is generally straightforward, as most platforms today support it as part of their security features. Take this example, popular cloud services like Microsoft 365 and Google Workspace offer built-in MFA options that can be activated with minimal effort. By enabling these features across all critical accounts, you create multiple barriers for potential intruders.

Education plays a crucial role in the successful adoption of MFA. Employees need to understand the importance of this additional layer of protection and how it works. Regular training sessions should include demonstrations on setting up MFA on their accounts and recognizing signs of phishing attempts aimed at compromising credentials. Sharing real-life scenarios where MFA has successfully thwarted attacks can emphasize its significance.

Establishing clear guidelines regarding when and where MFA is required is equally important. Critical systems containing sensitive data should always enforce multi-factor verification, while less critical applications may not necessitate such stringent measures. This risk-based approach helps strike a balance between user experience and essential security protocols.

Regular reviews of your MFA policies are essential to ensure they remain effective against emerging threats. Periodic audits can help identify gaps in implementation or compliance issues that need attention. For example, if certain employees consistently bypass MFA due to system misconfigurations, prompt corrective actions should be taken to reinforce security standards.

Challenges may arise during implementation, particularly if employees view MFA as an inconvenience. Addressing these concerns directly is crucial; emphasizing the role of MFA in protecting both company and personal data can help shift perceptions, encouraging employees to see it as an indispensable tool rather than an added burden.

And, consider extending MFA requirements beyond internal users. Clients accessing sensitive information online should also be encouraged—or even required—to use MFA for their accounts whenever possible. This not only secures their interactions with your business but also builds trust and demonstrates your commitment to cybersecurity.

In today's landscape of digital threats, embracing Multi-Factor Authentication positions your small business as a proactive leader in cybersecurity practices. As you implement these strategies, remember that each step you take fortifies your organization's defenses against potential breaches while fostering an environment where security is prioritized at every level.

 integrating MFA transcends mere technology; it's about cultivating a culture where security awareness becomes second nature among both employees and clients. By taking these steps now, you are investing in a safer future—one where robust authentication processes safeguard not just data but also the very foundation of your business operations against evolving threats.

Role-Based Access Control (RBAC)

Role-Based Access Control (RBAC) is a crucial strategy for managing user permissions and securing sensitive information in small businesses. By assigning access rights based on an individual's role within the organization, RBAC simplifies security protocols and reduces the risk of unauthorized access to critical data and systems.

To implement RBAC effectively, it is essential to first understand your organization's structure and job functions. Begin by identifying all roles within your business and their corresponding responsibilities. Roles can range from specific titles like "marketing coordinator" to broader categories such as "executive." Once these roles are established, define the resources each one requires to perform its functions effectively.

For practical implementation, consider adopting a centralized identity and access management system that supports RBAC. Many cloud services offer this functionality, allowing you to create roles and assign permissions through an intuitive interface. Platforms like Okta or Azure Active Directory provide robust tools for seamlessly managing user identities and permissions across applications.

After assigning access rights based on roles, it's vital to regularly review these assignments. Changes in personnel—whether through promotions, role shifts, or departures—can lead to outdated permissions that may expose your business to risk. Conduct periodic audits of user access rights, with quarterly reviews being a common practice, to ensure that permissions remain aligned with current responsibilities.

Education plays a critical role in successfully implementing RBAC. Employees need to understand why certain restrictions are in place and how they contribute to overall organizational security. A well-informed team is less likely to seek workarounds that could compromise data integrity. Consider hosting training sessions that emphasize the importance of data protection while providing practical demonstrations on securely accessing resources.

Challenges may arise during the implementation of RBAC, particularly in companies with limited resources or less formalized structures. Employees might feel frustrated by what they perceive as barriers to accessing necessary information for their roles. Addressing these concerns openly is essential; clearly communicate how RBAC safeguards sensitive data while facilitating efficient workflows.

To further bolster security measures, incorporate automated tools that alert administrators about suspicious access patterns. For example, if an employee attempts to access sensitive files outside of regular hours or from an unusual location, an alert can trigger an investigation before any potential damage occurs. This proactive approach not only reinforces the effectiveness of RBAC but also demonstrates your commitment to maintaining a secure environment.

Extending RBAC beyond internal staff can also enhance your cybersecurity posture. If external partners or vendors require limited access for collaboration, configure temporary roles with specific permissions tailored for those situations. This approach allows you to maintain control over your systems while still enabling necessary business interactions without compromising security.

Integrating Role-Based Access Control represents a strategic investment in protecting your small business's most valuable assets: its data and reputation. By establishing clear boundaries around who can access what information, you are not only adhering to best practices but also fostering a culture of security awareness throughout your organization.

As cyber threats continue to evolve, having robust access controls in place offers peace of mind and positions your business as one that prioritizes accountability and responsibility in safeguarding sensitive information. With clearly defined and monitored roles, you pave the way for a more resilient organizational structure—one prepared to tackle today's challenges and tomorrow's uncertainties head-on.

Identity Verification Techniques

Identity verification techniques are essential for establishing a strong cybersecurity framework in any small business. By ensuring that only authorized individuals can access sensitive data and systems, these methods significantly reduce the risk of unauthorized breaches and help maintain the integrity of your operations. As organizations increasingly transition to digital frameworks, effective identity verification has become a critical necessity rather than an optional measure.

The first step in strengthening identity verification is to adopt robust authentication methods. Relying solely on a single password can leave your business vulnerable to breaches. Multi-Factor Authentication (MFA) adds layers of security that require more than just a username and password for access. Take this example, combining something you know (like a password), something you have (such as a mobile device), and something you are (like biometric data) greatly enhances security. Tools like Google Authenticator or Authy can generate time-sensitive codes for an extra layer of verification.

Transitioning from traditional username/password

combinations to MFA may seem intimidating at first. To ease this process, begin by identifying which systems need enhanced security measures most urgently—prioritize high-value areas such as financial accounts or sensitive client databases. Implement MFA in these critical areas before expanding it to less sensitive systems. This phased approach allows for troubleshooting and feedback, preventing users from feeling overwhelmed.

In addition to MFA, biometric authentication offers a cutting-edge layer of security that utilizes unique physical traits, such as fingerprints or facial recognition, for identity verification. Technologies like Apple's Face ID or fingerprint sensors provide seamless user experiences while significantly bolstering security protocols. The strength of biometrics lies in their uniqueness; even if unauthorized parties gain access to user credentials, they cannot replicate physical characteristics.

To effectively implement biometric solutions, conduct a thorough evaluation of available technologies that meet your organization's needs and budget. Considerations should include not only hardware investments but also privacy regulations—securing user consent and protecting data associated with biometric identifiers is crucial.

Another effective method of identity verification involves using digital certificates. These electronic credentials verify the identities of users and devices within your network. Digital certificates utilize public key infrastructure (PKI) to secure communications by enabling encryption and authentication during transactions or information exchanges. For example, when employees log into secure applications using digital certificates instead of passwords, you reduce reliance on easily compromised access methods.

Establishing internal policies around identity verification is vital for consistency throughout your organization. Clear guidelines should outline how identity verification occurs at various levels—from employee onboarding procedures to regular access reviews for existing staff members. This structured approach not only promotes adherence to security standards but also prepares your team for audits or regulatory compliance checks.

Ongoing education about identity verification techniques is crucial for fostering a culture where cybersecurity practices are understood and embraced by all employees. Regular training sessions should cover how identity theft occurs, the importance of strong authentication practices, and the potential impacts on both personal and organizational levels when security measures are neglected.

Additionally, consider conducting simulated phishing attacks within your organization to raise awareness about common tactics employed by cybercriminals targeting identity credentials. Demonstrating how quickly an attack can occur and its repercussions on individual roles and overall business operations will help employees understand the necessity of robust identity verification measures.

As small businesses navigate an increasingly complex digital landscape rife with cybersecurity threats, adopting comprehensive identity verification techniques is imperative —not merely as a compliance requirement but as a proactive strategy for safeguarding against evolving risks. By layering different methods such as MFA, biometric solutions, and digital certificates while embedding education into your organizational culture, you strengthen your defenses against unauthorized access.

The measures taken today to enhance identity verification do more than protect data; they cultivate trust among clients who expect businesses to prioritize their privacy and sensitive information rigorously. This trust, in turn, translates into stronger business relationships and reputational integrity —critical elements for thriving in today's competitive marketplace where every advantage matters.

Privileged Access Management (PAM)

Privileged Access Management (PAM) plays a vital role in protecting your organization's sensitive data and systems. A key aspect to understand as we explore this concept is that not all users require the same level of access. The principle of "least privilege" is fundamental in cybersecurity; it ensures that users are granted only the access necessary to perform their job functions. This approach not only minimizes the potential attack surface but also reduces the risk of data breaches.

To implement PAM effectively, start by identifying your organization's most sensitive data and systems. For example, if you manage customer financial information or proprietary business data, these assets demand enhanced security measures. Next, classify users according to their roles and responsibilities to determine who genuinely needs elevated privileges. Regular user accounts should handle day-to-day operations, while administrative tasks should be conducted under controlled conditions.

With a clear understanding of access requirements, the next step is to establish strong authentication mechanisms. Multi-Factor Authentication (MFA) is crucial, as it adds an essential layer of security by requiring users to provide multiple forms of verification before accessing sensitive information. This can include something they know (like a password), something they have (like a smartphone for an authentication app), or something they are (like biometric verification). Implementing MFA for accounts with elevated privileges significantly reduces the risk of unauthorized access.

Once user authentication is secured, focus on session management. With PAM solutions in place, you can monitor and control privileged sessions in real time. Take this example, when a system administrator logs into a server for configuration changes, it's important to have the capability to actively observe that session. This monitoring allows for immediate intervention if any suspicious activity arises. Additionally, session recording serves dual purposes: it aids in compliance and offers valuable training insights. Reviewing recorded sessions helps establish best practices among employees and highlights common mistakes that could lead to vulnerabilities.

Another crucial element of PAM is implementing a privileged access vault—a secure repository for credentials associated with elevated access rights. This eliminates the need for users to remember complex passwords or keep them written down insecurely. When access to these credentials is required, users must request permission through an auditable workflow, ensuring that every action is tracked and logged. By centralizing password management, you significantly reduce the likelihood of weak passwords being used across accounts.

Regular audits are essential to maintaining an effective PAM strategy. These reviews should assess not only who has access but also how that access is being utilized. Establish a routine for reviewing permissions—ideally quarterly or biannually— so that if certain accounts show signs of inactivity or are not being used as intended, their privileges can be revoked promptly.

Equally important is educating your team about PAM policies and practices. Conducting training sessions that emphasize the principles of least privilege and the risks associated with over-privileged accounts can help foster a culture of security awareness within your organization. Using real-world case studies can make these risks more tangible by illustrating scenarios where improper access could lead to significant consequences.

Integrating PAM solutions with other security measures can further enhance your organization's overall cybersecurity posture. For example, linking PAM tools with Security

Information and Event Management (SIEM) systems provides better visibility into user behavior and incident response capabilities. These systems work together seamlessly; if an anomalous action occurs under a privileged account—such as an unusual login time or location—automatic alerts can be triggered.

By prioritizing Privileged Access Management within your cybersecurity framework, you are proactively addressing one of the most significant threats facing businesses today: insider threats and misuse of elevated privileges. Implementing robust PAM practices not only protects sensitive data but also cultivates trust among customers and partners by demonstrating a commitment to security.

Managing User Access Life Cycle

Managing the user access life cycle is essential for effective cybersecurity, especially in small businesses where resources and personnel are often limited. This process involves everything from creating user accounts to eventually deactivating access, all while safeguarding sensitive information. To build a strong user access life cycle management system, it's important to understand the key stages: provisioning, modifying, and de-provisioning.

The first stage, provisioning, requires a standardized procedure for creating user accounts. New hires should go through an onboarding process that sets up their accounts with appropriate permissions tailored to their roles. This can be facilitated through a simple questionnaire or checklist outlining the resources and data they need access to. For example, a marketing associate may require access to customer relationship management (CRM) software but not to financial records. Automating this process can save time and enhance accuracy; identity management software can expedite user account deployment while ensuring compliance with your organization's security policies.

Next comes the modification stage, which is vital when employees change roles within the company. Take this example, a software developer transitioning to a project manager will need different access levels than they had as a coder. Conducting regular reviews of user roles is essential —if access rights aren't updated promptly, it could create unnecessary vulnerabilities. Clear communication between departments is crucial here; HR should work closely with IT to ensure that any personnel changes are swiftly reflected in user permissions. Implementing role-based access control (RBAC) can further streamline this process by linking specific roles directly to pre-defined permissions.

The final stage of managing the user access life cycle is de-provisioning, which becomes especially critical when employees leave the organization or undergo significant role changes. Delays in revoking access can lead to significant risks, such as former employees accessing sensitive data long after their departure. Establishing an exit protocol that triggers automatic account deactivation upon termination or resignation is advisable. A thorough offboarding checklist should include tasks like recovering company-issued devices and ensuring all digital access is revoked before the employee's last day.

Throughout these stages, meticulous documentation is vital. Keeping track of who has access to what—and why—is not just about compliance; it's about creating an auditable trail that can quickly identify potential security gaps. Take this example, conducting regular audits of user accounts can uncover anomalies such as inactive accounts retaining elevated privileges or users assigned unnecessary permissions over time.

In addition to these practices, leveraging technology solutions can significantly enhance your ability to manage user access effectively. Single Sign-On (SSO) systems simplify the login process while maintaining robust security controls across various platforms—employees need only one set of credentials for multiple services. Also, integrating Multi-Factor Authentication (MFA) ensures that even if credentials are compromised, unauthorized access remains difficult.

Training staff on the importance of managing user access is equally crucial. Regular sessions that emphasize the risks associated with poor account management—such as social engineering attacks or data breaches—reinforce the importance of adhering to established protocols. By fostering a culture where every team member understands their role in safeguarding sensitive information, you reduce the likelihood of human error leading to security breaches.

As organizations grow and evolve, so must their approach to managing user access life cycles. Staying proactive in reviewing policies and utilizing technology not only strengthens security but also enhances operational efficiency within your business ecosystem. By implementing these measures, you'll create a resilient infrastructure that protects against unauthorized access while enabling your team members to perform their jobs effectively and securely.

Regular IAM Audits

Regular IAM audits are essential for sustaining an effective identity and access management system. These audits act as checkpoints to ensure that access controls remain relevant and secure over time. In a small business, where personnel changes can occur frequently and resources may be limited, establishing a routine for these evaluations is critical to mitigating risks associated with unauthorized access.

A successful IAM audit begins with clear criteria for assessing user access. Start by defining what constitutes appropriate access for each role within your organization. This process involves mapping out job functions and identifying the data necessary for employees to perform their duties effectively.

For example, a financial analyst requires access to budgeting software and sensitive financial reports but should not have permissions related to marketing campaigns. Regularly updating these role definitions ensures that access rights align with current business needs.

Conducting the audit involves collecting data on all user accounts, their assigned roles, and the resources they can access. Automation tools can simplify this process by tracking permissions across systems and generating reports that reveal who has access to what. This makes it easier to identify discrepancies or outdated permissions. Take this example, if a user retains access to confidential documents after changing departments, this could present a significant security risk. Regular audits help identify such anomalies quickly.

An important aspect of IAM audits is reviewing compliance with policies regarding role changes and terminations. When employees switch roles or leave the company, their access must be adjusted accordingly. Failure to do so can result in lingering permissions that unnecessarily expose sensitive information. Implementing automated alerts for changes in employment status can streamline this process; notifying IT or HR teams when updates are needed allows for prompt action and minimizes oversight.

Additionally, verifying compliance with regulations and industry standards relevant to your business is critical during the audit process. Many organizations must adhere to specific legal requirements concerning data protection and user privacy. For example, if your business handles personal data under GDPR guidelines, ensuring that only authorized personnel have access to such information is not only best practice but also a legal obligation. Regular audits help confirm compliance and provide documentation in case of regulatory inquiries.

Post-audit analysis is equally important. After reviewing

user accounts and permissions, convene stakeholders from various departments to discuss findings. This collaboration fosters a security-first culture within your organization while facilitating knowledge sharing about best practices and potential vulnerabilities identified during the audit. Encourage open dialogue about how users perceive current access policies; insights from front-line employees often highlight practical concerns that may not be evident from data alone.

In addition to formal audits, integrating continuous monitoring into your IAM strategy can offer real-time insights into user behavior patterns and anomalies that may signal security threats. Tools leveraging machine learning can analyze login attempts and flag unusual activities—such as an employee logging in from an unfamiliar location at odd hours —which may warrant further investigation.

Finally, using the results of your IAM audits as a foundation for training initiatives is vital for enhancing cybersecurity awareness throughout your organization. After each audit cycle, consider hosting workshops or briefings to share findings with staff members. Discussing the real-world implications of improper access management reinforces the importance of vigilance among employees at every level.

Establishing regular IAM audits is not merely about compliance; it's about fostering a culture of accountability surrounding data security within your small business. By implementing systematic evaluations of user access rights, engaging employees in discussions about their roles in safeguarding information, and utilizing technology effectively, you create an environment where cybersecurity becomes an integral part of daily operations—not just an afterthought or a box-checking exercise.

CHAPTER 8: DEVELOPING A COMPREHENSIVE SECURITY AWARENESS PROGRAM

Importance of Security Awareness

S ecurity awareness is more than just a technical necessity; it's a cultural imperative that lays the groundwork for a resilient organization. For small businesses, where each employee plays a vital role in cybersecurity, grasping the importance of security awareness can mean the difference between vulnerability and strength. Employees often serve as the first line of defense against cyber threats, and their actions—or lack thereof—can significantly impact the business.

To illustrate this point, consider that nearly 90% of data

breaches result from human error, according to a recent study. This statistic highlights the need to cultivate an environment where security is prioritized and woven into daily routines. When employees are aware of potential threats and understand their role in mitigating risks, they become proactive participants in your cybersecurity strategy rather than passive observers. This shift not only enhances overall security but also fosters a sense of ownership among team members.

Building this culture effectively begins with integrating security awareness into the onboarding process for new hires. During orientation, share not only the company's mission but also its commitment to cybersecurity. Discuss real-life incidents that have affected other businesses, focusing on how human actions or lapses led to those breaches. By making these stories relatable, you create context that resonates with employees and emphasizes why their vigilance matters.

In addition to onboarding, ongoing training sessions are crucial. Regular workshops can cover various topics such as phishing attacks, password management, and safe internet practices. Each session should blend theoretical knowledge with practical exercises; for example, simulating phishing attempts allows employees to recognize suspicious emails firsthand. One company implemented quarterly phishing tests and observed a 60% reduction in susceptibility over six months as employees honed their ability to spot red flags.

Beyond structured training, creating an easily accessible repository of resources related to cybersecurity best practices is beneficial. This could include infographics on identifying phishing scams or checklists for safe online behavior. Such resources empower employees to seek guidance independently when faced with something suspicious or confusing.

Fostering open dialogue about cybersecurity is equally

essential. Establishing channels for employees to report potential threats or share concerns promotes transparency and trust within your organization. An anonymous reporting system allows employees to voice worries without fear of repercussions and can lead to valuable insights about vulnerabilities you might not have identified otherwise.

Engaging leadership in promoting security awareness is another key component. When management visibly prioritizes cybersecurity—whether through regular updates at team meetings or participation in training—it signals that security is not solely an IT issue but a collective responsibility shared by everyone.

Feedback mechanisms following training sessions can further enhance your efforts by assessing understanding and identifying areas that need reinforcement. Surveys or informal discussions can reveal which topics resonated most with employees and which ones require further clarification or deeper exploration.

Instilling security awareness requires continuous reinforcement through real-world application and discussions about current threats facing your industry. Highlighting recent breaches involving competitors serves as a powerful reminder of why vigilance is necessary; linking these incidents back to specific actions employees can take reinforces their learning.

As your organization matures its approach to security awareness, consider developing internal champions— employees passionate about cybersecurity who are willing to advocate for best practices among their peers. These advocates can help bridge gaps between IT departments and other teams, ensuring that everyone understands their role within the broader context of organizational security.

 fostering a culture of security awareness transforms your workforce into active defenders against cyber threats rather than passive victims waiting for an incident to occur. A well-informed team that recognizes its responsibility plays an invaluable role in safeguarding sensitive information while simultaneously enhancing customer trust—a critical component for any thriving small business today.

Embracing this mindset creates an atmosphere where everyone feels empowered and equipped to contribute toward robust cyber hygiene practices every day—a necessity as digital threats continue evolving at unprecedented speeds.

Designing Training Programs

Designing an effective security training program requires a multifaceted approach that not only imparts essential information but also engages employees in a meaningful way. By tailoring the training to the specific context of your business and its unique threats, you ensure that the material resonates with staff, empowering them to take proactive measures. The aim is not merely to achieve compliance; rather, it is to cultivate a mindset in which security is integrated into everyday decision-making.

Begin by assessing your organization's specific needs. Consider factors such as employee roles, existing knowledge levels, and inherent vulnerabilities related to your business model. Take this example, a retail company may prioritize protecting customer data, while a tech startup might focus on safeguarding intellectual property. Involving employees in this assessment can reveal insights that a top-down approach might overlook; they can share challenges they face daily that may not be immediately apparent to management.

Once you've identified these needs, curate training content that is both relevant and engaging. Storytelling is particularly effective in this context—real-world examples of security breaches can vividly illustrate the consequences of inadequate cybersecurity. For example, discussing high-profile incidents like the 2013 Target breach highlights how seemingly minor oversights can lead to significant repercussions. Such stories capture attention and create memorable lessons.

To accommodate diverse learning styles, vary your training formats. Combine traditional presentations with interactive workshops, gamified learning modules, and online courses designed for remote teams. Take this example, a gamified approach might include simulations where employees identify phishing attempts or respond to cyber incidents. This not only reinforces key concepts but also fosters teamwork as employees collaborate to solve scenarios together.

Hands-on activities are invaluable for deepening understanding. Consider organizing "hackathons" where staff can learn about vulnerabilities by attempting to breach simulated systems in a controlled environment. This practical experience demystifies cybersecurity concepts and provides participants insight into the mindset of potential attackers.

Another innovative strategy involves peer-led training sessions. Identify individuals within your organization who possess strong knowledge of cybersecurity topics and empower them to lead discussions or workshops for their colleagues. Peer learning nurtures camaraderie and provides relatable perspectives—employees may feel more comfortable discussing challenges with someone who understands their daily routines.

Effective training programs should also include regular updates to keep content fresh and responsive to emerging threats. Given that cybersecurity is an ever-evolving landscape, short modules focusing on current issues should supplement foundational knowledge established earlier in training sessions. Monthly newsletters summarizing new types of threats or recent breaches relevant to your industry can efficiently reinforce awareness without overwhelming employees.

Assessing the effectiveness of your training is crucial for

continuous improvement. Utilize metrics such as employee quiz scores after trainings or track incident reports before and after implementing new strategies; this will provide tangible evidence of success or reveal areas needing further attention. Conducting anonymous surveys about comfort levels with various topics allows you to refine focus areas based on employee feedback.

Finally, integrating cybersecurity discussions into regular team meetings underscores its importance beyond dedicated training sessions alone. When managers address security practices alongside project updates or performance reviews, it signals that cybersecurity is a core component of overall business health.

An engaging training program does more than inform—it transforms employees into advocates for security awareness within your organization, turning them from passive recipients of information into active participants in protecting sensitive data against evolving threats each day. Establishing this culture fosters resilience while simultaneously enhancing trust among customers who rely on your commitment to safeguarding their information.

successful design lies not only in imparting knowledge but also in fostering a community where every member feels equipped and responsible for maintaining strong security practices—essential elements as small businesses navigate an increasingly complex digital landscape filled with potential pitfalls waiting around every corner.

Cybersecurity Workshops and Seminars

Cybersecurity workshops and seminars are vital tools for enhancing your team's security awareness. These events not only deliver essential information but also create an interactive environment that encourages employees to engage with the material actively. The objective is to foster an immersive experience that cultivates a deep understanding of cybersecurity principles, integrating them into the organizational culture.

To begin planning an effective workshop, it's crucial to clarify your specific objectives. Are you focusing on phishing awareness, data protection, or incident response? Defining these goals will guide your content development. For example, if phishing poses a significant risk to your business, you might design the seminar around real-life examples of successful phishing attempts in other organizations. Incorporating interactive exercises that allow employees to identify suspicious emails can make the training both relevant and impactful.

Choosing the right speakers can significantly boost the effectiveness of your workshops. Consider inviting external experts who can share insights based on their field experiences. A cybersecurity consultant, for instance, may offer a fresh perspective on emerging threats or best practices tailored to your industry. Additionally, having internal team members share their experiences can enhance relatability; an employee recounting how they identified a potential security threat can inspire others to remain vigilant.

Structuring your workshops in a variety of formats can cater to different learning preferences and maintain participant engagement. Combining presentations, group discussions, and hands-on activities creates a dynamic learning environment. For example, after a brief lecture on data encryption, participants could break into small groups to practice encrypting and decrypting sample files using tools like VeraCrypt or AxCrypt. This practical application reinforces theoretical concepts and builds confidence in using these tools effectively.

Utilizing technology can expand your reach further. Virtual seminars allow remote teams or employees from various locations to participate without the need for travel. Platforms like Zoom or Microsoft Teams enable breakout sessions where smaller groups can delve into specific topics or engage in role-playing exercises related to incident response scenarios. Incorporating polls and quizzes during these sessions not only adds an element of fun but also helps gauge understanding in real-time.

Providing attendees with actionable takeaways is essential for ensuring immediate implementation of what they've learned. Create checklists or quick-reference guides summarizing key points discussed during the event. Take this example, after a session on strong password policies, distribute handouts outlining best practices for creating and managing passwords —complete with tips on effectively using password managers like LastPass or Dashlane.

Gathering feedback is critical for continuous improvement and enhancing the impact of future workshops. Distributing anonymous surveys at the end of each session allows you to collect participants' thoughts on content relevance and delivery effectiveness. Questions might include "What was the most valuable aspect of this workshop?" or "What topics would you like us to cover next?" This feedback loop demonstrates that you value employee input and helps refine future training initiatives.

Establishing follow-up activities can further reinforce what was learned during workshops and seminars. Implementing monthly cybersecurity challenges encourages employees to apply their knowledge creatively—through simulated phishing attempts or by identifying security vulnerabilities in mock scenarios tailored to your organization's context.

By cultivating a community around cybersecurity within your organization, you transform each employee into an advocate for security awareness. As they gain confidence in their understanding of cyber threats and protective measures, they shift from passive recipients of information to proactive defenders against potential attacks. This cultural shift not only enhances overall resilience but also reassures customers that their data is protected by a knowledgeable and committed team.

hosting regular workshops strengthens individual skill sets while significantly contributing to building a robust cybersecurity framework within your business—one where every team member feels empowered to actively contribute toward creating a safer digital environment as threats continue to evolve.

Phishing Simulations

Phishing simulations are an effective way to enhance your organization's cybersecurity posture. They provide an interactive and practical method for training employees to recognize and respond to phishing attempts, which are among the most prevalent and damaging cyber threats faced by small businesses today. By integrating these simulations into your training program, you create an engaging learning experience that translates into real-world vigilance.

To implement effective phishing simulations, begin by defining the exercise's parameters. Identify your target audience within the organization, which may include everyone from new hires to seasoned employees. Tailoring the complexity of the simulation according to experience levels ensures that all participants find value in the exercise. Take this example, junior employees might engage with simpler scenarios focused on recognizing basic phishing techniques, while more experienced staff could encounter sophisticated schemes that employ social engineering tactics.

One practical approach is to utilize phishing simulation software, such as KnowBe4 or PhishMe. These tools allow you to design custom phishing emails that mimic real threats your employees might encounter. Start by crafting a series of emails incorporating common elements of phishing attempts, such as urgency or fear-based messaging. For example, you might send an email that appears to be from IT requesting urgent password updates or a notification about an overdue invoice requiring immediate attention. The aim is to assess how many employees fall for these traps and how they react upon realizing they've been targeted.

After executing the simulations, it's essential to analyze the results thoroughly. Track metrics such as open rates, click-through rates, and reporting behavior. If a significant percentage of employees fail to identify the phishing attempts, it signals a need for further training. This data not only provides insights into individual performance but also highlights broader organizational weaknesses in cybersecurity awareness.

Following each simulation, conduct debriefing sessions to discuss outcomes and lessons learned. These meetings should foster a constructive atmosphere rather than a punitive one. Focus on providing feedback and encouraging knowledge sharing. Highlight specific phishing techniques used in the simulations, analyze why certain employees were deceived, and promote open discussions on recognizing similar threats in the future. This collaborative learning experience can cultivate a culture of awareness where employees feel safe discussing their mistakes without fear of reprimand.

To enhance engagement during these debriefing sessions, consider incorporating gamification elements. You could create friendly competitions where teams earn points for correctly identifying phishing emails or promptly reporting simulated attacks. This approach reinforces learning while motivating employees to remain vigilant in real-world situations.

For lasting effectiveness, regular phishing simulations should become a cornerstone of your security awareness program. The frequency can vary; some organizations conduct them monthly while others opt for quarterly exercises. The key is consistency—regular exposure keeps phishing awareness fresh in employees' minds and reinforces best practices over time.

After each simulation cycle, update your training materials based on emerging trends observed during the exercises. Phishing tactics evolve rapidly; keeping your content relevant ensures your team remains equipped to tackle new threats head-on. For example, if you notice an increase in spear-phishing attempts targeting high-level executives, consider developing specialized training focused on protecting sensitive information at that level.

 phishing simulations do more than teach employees how to recognize threats—they empower them with the confidence to act decisively when confronted with suspicious communications. As they become more adept at spotting red flags, they play a crucial role in building a security-conscious culture within your organization.

By integrating these simulations into your cybersecurity framework, you create an environment where every employee participates in safeguarding sensitive information. As you nurture this sense of ownership over security practices, you are not just mitigating risks; you're fostering a proactive stance against cyber threats that could jeopardize your business's success and reputation.

Creating an Incident Reporting Culture

Establishing a culture of incident reporting is essential for an effective cybersecurity strategy. When employees feel empowered to report incidents without fear of repercussions, security transforms into a shared responsibility. This culture not only encourages transparency but also fosters proactive engagement—both critical elements for any organization seeking to strengthen its defenses against cyber threats.

To cultivate this culture, begin by clearly defining what

constitutes a cyber incident within your organization. Your definition should encompass everything from minor phishing attempts to significant data breaches. Providing specific examples will help employees recognize the types of incidents they might encounter in their daily tasks. Take this example, if an employee receives a suspicious email requesting sensitive information, they should understand that this is a reportable incident.

Once you've outlined what incidents to report, it's important to streamline the reporting process itself. An accessible and straightforward mechanism for reporting is crucial. Consider establishing multiple channels for reporting—such as an online form, a dedicated email address, or even a direct line to the IT department. These channels should be user-friendly and encourage prompt reporting. For those hesitant to come forward due to fear of judgment or repercussions, implementing an anonymous reporting system can provide reassurance.

Effective communication plays a vital role in promoting this culture. Regularly remind employees of the importance of incident reporting through internal communications like newsletters, team meetings, and training sessions. Use these opportunities to highlight real-world incidents that have affected similar organizations and illustrate their operational impact. Sharing such stories raises awareness and underscores the necessity of immediate reporting.

Training is another crucial component in nurturing an incident reporting culture. Conduct workshops that focus on identifying potential threats and understanding the correct procedures for reporting them. Role-playing scenarios can be particularly beneficial; they allow employees to practice recognizing suspicious activities in a supportive environment. For example, simulate a scenario where an employee encounters malware during their workday—how should they respond? What steps should they take?

Following up on reported incidents further reinforces this culture. When employees see that their reports lead to meaningful action—such as improved security measures or new protocols—they are more likely to continue reporting in the future. Communicate the outcomes of investigations into reported incidents and provide updates on any changes made as a result of employee feedback. This transparency builds trust and encourages ongoing participation.

Additionally, consider incentivizing timely reports as part of your strategy. Recognition programs can motivate employees who actively report incidents or contribute positively to cybersecurity practices within your organization. Take this example, you might implement monthly awards for individuals or teams demonstrating exceptional vigilance regarding security measures.

Establishing metrics can also help gauge the effectiveness of your incident reporting culture over time. Track how many incidents are reported, and analyze response times and outcomes associated with those reports. If you notice an increase in reported incidents following these initiatives, it indicates that employees feel more comfortable coming forward—a positive sign that your efforts are making an impact.

Finally, regularly review and refine your approach based on staff feedback and changes in the cybersecurity landscape. As threats evolve, your policies and training materials must also reflect new risks and realities facing your organization.

When every employee actively participates in fostering this culture of incident reporting, you create a robust framework that significantly enhances your organization's overall security posture while promoting a shared commitment to safeguarding sensitive information against cyber threats.

Engaging Management in Awareness

Engaging management in cybersecurity awareness is crucial for fostering a company-wide commitment to security practices. Leadership plays a pivotal role in shaping how cybersecurity is viewed within the organization. When executives prioritize security awareness, it reverberates throughout the workforce, encouraging every employee to recognize their responsibility in maintaining security.

To begin, involve management in the development of cybersecurity training programs. When leaders take part in crafting these initiatives, they lend credibility to the message and underscore its importance. For example, consider organizing a brainstorming session with your executive team to identify key areas of concern and relevant scenarios specific to your industry. This approach not only empowers management but also enriches the training content with insights drawn from real threats faced by the organization.

Additionally, integrating cybersecurity discussions into regular management meetings reinforces its significance. Allocate specific time on the agenda for cybersecurity updates and concerns. During these discussions, share recent developments regarding cyber threats, internal incidents, and improvements in security measures. Presenting data on phishing attempts targeting your sector can illustrate the necessity of vigilance among all staff members. This ongoing dialogue keeps security at the forefront of managerial priorities and encourages leaders to champion these initiatives within their teams.

Leadership should also model desired behaviors related to cybersecurity. When managers consistently adhere to security protocols—such as using strong passwords or participating in training sessions—they send a powerful message to their teams. Their actions set a benchmark for employees, helping to cultivate a culture where security best practices are integrated into daily routines. Take this example, if department heads regularly remind their teams about password hygiene or secure file-sharing methods, these behaviors become normalized and are established as organizational standards.

Recognizing and rewarding management involvement can further enhance engagement in cybersecurity initiatives. Consider developing an incentive program that acknowledges leaders who actively promote cybersecurity awareness within their departments. This could include recognition during company-wide meetings or awards for innovative initiatives that strengthen security practices. By creating positive reinforcement around management-level efforts in cybersecurity, you encourage sustained commitment across all leadership tiers.

Effective communication is essential for aligning managerial priorities with organizational goals related to cybersecurity awareness. Utilize various channels—such as emails, newsletters, and intranet postings—to disseminate important information in a way that resonates with managers' specific contexts. Tailor messages to emphasize how cybersecurity impacts overall business performance and operational continuity; for instance, highlight how a strong security posture can prevent costly breaches that might disrupt operations or harm reputations.

Encouraging management to participate in cybersecurity workshops and seminars alongside employees fosters a sense of unity around security initiatives and reinforces shared responsibility for safeguarding the organization's assets. Scenario-based training can be particularly effective; it allows leaders to see firsthand how decisions impact security outcomes while equipping them with tools to guide their teams effectively.

Also, addressing incidents that arise from employee reports is vital for broader awareness efforts led by management.

When leaders openly discuss reported issues—explaining what occurred and what corrective actions were taken—they not only inform employees but also reinforce that their input is valued and contributes to meaningful change.

To maintain momentum, consider integrating cybersecurity metrics into overall business performance evaluations for managers. Metrics such as incident response times or completion rates for mandatory training can serve as tangible indicators of how well teams engage with security protocols under their leadership.

creating a culture that values cybersecurity begins with engaged management; this commitment influences every aspect of an organization's approach to risk mitigation and responsiveness to threats. By embedding these principles into daily operations and decision-making processes at all leadership levels, you foster an environment where every employee feels empowered to take proactive measures against cyber risks. This collective mindset not only enhances resilience against attacks but also promotes a commitment to protecting sensitive information throughout the organization.

Measuring Training Effectiveness

Measuring the effectiveness of your cybersecurity training program is essential for enhancing your organization's resilience against cyber threats. Conducting training sessions alone is insufficient; evaluating their impact is crucial to ensure that employees are not only absorbing information but also applying it in their daily tasks. A well-structured measurement strategy not only highlights successes but also identifies areas for improvement, fostering a culture of continuous learning.

To start, establish clear, measurable objectives for your training initiatives. Consider what you want employees to achieve after the training, whether it's recognizing phishing attempts, adhering to proper password protocols, or understanding data protection policies. These goals should align with your overall cybersecurity strategy and address the specific risks your organization faces. Take this example, if recent assessments indicate a high prevalence of phishing attempts within your industry, your training objectives should prioritize awareness and response strategies related to these threats.

One effective method for measuring the impact of your training is through pre- and post-training assessments. These evaluations can take the form of quizzes or scenario-based questions tailored to the content covered in the training sessions. By comparing results from before and after the training, you can quantitatively gauge how much knowledge has been gained. For example, if a group of employees scores an average of 60% on a quiz before training and improves to 85% afterward, this suggests that the session successfully imparted knowledge.

Real-world simulations are another powerful tool for evaluating training outcomes. Conduct phishing simulation exercises where employees receive mock phishing emails designed to mimic actual threats. Track metrics such as the percentage of employees who clicked on links or reported suspicious emails. This method provides valuable insight into employee awareness and helps refine training content based on observed behaviors. If a significant number of employees fall for simulated phishing attempts, it indicates a need for increased focus in this area.

Feedback surveys following training sessions can yield qualitative data about participants' experiences and perceptions. Ask employees about the clarity of the information presented, any challenges they encountered, and suggestions for improvement. This direct feedback can inform future training iterations and help tailor programs to better meet employee needs. Additionally, consider conducting focus groups to explore specific topics or challenges that arise frequently during discussions.

Engagement metrics are also crucial in assessing effectiveness. Monitor attendance rates at training sessions and participation levels during workshops or discussions. While high attendance may indicate interest, low engagement during activities—evident through minimal interaction or feedback—can reveal a disconnect between content delivery and employee comprehension or interest.

Beyond individual performance assessments, it's important to evaluate broader organizational impacts by analyzing security incident reports over time. A decrease in incidents following a comprehensive training program focused on specific vulnerabilities suggests that employees are effectively applying their knowledge in real-world scenarios. Conversely, if incidents remain steady or increase despite ongoing training efforts, it may be necessary to revisit your content or delivery methods.

Establishing benchmarks is key to measuring ongoing effectiveness. Regularly review metrics such as incident response times and compliance rates with security protocols; these indicators can reveal whether your cybersecurity culture is improving over time. Setting goals for these metrics— such as reducing response times by 20% within six months —creates accountability within teams while emphasizing the importance of continual vigilance.

An effective cybersecurity training program should evolve alongside technology and emerging threats; regular assessments ensure that it remains relevant and impactful. By integrating evaluation practices into routine operations, you foster a proactive approach to learning and reinforce the idea that cybersecurity is an ongoing commitment shared across all levels of your organization.

By consistently measuring and refining your training efforts based on data-driven insights and employee feedback, you cultivate an environment where awareness becomes second nature—a crucial asset in effectively navigating today's complex cyber landscape.

Updating Programs Regularly

As your organization evolves, so too must your cybersecurity training programs. Regular updates to these initiatives are not merely advisable; they are essential. The cyber threat landscape is in constant flux, with new vulnerabilities and attack methods emerging frequently. To effectively combat current threats, your training program must adapt, ensuring that employees are equipped with the latest knowledge and skills.

Begin by identifying specific areas where your training could use a refresh. Analyzing recent security incidents within your industry or organization can provide valuable insights. Take this example, if a new type of malware becomes widespread, it's crucial to include information on how to recognize and respond to it in your training. Staying informed through cybersecurity news sources and industry reports will help you keep abreast of these developments. Regularly updating content not only reinforces existing knowledge but also instills confidence in your team, assuring them that they are armed with relevant information.

A practical approach to implementing updates is to conduct periodic reviews of training materials—ideally on a quarterly basis. Involving various stakeholders, such as IT personnel, management, and frontline employees who participate in the training, can uncover gaps or highlight outdated elements. For example, if there are changes in password management policies due to technological advances or new regulatory requirements, ensure that employees receive timely training on the updated protocols.

Incorporating lessons learned from real-world incidents can also enhance the learning experience. Case studies of notable breaches—like the Target data breach—can help contextualize theoretical concepts for employees, illustrating the potential consequences of inadequate cybersecurity practices. Sharing these stories during training sessions emphasizes the real-world implications of their actions.

To further engage employees and improve retention, consider integrating interactive training methods. Gamification elements can make learning more enjoyable; for instance, quizzes that award points for correct answers or friendly competitions among departments based on response times during simulated phishing attempts foster teamwork and active participation.

Additionally, varying the formats of your training sessions can keep content fresh and engaging. While traditional presentations have their place, incorporating multimedia elements—such as videos or podcasts—can cater to different learning styles. A concise video explaining the importance of two-factor authentication may resonate more with employees than a lengthy lecture on its technical details.

As you update content, ensure that post-training assessments evolve as well. Pre- and post-assessment questions should reflect any new threats or changes in policies. These assessments should not only measure knowledge retention but also evaluate employees' abilities to apply what they've learned in practical scenarios. Well-designed scenario-based assessments can reveal whether employees understand how to recognize and respond appropriately in various situations.

Maintaining an ongoing feedback loop is critical for ensuring your programs remain relevant. After each session, solicit employee feedback regarding clarity, engagement levels, and applicability of the content to their daily tasks. Analyzing trends over time will help you identify areas that may need adjustment; if feedback consistently highlights certain aspects as ineffective or confusing, make those changes promptly.

Finally, emphasize that cybersecurity awareness is an ongoing journey rather than a one-time event. Encourage discussions around cybersecurity topics through forums or newsletters where recent threats can be openly discussed and lessons shared across teams.

By keeping your cybersecurity training programs up-to-date, you not only ensure compliance with evolving regulations but also cultivate a culture of vigilance within your organization —a culture where every employee feels empowered to actively contribute to a secure digital environment. This continuous evolution strengthens overall organizational resilience against emerging threats while fostering a proactive workforce capable of navigating today's complex cyber landscape effectively.

CHAPTER 9: INCIDENT RESPONSE AND MANAGEMENT

What Constitutes a Cyber Incident?

A cyber incident is more than just a technical glitch; it can severely disrupt business operations, tarnish reputations, and result in substantial financial losses. For small business owners, grasping the essence of what constitutes a cyber incident is essential. Being proactive in cybersecurity strategies is far more effective than waiting for an incident to occur. Essentially, a cyber incident arises when there is an unauthorized access attempt or a security breach that compromises the confidentiality, integrity, or availability of information systems.

The range of cyber incidents is vast. On one end of the spectrum are minor breaches—like an employee inadvertently clicking on a phishing email that exposes login credentials. On the other end are major incidents, such as ransomware attacks, where hackers encrypt your data and demand payment for its release. Each type of incident carries varying degrees of severity and requires distinct responses. Take this example, while an unintentional data exposure may call for immediate internal communication and monitoring, a ransomware attack necessitates a far more comprehensive response involving law enforcement and possibly legal counsel.

Recognizing the signs of a cyber incident can be intricate. Symptoms can manifest in various ways, from sluggish system performance to unusual network activity or unexplained access attempts on accounts. These red flags often indicate something is wrong. For example, if your team discovers files that are missing or altered without explanation, it could signal unauthorized access. Establishing a baseline for normal network activity can significantly enhance your ability to detect any deviations that may suggest a potential incident.

It's also crucial to differentiate between incidents and events. An event refers to any observable occurrence within a network or system—whether it's routine user login activity or the failure of hardware components. Not every event qualifies as an incident; however, if an event raises concerns about potential harm to your systems or data, further investigation is warranted. For example, multiple failed login attempts from an unknown IP address should prompt scrutiny and possibly immediate security measures.

Once an incident has been identified, timely response becomes critical. It's not just about acknowledging that something has gone wrong; it's about having established protocols to address the situation effectively. This includes crafting an incident response plan tailored to your business needs—a document that delineates roles and responsibilities during an incident while outlining steps for containment and recovery.

A well-prepared small business should conduct regular training sessions for employees on recognizing and reporting potential incidents. This proactive approach empowers staff to remain vigilant and informed, effectively making them the first line of defense against cyber threats. Take this example, conducting phishing simulation exercises can help train employees to identify fraudulent emails and suspicious links.

Additionally, staying informed about industry trends related to cyber threats enhances your ability to spot potential incidents as they emerge. Subscribing to cybersecurity newsletters or participating in local business forums can provide valuable insights into new threats specific to your sector. Awareness fosters preparedness; when employees understand evolving threats, they become more skilled at identifying indicators of potential incidents.

Having a clear communication strategy for both internal and external stakeholders following a cyber incident is also vital. Transparency plays a crucial role; informing affected parties can help mitigate damage to your reputation while building trust post-incident. It's essential to communicate with clients regarding what occurred, how their information may have been affected, and what steps are being taken to resolve the issue.

defining what constitutes a cyber incident extends beyond technical terminology—it encompasses understanding the broader implications for your business. Each incident represents both a challenge and an opportunity for growth in your cybersecurity practices. By actively engaging with the concept of cyber incidents and implementing robust measures for managing them, you position your business not only to withstand potential threats but also to thrive in an increasingly digital landscape. The journey toward resilience begins with awareness; by recognizing what defines a cyber incident today, you equip yourself better to protect your business tomorrow.

Building an Incident Response Team

Creating an effective incident response team is not just a reactive measure; it's a strategic investment in your business's resilience. As cyber threats grow increasingly sophisticated, having a dedicated team with clearly defined roles prepares your organization to respond swiftly and effectively when incidents arise. This proactive stance cultivates a culture of readiness that can significantly mitigate the potential impact of cyber incidents.

To start this process, assess the specific needs of your organization. Take into account factors such as the size, nature, and industry of your business, along with the types of data you manage. For example, a small retail business processing credit card transactions may face different threats than a healthcare provider handling sensitive patient information. Tailoring your incident response team to meet these unique challenges is essential for effective risk management.

Recruiting the right individuals is crucial. An effective incident response team should consist of members from various departments—such as IT, human resources, legal, and communications—each contributing distinct perspectives and expertise. The IT team will likely lead in technical analysis and containment strategies, while HR can manage employee communications and provide support during stressful situations. Including a legal representative ensures compliance with regulations, especially during incidents involving customer data breaches.

Training these team members is equally vital. Regular drills simulating various scenarios—from phishing attempts to full-blown ransomware attacks—help prepare the team for real incidents. Take this example, conducting a tabletop exercise allows team members to discuss their roles in a hypothetical situation, revealing potential gaps in your strategy and highlighting areas for improvement. This collaborative approach not only enhances individual skills but also strengthens team cohesion, creating an environment where everyone understands their responsibilities during an actual incident.

Clear communication channels within the team are paramount for effective coordination during an incident. Each member should know who to report to and how information will flow throughout the process. Developing a communication plan that includes contact lists, escalation protocols, and notification templates can streamline this process. For example, if an employee detects unusual network activity, they should know exactly whom to alert and what details need to be included in that alert.

Equally important is crafting an Incident Response Plan (IRP) that outlines the steps your organization will take when an incident occurs. The IRP should specify processes for detection, containment, eradication, recovery, and post-incident review. Consider including tailored procedures for different types of incidents; having specific responses can drastically improve reaction times. Take this example, if ransomware encrypts files, pre-defined steps for isolating affected systems while preserving evidence for forensic analysis are crucial.

Post-incident reviews play a vital role in refining both your team's performance and your overall cybersecurity posture. After managing any incident, conducting a debriefing session allows you to evaluate what went well and what could be improved. These discussions yield invaluable insights into the strengths and weaknesses of your response strategy—leading to enhancements in training and procedures moving forward.

And, fostering a culture of awareness within your organization enhances overall preparedness against cyber threats. Encourage all employees—not just those on the response team—to regularly engage with cybersecurity training. Everyone should understand basic security protocols like identifying phishing emails or using secure passwords. This widespread knowledge creates additional layers of defense against incidents before they escalate into major breaches.

building an incident response team transcends simply assembling personnel; it's about instilling a mindset of proactive readiness throughout your organization. Investing in training, establishing clear communication pathways, and comprehensive planning transforms your business into one that anticipates rather than merely reacts to cyber threats. By strengthening this critical component of your cybersecurity strategy, you empower not just the response team but all employees—turning them into vigilant defenders against the ever-evolving landscape of cyber threats.

Creating an Incident Response Plan

Creating an incident response plan (IRP) is essential for strengthening your organization against cyber threats. This plan serves as a roadmap for your response team, outlining effective and efficient strategies to manage various incidents. A well-designed IRP can help minimize damage from security breaches, reduce recovery time, and protect your business's reputation.

Begin by defining the scope of your plan. Identify the types of incidents most relevant to your organization, drawing insights from previous risk assessments and threat analyses. For example, if phishing is a common threat you've identified, incorporate specific procedures for addressing phishing attacks within your IRP. Similarly, if ransomware poses a risk, outline steps for isolating infected systems and restoring data from backups. This targeted approach makes your plan more actionable during high-pressure situations.

With relevant incident types identified, structure your IRP around the key phases of incident management: preparation, detection and analysis, containment, eradication, recovery, and post-incident review. Each phase should detail specific actions and designate responsible personnel to ensure accountability throughout the process.

In the preparation phase, prioritize training and awareness initiatives that empower employees to recognize potential threats early. Take this example, conducting workshops on social engineering tactics can help staff identify suspicious activities before they escalate into serious incidents.

Next comes detection and analysis. Establish clear criteria for identifying incidents along with methods for analyzing them. This could involve implementing tools that monitor network traffic for anomalies or systems that log user activity for forensic investigations. Encourage team members to actively utilize these tools; their insights will be crucial for prompt responses.

During the containment phase, focus on immediate actions to limit the impact of an incident. For example, if malware is detected on a workstation, isolate that device from the network while maintaining communication with other systems to protect data integrity. Your IRP should clearly define who has the authority to make such decisions—this clarity helps avoid delays that could worsen the situation.

Eradication involves thoroughly removing threats from your environment. Define processes for cleaning infected systems or rebuilding them entirely if necessary. While often overlooked, this phase is critical to ensure all malware or vulnerabilities are addressed before proceeding.

The recovery phase focuses on restoring services and operations while vigilantly monitoring systems for any signs of re-infection. Having predetermined strategies simplifies this process; established backups of essential data facilitate smoother restoration efforts.

Post-incident reviews play a crucial role in refining both your plan and team performance. After resolving an incident, gather the response team to discuss what transpired: What worked well? What fell short? Take this example, if communication broke down during a critical moment, brainstorm ways to enhance messaging protocols or clarify team roles. Documenting these insights will help you update your IRP accordingly.

Regularly testing your incident response plan is equally important. Simulated incidents can expose weaknesses in your response strategy while providing hands-on experience for team members. Whether through tabletop exercises or live drills that mimic real-world scenarios like data breaches or denial-of-service attacks, these practices reinforce preparedness.

Incorporating continuous improvement into your cybersecurity framework is vital as threats evolve rapidly. Treat your IRP as a living document—review it at least annually or whenever significant changes occur in technology or business operations.

To wrap things up, developing a comprehensive incident response plan equips not just your response team but also your entire organization with a proactive stance against cyber threats. By clearly defining procedures across all phases of incident management and emphasizing training along with regular reviews, you foster resilience and readiness within your business framework—transforming uncertainty into confidence when navigating the challenges of the digital landscape.

Detection and Analysis of Incidents

Detection and analysis of cyber incidents is a vital phase that significantly influences the effectiveness of your incident response plan. The distinction between a successful response and a damaging oversight often hinges on how quickly and accurately you can identify an issue as it arises. This phase lays the foundation for your organization's ability to mitigate threats before they escalate into major crises.

To begin, it is essential to establish a robust detection framework. This means leveraging technology that continuously monitors your systems. Intrusion Detection Systems (IDS) are crucial in this regard, as they can flag suspicious activities in real-time, prompting immediate investigation. Take this example, if a user attempts to access sensitive files outside their usual behavior patterns, the IDS can alert your security team, enabling swift action.

Enhancing your detection capabilities with Security Information and Event Management (SIEM) solutions further bolsters your ability to identify anomalies. These systems collect and analyze data from various sources across your network, creating a comprehensive view that facilitates the spotting of unusual patterns indicative of security incidents. A practical application could involve setting up alerts for excessive login attempts on user accounts, which may signal a brute-force attack. By automating these alerts, you allow your team to concentrate on analyzing potential threats instead of sifting through vast amounts of data manually.

Once an incident is detected, the next step is thorough analysis. This requires a systematic approach to understanding what has occurred, how it transpired, and its potential impact on your organization. Developing a checklist for incident analysis is beneficial; it should include identifying affected systems, gathering logs, and examining user activity leading up to the incident. For example, if malware is detected on a device, your team should isolate that device while also reviewing logs to ascertain how the malware infiltrated the system.

Incorporating forensic tools can significantly enhance this analysis phase. Tools like Wireshark facilitate deep packet inspection; if you suspect data exfiltration during an incident, capturing network traffic with Wireshark can help you ascertain what information was compromised and how it was taken. This level of insight proves invaluable not just for addressing current incidents but also for strengthening future defenses.

After assessing the incident's impact and origin, effective communication within your response team and throughout the organization becomes paramount. Establishing clear reporting structures is essential; define specific roles that designate who communicates with stakeholders and who investigates the technical aspects of the breach. An internal communication protocol minimizes confusion during high-stress situations—clarity breeds efficiency.

Additionally, it's crucial to establish metrics for evaluating the effectiveness of your detection and analysis efforts. Regularly review how many incidents were successfully identified compared to those that went undetected until later stages. For example, tracking metrics such as Mean Time to Detect (MTTD) offers insights into how quickly your organization responds to potential threats. If prolonged detection times emerge as a trend, use this information as a catalyst for implementing training programs aimed at enhancing staff awareness.

However, detecting and analyzing incidents transcends technology; it also involves people and processes. Training employees to recognize early warning signs can substantially improve detection rates. Consider conducting workshops or simulated phishing attacks that educate staff about identifying phishing emails—this empowers them to proactively report suspicious activities.

 effective detection and analysis serve as the backbone of your cybersecurity strategy by providing actionable insights when time is critical. When combined with advanced technologies and ongoing employee training initiatives, you cultivate a resilient infrastructure capable not only of surviving incidents but also of learning from them.

This proactive approach transforms experiences into valuable knowledge while fostering a culture that prioritizes preparedness over panic—a crucial shift in today's volatile cyber landscape characterized by increasingly sophisticated threats. By focusing on continuous improvement in these areas, you strengthen both your immediate defenses and long-term resilience against emerging cyber threats.

Containment, Eradication, and Recovery

As an incident unfolds, the next critical phase involves containment, eradication, and recovery. Efficient management during this stage is vital; without it, the damage from a cyber incident can escalate rapidly, leading to significant losses. This phase focuses on stopping the threat in its tracks, eliminating it from your systems, and restoring normal operations—all while extracting lessons to strengthen future defenses.

Containment strategies must be tailored to the nature and severity of the incident. For example, if a data breach is detected within your network, immediately isolating the affected systems is crucial. Disconnecting these systems from the network can limit further unauthorized access. In the case of an ongoing ransomware attack, shutting down specific segments of your infrastructure may prevent the malware from encrypting additional files or spreading further. This emphasizes the importance of having a well-defined containment plan that outlines specific actions for various incidents and ensures that all team members are trained in these procedures.

Once containment measures are in place, the next step is eradication. The objective here is to remove all traces of the threat from your environment. This may involve conducting comprehensive malware scans across your network and applying updates or patches to vulnerabilities that were exploited. Take this example, if an employee inadvertently installed malware through a phishing email, it's essential not only to remove that malware but also to address any underlying weaknesses in security awareness training.

Utilizing endpoint detection solutions can be particularly helpful during this phase, as they provide detailed information on compromised devices, enabling your security team to neutralize threats effectively.

Recovery extends beyond simply restoring systems to operational status; it requires thorough validation that all malicious components have been eradicated and that systems are secure before being brought back online. Testing restored systems for vulnerabilities is essential—this might include running penetration tests or conducting security audits to identify any gaps that could be exploited again.

Documentation throughout this process plays a crucial role. Maintaining detailed records helps track actions taken during containment and eradication efforts and serves as a resource for post-incident analysis. For example, after addressing a cyberattack on customer data, documenting how you contained the breach can provide valuable insights into what strategies were effective and what areas need improvement for future responses.

Clear and transparent communication during the containment and recovery phases is equally important. Keeping internal teams informed about actions taken— and their rationale—fosters an atmosphere of trust and collaboration as employees come together to address potential fallout from an incident. This might involve ongoing updates about system statuses or reinforcing best practices moving forward.

Once operations are recovered, it's essential to conduct a thorough review of the incident itself: What vulnerabilities were exploited? Was there inadequate monitoring? Did employees fall victim to social engineering tactics? Performing a root cause analysis not only helps clarify how to prevent future incidents but also promotes a culture of continuous improvement within your organization.

Looking ahead, integrating lessons learned into your broader cybersecurity strategy is crucial. Use findings from the incident to create new protocols; implement additional training sessions aimed at addressing identified weaknesses in your team's cybersecurity knowledge and skills.

Strengthening relationships with external partners also contributes to enhancing recovery processes. Collaborating with forensic experts or cybersecurity consultants can provide further insights into securing your environment against similar threats in the future.

successful containment, eradication, and recovery reflect not only tactical responses but also an organizational commitment to resilience against cyber threats. By prioritizing preparation through comprehensive planning and proactive training initiatives while maintaining open lines of communication throughout each phase of response, you position your business not just as one that reacts but as one that evolves continuously in an ever-changing digital landscape.

Post-Incident Evaluation

Post-incident evaluation lays the foundation for future resilience. After successfully containing, eradicating, and recovering from an incident, this step becomes a vital opportunity for reflection and strategy refinement. Each incident provides valuable insights that can enhance your organization's cybersecurity posture, turning setbacks into opportunities for growth.

Start with a thorough review of the incident by convening all relevant stakeholders—IT staff, management, and involved third parties—to analyze the events in detail. Document every aspect of the incident, from its initial detection to the steps taken during containment and recovery. This documentation should include timelines of events, actions executed, and decisions made, creating a comprehensive narrative that highlights both what went wrong and what went right.

Next, examine the vulnerabilities that were exploited during the attack. Were there specific security measures that failed? Take this example, if a particular firewall configuration allowed unauthorized access, it's crucial to understand how this oversight occurred. Utilize tools like vulnerability scanners to identify additional weaknesses in your infrastructure that may have previously gone unnoticed. This analysis can help prioritize future investments in security technology and personnel training.

As you dissect the incident, pay close attention to the communication strategies used during and after the breach. Did your team receive timely updates? How effectively was information shared across departments? Open communication fosters an environment where employees feel secure reporting potential threats without fear of repercussions. It also plays a vital role in mitigating panic and confusion following an incident.

Incorporating lessons learned into ongoing training programs is another essential aspect of post-incident evaluation. Tailor training sessions to address specific gaps identified during your review. For example, if employee susceptibility to phishing was noted as a contributing factor in the breach, consider implementing more rigorous security awareness training aimed at helping staff recognize such threats.

Additionally, review your response plan against real-world events. Did your incident response team adhere to established protocols efficiently? If there were deviations, assess whether these arose from ambiguities in procedures or unforeseen complications. Updating your incident response plan to reflect these lessons ensures that your organization becomes more resilient in preparing for future incidents.

It's also wise to evaluate relationships with external partners during this phase. If third-party vendors were implicated in the breach—either through their systems or connections —revisit service level agreements (SLAs) and security requirements. Establishing clearer expectations and security practices can strengthen defenses against supply chain vulnerabilities.

The post-incident evaluation serves not only as an internal reflection but also as an opportunity for external engagement. Sharing insights with industry peers or participating in cybersecurity forums can broaden perspectives on emerging threats and effective mitigation strategies. Collaborative efforts help foster a community-oriented approach to cybersecurity where businesses learn collectively.

Finally, approach this evaluation phase with a mindset geared toward continuous improvement. Cybersecurity is not static; threats evolve rapidly, necessitating an adaptive defense strategy. Schedule regular reviews of incident responses across various scenarios—tabletop exercises can simulate breaches based on real experiences and encourage proactive thinking among teams.

By embedding these evaluations into your organizational culture, you cultivate resilience against cyber threats while empowering your team to become proactive defenders rather than reactive responders. This cycle of learning from each incident strengthens your business, transforming vulnerabilities into informed defenses poised to tackle future risks head-on.

Communicating with Stakeholders

The effectiveness of your incident response hinges significantly on how well you communicate with stakeholders during and after a cyber incident. This communication goes beyond simply relaying facts; it is about building trust and ensuring that everyone involved understands their roles and the steps being taken. Clear and transparent communication can help mitigate confusion, reduce panic, and lay a stronger foundation for recovery.

Begin by identifying key stakeholders, which may include employees, customers, suppliers, and regulatory bodies. Each group will have different information needs and concerns, making it crucial to tailor your messages accordingly. For example, employees may require detailed instructions on their immediate responsibilities, while customers might seek reassurance about the safety of their data and the measures being implemented to rectify the situation. Prompt and sincere engagement with these groups can help maintain confidence in your organization.

Establishing a communication protocol during an incident is essential. Designate a spokesperson or a team responsible for managing all communications. This approach helps prevent conflicting messages from circulating and ensures that the information shared is accurate and consistent. Utilize multiple channels for dissemination—emails, company intranet updates, and social media can effectively reach different audiences. Take this example, real-time updates on social media can keep customers informed without overwhelming them with technical jargon.

Once the dust settles, maintaining transparency remains critical. After containing the incident and beginning recovery efforts, share what transpired with all stakeholders. Outline the timeline of events, actions taken, and future preventive measures. Providing this context not only demonstrates accountability but also reflects your organization's commitment to safeguarding its assets and people.

Consider organizing post-incident meetings with employees to discuss lessons learned openly. This supports a culture of learning rather than blame, allowing staff to feel safe discussing what went wrong without fear of repercussion. Encourage feedback during these discussions; employees often have insights into vulnerabilities that management might overlook.

Additionally, informing customers about how their data was affected—and what you are doing to protect it moving forward —can strengthen loyalty. For example, if personal data was compromised during a breach, offering credit monitoring services or identity theft protection can demonstrate proactive care for their security beyond the immediate crisis.

Communicating with third-party vendors who play a role in your cybersecurity ecosystem is equally important. If they were involved in or affected by the breach, clear communication will be vital in addressing potential vulnerabilities within those partnerships. Engaging them in discussions about enhanced security measures reinforces collaborative efforts to protect against future risks.

Regulatory compliance also necessitates specific communication strategies. Following incidents that impact personal data or financial information, companies must notify relevant authorities within set timelines to remain compliant with laws such as GDPR or PCI DSS. Keeping meticulous records of communications throughout the incident will aid in fulfilling these obligations efficiently.

Also, utilize these opportunities for community engagement post-incident by sharing anonymized case studies in industry forums or webinars. This not only positions your organization as a leader in cybersecurity awareness but also contributes to broader industry knowledge-sharing efforts that benefit everyone involved.

 remember that communication is not just about relaying information—it's about building relationships founded on trust and integrity. Your response during crises speaks volumes about your organizational values; effective communication can reinforce those values and help turn challenges into opportunities for deeper connections with stakeholders.

By prioritizing stakeholder communication throughout the incident management lifecycle—from detection through recovery—you foster an environment where transparency thrives and mutual trust flourishes. This proactive approach equips your business not only to respond effectively but also to emerge stronger and more resilient against future threats.

Legal and Regulatory Implications

Legal and regulatory implications are crucial in shaping how small businesses approach cybersecurity. Rather than being an afterthought, these considerations should be woven into the strategic planning and risk management processes that protect your organization. A thorough understanding of the legal landscape helps ensure compliance and mitigates potential liabilities associated with cyber incidents.

To begin, it's essential to familiarize yourself with the regulations that govern your industry. For example, if your business handles personal data, laws like the General Data Protection Regulation (GDPR) or the California Consumer Privacy Act (CCPA) impose strict requirements regarding data protection and breach notifications. Non-compliance can result in significant fines and damage to your reputation. Therefore, a proactive approach involves integrating these legal requirements into your cybersecurity policies, ensuring that every employee understands their compliance responsibilities.

In addition to regulatory compliance, it's important to consider the contractual obligations you may have with customers and partners concerning data security. Many organizations include specific cybersecurity clauses in their contracts that outline expectations for data handling, incident response times, and liability in the event of breaches. Regularly reviewing these contracts helps ensure alignment with evolving standards and customer expectations.

Awareness of reporting requirements associated with various

regulations is also critical. Take this example, GDPR mandates that organizations report significant breaches within 72 hours of discovery. This necessitates established protocols for promptly identifying and escalating incidents. Understanding these timelines empowers your team to act swiftly when issues arise.

Establishing a dedicated compliance team can enhance your ability to navigate this complex landscape effectively. This team should focus on staying informed about emerging laws and best practices while ensuring that cybersecurity strategies align with legal obligations. Regular audits and assessments can help identify potential compliance gaps, providing opportunities for improvement before issues escalate.

Training is another vital component in maintaining compliance. All employees need to be aware of not only cybersecurity best practices but also their specific roles within the framework of legal obligations. Conducting regular training sessions ensures that everyone understands how their actions contribute to compliance efforts, fostering a culture where security is prioritized throughout the organization.

The consequences of failing to meet legal requirements extend beyond financial penalties; they can also undermine customer trust. In an era where consumers are increasingly concerned about their privacy, demonstrating a commitment to protecting their data can set your business apart from competitors. Implementing robust encryption measures or engaging third-party audits can reinforce your dedication to transparency and accountability.

Engaging with law enforcement is another important aspect when necessary. In cases of significant breaches or cybercrimes, timely reporting can aid investigations that protect not only your business but potentially others in your industry as well.

It's equally important not to overlook industry-specific standards; sectors like healthcare and finance often have additional regulatory frameworks governing data security practices. Understanding these nuances allows you to tailor your strategies appropriately—considering HIPAA for healthcare providers or PCI DSS for businesses that handle credit card transactions.

Finally, keep in mind that regulations evolve over time in response to emerging threats and public concerns regarding privacy and security. Staying engaged with industry groups or participating in forums focused on cybersecurity legislation enables you to anticipate changes rather than react after they occur.

Navigating legal and regulatory implications goes beyond merely avoiding penalties; it's about fostering resilience within your organization through strategic foresight and seamless integration of compliance into daily operations. By embracing these considerations as foundational elements of your cybersecurity strategy, you create a framework that not only protects against current threats but also prepares you for future challenges in an ever-evolving digital landscape.

CHAPTER 10: PHYSICAL SECURITY AND ITS ROLE IN CYBERSECURITY

What is Physical Security?

Physical security is a critical cornerstone of a comprehensive cybersecurity strategy. It extends beyond just locks and cameras; it involves a multifaceted approach aimed at protecting your assets, personnel, and data from unauthorized access and potential damage. In our increasingly digital landscape, where cyber threats are ever-present, the significance of physical security can often be overlooked. However, neglecting this aspect can create vulnerabilities that cybercriminals are eager to exploit.

Begin by examining your business premises. The design and layout of your physical space are essential for safeguarding sensitive information. Start with an assessment of access points—doors, windows, and other entries. Are they secure? While high-quality locks are fundamental, consider implementing advanced systems like keycard access or biometric scanners. These technologies not only deter unauthorized entry but also allow you to track who accesses sensitive areas within your organization.

Surveillance systems also play a vital role in physical security. Strategically placed cameras serve dual functions: they monitor activities around your business and act as deterrents against potential intruders. When deploying surveillance systems, it's important to comply with local laws regarding privacy and data collection. Be sure to communicate clearly with employees about the presence of cameras and their intended use.

While monitoring external threats is crucial, protecting critical internal assets is equally important. Server rooms and data centers should be restricted to authorized personnel only. Implement controlled access measures, such as electronic locks, to ensure that only those who need entry can gain access to these sensitive areas. Additionally, physical barriers like security doors or cages can provide an extra layer of protection for servers and networking equipment.

Environmental factors also warrant attention; natural disasters can pose significant risks to both physical infrastructure and data integrity. Consider preventive strategies like flood barriers for vulnerable areas or specialized fire suppression systems for server rooms. Regular assessments of these measures will help ensure their ongoing effectiveness.

Employee training is essential in reinforcing physical security protocols. Even the most robust systems can be compromised by human error. Conduct regular training sessions to foster a culture in which employees understand the importance of securing their workspaces—simple actions like locking doors behind them or promptly reporting suspicious activity can prevent many incidents before they escalate.

Establishing clear security policies for visitors and contractors is also wise. Develop protocols that include visitor logs and escorted access to sensitive areas. This not only helps track who is on-site but also verifies that individuals have legitimate reasons for being there.

As you enhance your physical security measures, consider integrating cybersecurity practices into this framework. Take this example, ensure that any networked devices within your premises—such as IP cameras—are safeguarded against cyber threats through strong passwords and regular software updates. This convergence creates a more holistic approach to protecting your business.

Regular audits are vital for maintaining effective physical security over time. Schedule assessments that evaluate not just the effectiveness of locks and cameras but also employee adherence to established policies. These audits can highlight weaknesses in both infrastructure and training efforts while providing actionable insights for necessary improvements.

Engaging with local law enforcement can further strengthen your overall security posture. Building relationships with officers familiar with your business can facilitate quicker response times during emergencies and offer invaluable advice on enhancing safety protocols based on their experiences within the community.

To wrap things up, physical security is an indispensable element of your cybersecurity strategy. By recognizing its multifaceted nature—from safeguarding infrastructure to training employees—you lay a solid foundation that protects tangible assets while bolstering resilience against cyber threats. As you implement these practices, remember that every measure taken today fortifies your business's defenses for tomorrow, preparing you for an evolving landscape filled with challenges yet abundant in opportunities for growth and innovation.

Securing Server Rooms and Data Centers

Securing server rooms and data centers is essential for protecting your business against both physical and cyber threats. These areas store sensitive data and critical infrastructure, making them attractive targets for unauthorized access. To create a secure environment, the first step is to establish strict access control protocols, allowing entry only to employees who genuinely need it for their job functions.

Implementing keycard systems or biometric scanners significantly enhances security by ensuring that only authorized personnel can access these areas. Unlike traditional locks, these technologies create a digital trail, enabling you to monitor who enters and exits. When considering these systems, it's important to evaluate their cost in relation to the risks posed by leaving sensitive areas vulnerable. A breach in your server room could result in catastrophic data loss or theft, far outweighing the initial investment in robust security measures.

In addition to access controls, physical barriers act as effective deterrents. Security doors and cages designed specifically for servers can prevent unauthorized individuals from tampering with equipment. While high-security locks are essential, pairing them with reinforced doors provides an additional layer of protection. It's also wise to place servers in climate-controlled environments equipped with alarms for temperature and humidity changes; maintaining the operational integrity of your hardware is just as crucial as safeguarding it from intruders.

Surveillance systems should be an integral part of your security strategy. Installing cameras both inside and outside your server room allows for continuous monitoring of activities. Opt for models that offer remote viewing capabilities so you can oversee your facilities from anywhere. However, it's vital to maintain transparency about surveillance practices. Informing employees about monitoring policies fosters trust and ensures compliance with privacy regulations.

Regular maintenance checks of your physical security measures are equally important. Schedule periodic reviews of access controls, surveillance equipment, and environmental protections such as fire suppression systems or water leak detectors. These assessments help identify potential issues before they escalate into serious problems, providing peace of mind that your physical infrastructure remains secure.

Training your team on physical security protocols is critical. Employees should understand the procedures for reporting suspicious activity or breaches in security protocol. For example, if someone notices a door left ajar or sees another individual attempting to use a card key that doesn't belong to them, they should know how to respond promptly. This vigilance can help prevent unauthorized access before it becomes a significant issue.

Visitor management is another essential element of securing server rooms and data centers. Establish clear guidelines for how visitors interact with these sensitive areas—require visitor logs and ensure they are always accompanied by authorized personnel while on-site. This practice not only monitors who enters but also creates accountability for everyone within your secure spaces.

To effectively integrate cybersecurity with physical security practices, ensure that all networked devices within the server room have strong passwords and are regularly updated to mitigate vulnerabilities that hackers may exploit through digital means. As technology evolves, so do the tactics used by cybercriminals; staying ahead necessitates ongoing vigilance.

Collaborating with local law enforcement can further enhance your security efforts. Building relationships with police officers familiar with your business's layout and operations allows you to leverage their expertise during routine assessments or emergencies. They can provide valuable insights based on trends they observe in the community.

As you develop these strategies, remember that securing your server rooms and data centers is not just about preventing breaches; it's about fostering a culture of security awareness within your organization. Every employee has a role in maintaining this environment—empowering them with knowledge about potential risks promotes collective responsibility.

Investing time and resources into these aspects will bolster your resilience against both physical and digital threats. By safeguarding what lies behind locked doors, you're not merely protecting hardware; you're preserving the very heart of your business—the data that drives decisions, innovation, and ultimately success in the marketplace.

Access Control Systems

Access control systems serve as the guardians of your organization's sensitive information and physical assets. They play a crucial role in defining who can access specific resources and under what circumstances, ultimately contributing to a secure environment. By adopting robust access control measures, you not only protect valuable data but also enhance your organization's overall security posture.

Essentially of an effective access control system is the principle of least privilege. This concept asserts that users should have access only to the resources essential for their specific roles. Take this example, a marketing intern should not be granted access to financial databases or sensitive customer information. To achieve this, conduct a comprehensive audit of organizational roles and their corresponding access needs, ensuring that each employee's permissions align with their job functions.

Selecting the right technology for access control is equally vital. Options such as card-based systems, biometric scanners, and mobile credentialing solutions offer varying levels of security. Biometric systems, including fingerprint or facial recognition technology, provide enhanced security due to their reliance on unique personal identifiers that are challenging to replicate. In contrast, card-based systems can be susceptible to loss or theft. Therefore, consider implementing a layered security approach by combining multiple methods; for example, using a two-factor authentication (2FA) system that requires both a card and biometric verification can significantly bolster defenses against unauthorized access.

As you roll out these technologies, it's important to maintain an up-to-date database of user permissions. Regularly reviewing and updating this list ensures that it reflects any changes in personnel or job responsibilities. For example, when an employee transitions to a new role or departs from the company, promptly adjusting their access rights prevents lingering permissions that could pose security risks. Neglecting this step may lead to vulnerabilities that malicious actors could exploit.

Another key aspect of an effective access control system is the logging and monitoring of activity within your facilities. Keeping detailed records of who accessed which areas and when allows you to identify unusual patterns or unauthorized attempts at entry. This information is invaluable during audits or investigations following security incidents. Many advanced systems offer real-time alerts that notify administrators of suspicious activity as it occurs; timely action can mean the difference between averting a close call and experiencing a significant breach.

Even in today's digital landscape, physical barriers remain essential components of security strategies. High-security locks, reinforced doors, and turnstiles act as deterrents against unauthorized entry. Installing security gates at critical entry points where sensitive data is stored or processed further strengthens your defenses. These physical elements complement electronic access controls, creating an environment where only authorized personnel can operate.

In addition to safeguarding physical access, it is vital to ensure that networked devices are protected from internal threats as well. Devices such as printers or computers located in secured areas should have restricted network access consistent with the physical controls in place. By segmenting networks according to user roles and needs, you minimize the risk of intruders moving laterally within your organization after gaining initial access through less secure channels.

Training employees on the importance of these controls cannot be overstated. Regular workshops that emphasize strong password practices and awareness of social engineering tactics are crucial for fostering a culture of security throughout your organization. Employees must understand how their actions impact overall security; for example, sharing login credentials or propping open secure doors can inadvertently expose the organization to unnecessary risks.

Implementing an effective visitor management system adds another layer of protection to your access control strategy. Establish procedures for visitors entering sensitive areas—such as requiring them to sign in and provide identification while ensuring they are escorted by authorized personnel at all times. This not only safeguards your assets but also serves as a visual reminder that security is everyone's responsibility.

Also, conducting regular audits of your access control systems is essential for maintaining effectiveness over time. Schedule assessments at least biannually to evaluate whether current policies align with best practices and adapt them based on emerging threats or technological advancements. Engaging an external expert for these audits can provide valuable insights into vulnerabilities you may have overlooked.

 effective access control extends beyond merely preventing

unauthorized entry; it involves cultivating an organizational culture where everyone plays a part in safeguarding sensitive information and resources. Each layer you implement strengthens resilience against both internal missteps and external attacks alike. As you refine your strategies for implementing access control systems, remember that the strength of your defenses relies heavily on how well these controls are integrated into daily operations and employee awareness initiatives. Investing in this area not only protects vital assets but also fosters trust among employees and clients —a cornerstone of any successful business endeavor.

Surveillance Systems

Surveillance systems serve as the vigilant eyes of your organization, providing constant oversight of both physical premises and digital assets. In an era where cyber threats are continuously evolving, these systems offer a crucial layer of security that complements measures such as access control and network security. By monitoring activities around your facilities effectively, you can deter potential intruders and collect vital evidence for incident investigations.

To establish an effective surveillance system, begin by assessing your organization's specific needs. Consider factors such as the size of your premises, the nature of your operations, and the types of assets that require protection. For example, retail businesses may prioritize monitoring high-traffic areas like entrances and cash registers, while offices might focus on securing critical access points to server rooms or sensitive data storage areas. Identifying these vulnerabilities allows you to determine optimal camera placements, ensuring comprehensive coverage without blind spots.

Modern surveillance technology offers a variety of options tailored to different environments. IP cameras, for instance, provide high-resolution imagery and can be accessed remotely through secure web interfaces. This feature enables real-time monitoring from anywhere in the world—a significant advantage for business owners who want to oversee operations while away. Conversely, traditional analog cameras might still be sufficient for smaller businesses with less complex security needs. Regardless of the choice, investing in quality equipment is essential; subpar cameras can result in grainy footage that fails to capture critical details during an incident.

Incorporating advanced features into your surveillance system can significantly enhance its effectiveness. Motion detection capabilities enable cameras to record only when movement is detected, which conserves storage space and simplifies footage review when needed. Some systems even leverage artificial intelligence (AI) to differentiate between normal activity and suspicious behavior—an invaluable tool for minimizing false alarms while maximizing genuine threat detection.

While installing surveillance systems is important, their efficacy heavily depends on proper management and maintenance. Regularly reviewing recorded footage ensures that any suspicious activity is promptly noted and addressed. Additionally, periodic checks on camera functionality are crucial; a malfunctioning camera can leave vulnerabilities unnoticed. Establishing a routine maintenance schedule allows technicians to check lenses for obstructions or dirt that may obscure visibility.

Data privacy also plays a significant role in implementing surveillance systems. Ensure that your policies comply with local regulations regarding video monitoring. Inform employees about the presence of cameras in the workplace and establish clear guidelines around data retention—specifying how long recordings will be stored and under what circumstances they may be reviewed or shared. Transparency fosters trust among staff members while demonstrating your organization's commitment to ethical practices alongside security.

Integrating surveillance into a broader security framework enhances overall effectiveness. Collaborate closely with access control measures; for instance, integrating video feeds with access logs can help verify who entered specific areas at particular times during incidents or breaches. This layered approach creates a comprehensive view of security events that aids investigations and supports legal proceedings if necessary.

Training staff on how to respond to incidents captured by surveillance systems is also essential. Employees should know whom to alert if they observe suspicious behavior on camera or what steps to take during an active threat situation. Establishing clear protocols minimizes confusion during emergencies and ensures swift action when it matters most.

Regular audits of your surveillance system keep it aligned with evolving best practices and technological advancements. Scheduling assessments at least once a year enables you to identify gaps in coverage or outdated technologies that may no longer address current threats effectively. Engaging external experts in these evaluations can provide fresh perspectives on potential improvements you may not have considered.

 surveillance systems represent more than just deterrents— they reflect a proactive commitment to fostering a culture of safety within your organization. When thoughtfully integrated with other measures such as access control, employee training, and regular audits, these systems create an environment where risks are minimized through vigilance and informed decision-making.

As you refine your approach to implementing robust surveillance strategies, recognize their power not only in protecting assets but also in cultivating an overarching culture of awareness within your organization—one where everyone plays a role in safeguarding both physical spaces and digital infrastructures alike. Your investment today lays the groundwork for enhanced resilience against future threats while building confidence among employees and clients who prioritize secure operations above all else.

Environmental Monitoring

Effective environmental monitoring serves as a vital foundation for strong physical security. It goes beyond traditional surveillance by fostering a deeper awareness of one's surroundings. Instead of merely observing, environmental monitoring empowers businesses to proactively identify threats before they escalate into serious issues. This multifaceted approach combines advanced technology with strategic human oversight, ensuring that your premises remain secure and resilient against potential intrusions.

Essentially of environmental monitoring are various systems designed to detect and respond to changes that may signal security risks. Take this example, temperature sensors can alert you to unusual fluctuations in server rooms or data centers, which could indicate equipment failure or unauthorized access. A well-configured system can send notifications if a door is left ajar or if movement is detected in restricted areas after hours. By incorporating such sensors into your security framework, you enhance not only physical safety but also the protection of valuable data assets.

Consider the example of a small business that successfully implemented an environmental monitoring system. A boutique marketing agency, having experienced several break-ins over the years, decided to invest in an integrated system featuring motion detectors, humidity sensors, and temperature control devices. Once installed, they found that their server room was maintained at optimal temperatures and monitored for unauthorized access through alerts sent directly to management's smartphones. This proactive approach allowed them to swiftly address potential issues before they led to significant losses.

Surveillance cameras are another critical component of environmental monitoring. While often seen solely as deterrents against theft, they also provide invaluable insights into the operational environment. When strategically positioned, these cameras can monitor high-risk areas like entrances and exits, capturing unusual behaviors in real-time. For example, if employees frequently access restricted areas without proper authorization during off-hours, management can intervene before these internal threats escalate into serious security breaches.

Maximizing the effectiveness of these cameras relies on their placement. Position them to capture clear images of faces and license plates while covering any blind spots on your premises. Additionally, ensure that all recordings are stored securely and regularly reviewed as part of routine security audits. Utilizing cloud storage solutions can facilitate easy access to footage while safeguarding it against physical damage or tampering.

Environmental factors also encompass physical barriers and access controls. Effective use of fencing, gates, and bollards creates a first line of defense against unauthorized entry. Establishing clear pathways for visitors while securing sensitive areas promotes both safety and operational efficiency.

And, conducting regular assessments of the physical environment is essential for maintaining a secure workspace. Routine checks help identify potential vulnerabilities—such as damaged fencing or malfunctioning locks—so they can be addressed promptly. Implementing a checklist for inspections can streamline this process, covering aspects like lighting conditions around entry points and the functionality of access control mechanisms.

Take this example, consider an architectural firm located in a bustling urban area with heavy foot traffic. The firm regularly uses a checklist to evaluate not only the physical condition of their premises but also how well their environmental monitoring systems perform under varying conditions—such as heavy rain or snow—that might affect visibility around the office's perimeter.

In addition to these tangible elements, cultivating a culture of awareness among employees significantly enhances the effectiveness of your environmental monitoring efforts. Training staff to recognize suspicious activity or potential hazards can greatly improve early detection. Regular meetings where employees share observations about their surroundings foster this culture—creating a shared responsibility among all team members contributes to a more secure environment.

 integrating comprehensive environmental monitoring systems with employee training creates an effective framework for physical security management within small businesses. By investing in technology while cultivating awareness among your team, you establish an agile defense mechanism capable of adapting to evolving threats without being burdensome or intrusive.

The benefits are clear: effective environmental monitoring not only mitigates risk but also fosters a safer environment for employees and clients alike—enhancing productivity and instilling confidence in operations. Each layer added fortifies the overall security posture while building resilience against both current threats and those yet unseen.

Security Policies for Employees

Establishing robust security policies for employees is vital to maintaining a secure work environment and safeguarding sensitive data. These policies form the foundation of your cybersecurity strategy, ensuring that every team member understands their role in protecting the organization from potential threats. By creating clear guidelines, you not only shield the company but also empower employees to act responsibly and take proactive measures regarding security.

A key first step in developing effective security policies is to involve employees in the process. Engaging your team can provide invaluable insights into the unique challenges they encounter daily. This collaborative approach fosters a sense of ownership over security measures, encouraging compliance with established protocols. Consider hosting brainstorming sessions that allow employees to voice concerns and propose improvements based on their experiences.

After gathering input from your team, focus on defining specific policies tailored to different aspects of cybersecurity. Begin with acceptable use policies that clarify how employees should manage company resources—such as computers, software, and internet access. Take this example, specify that personal devices should connect only to secure networks when accessing company data, and outline which websites and applications are permitted during work hours to minimize exposure to potential threats.

Next, address password management, a common vulnerability within organizations. Provide clear guidelines for creating strong passwords that emphasize complexity, length, and uniqueness. Encourage the use of passphrases instead of simple passwords and recommend regular updates. To streamline this process, consider adopting a password manager tool for the organization, and offer training on how to use these tools effectively. This not only enhances security but also simplifies credential management for employees.

Another crucial aspect of employee security policies is data handling protocols. Clearly outline how sensitive information should be stored, shared, and disposed of within the organization. For example, if employees need to transfer files containing sensitive data via email or cloud services, implement encryption practices to protect this information from unauthorized access during transmission.

Training plays a pivotal role in reinforcing these security policies among staff members. Regular training sessions —whether quarterly workshops or monthly briefings—can keep everyone informed about evolving threats and best practices in cybersecurity. Incorporating real-world scenarios into these sessions illustrates the potential consequences of non-compliance while providing practical steps for mitigating risks.

A notable example comes from a healthcare startup that faced significant challenges regarding patient data protection due to regulatory compliance requirements like HIPAA (Health Insurance Portability and Accountability Act). They rolled out a comprehensive training program alongside their security policy implementation, ensuring each employee received targeted training on recognizing phishing attempts and other cyber threats specific to the healthcare industry. The result was a remarkable decrease in data breaches attributed to human error within just six months.

In addition to training, it's essential to establish clear channels for reporting suspicious activities or potential breaches within your organization. Create an incident reporting policy that encourages employees to come forward without fear of reprisal when they suspect something is amiss. This transparent approach promotes accountability while making team members feel supported in their efforts to maintain a secure environment.

Monitoring compliance with these policies is just as important as developing them. Regular audits can identify lapses in adherence and provide opportunities for improving both procedures and employee understanding of security expectations. Setting up an anonymous feedback system can also encourage team members to express concerns or suggest modifications without hesitation.

Finally, periodically reviewing and updating your security policies ensures they remain relevant amid an evolving cybersecurity landscape. As technology advances and new threats emerge, revisiting these guidelines allows your organization to adapt accordingly while keeping your staff informed about necessary changes.

To wrap things up, creating effective security policies goes beyond merely fulfilling requirements; it involves fostering a culture of vigilance where every employee recognizes their critical role in protecting company assets. By engaging staff in the policy development process and investing in tailored training programs, you'll cultivate a workforce that not only complies with regulations but actively contributes to an environment where security is integral to daily operations. these proactive measures enhance resilience against cyber threats while building trust among clients who rely on your commitment to protecting their data.

Visitor Management

A comprehensive visitor management system goes beyond a simple checklist or sign-in sheet at the reception desk; it is a vital element of your organization's security framework. When visitors enter your premises, they introduce variables that can impact your security posture. Therefore, establishing a robust visitor management protocol is essential for protecting sensitive information, safeguarding assets, and maintaining operational integrity.

To begin, let's explore the significance of pre-visit screening. Gathering relevant information before any guest arrives is crucial. An online registration form can efficiently collect necessary details such as the visitor's name, contact information, purpose of the visit, and expected duration. This proactive approach not only helps you anticipate who will be on-site but also aids in verifying each visitor's identity.

Many organizations have successfully integrated visitor management software to automate this registration process, streamlining the workflow and sending confirmation emails. For example, a tech firm in Seattle utilizes a cloud-based platform that significantly reduces wait times at reception while ensuring accurate records.

Once visitors arrive, effective check-in procedures become critical for ensuring security. Implementing digital check-in kiosks can streamline this process, allowing visitors to input their details directly into the system and capturing their information in real-time. Adding photo ID scans enhances verification by enabling staff to cross-reference against pre-approved lists or alerts for known security risks. A retail chain that adopted this approach saw a marked improvement in identifying unauthorized individuals attempting access.

While guests are on-site, establishing clear guidelines regarding visitor behavior and movement is essential. Issuing temporary badges that indicate whether visitors have unrestricted access or are limited to specific areas helps maintain security. Take this example, if sensitive data is stored in particular departments, restricting access to those zones while allowing visitors to access public areas is vital. An architecture firm implemented color-coded badges—green for unrestricted access and red for limited zones—which improved overall safety and accountability.

Another important aspect involves assigning an employee liaison or host to accompany visitors throughout their stay. This measure ensures that guests are monitored and reduces the risk of wandering into restricted areas unintentionally. For example, a financial institution designated specific team members as "visitor coordinators," who not only welcomed guests but also educated them about relevant security policies during their visit. This personal touch not only enhances security but also strengthens client relations.

Post-visit procedures are equally important for closing the loop on visitor management. After guests leave, follow-up communications thanking them for their visit and reminding them of confidentiality protocols regarding any sensitive discussions are beneficial. A tech startup introduced a follow-up email template for this purpose and found that reinforcing security protocols helped maintain professionalism while heightening clients' awareness of data protection.

Incorporating technology into your visitor management strategy can yield significant benefits as well. Utilizing mobile applications allows employees to pre-register guests or notify security personnel when visitors arrive. This proactive approach ensures you maintain control over who is on-site while enhancing the overall visitor experience.

Regular audits of your visitor management practices should also be a part of your security routine. Assessing how effectively your policies are being implemented and whether they align with current threats and compliance requirements is essential. Take this example, conducting an annual review can identify gaps such as unregistered visitors or inconsistencies in badge issuance procedures, allowing you to make necessary adjustments.

Finally, training employees on visitor management protocols is paramount. Everyone in your organization should understand their responsibilities regarding visitor management, including recognizing suspicious behavior and promptly reporting anomalies. A leading manufacturing firm held workshops simulating various visitor scenarios, empowering employees with practical skills to enhance overall site safety.

Establishing an effective visitor management system not only safeguards your organization but also fosters trust with clients and partners by demonstrating a commitment to security measures. By integrating technology, clear protocols, and ongoing training into your approach, you create an environment where everyone—from employees to visitors —understands the importance of vigilance in maintaining cybersecurity defenses.

Implementing these strategies lays a strong foundation for creating a secure space that accommodates necessary business interactions without compromising safety or privacy —a balance that is crucial for any small business navigating today's complex landscape of cybersecurity threats.

Physical Security Audits

To effectively conduct physical security audits, small business owners must understand that these audits go beyond mere checklists; they are comprehensive assessments of their organization's vulnerabilities and strengths. A well-planned audit uncovers critical insights that inform broader security strategies, highlighting the relationship between the physical environment and potential cyber risks.

Begin by establishing the audit's scope. Identify the specific areas of your business to evaluate—this could include the main office, remote workspaces, and storage facilities. For example, a local retailer might focus on its storefront, storage area, and parking lot, while a tech company may assess server rooms and employee access points. The goal is to create a complete picture of where your assets are located and how accessible they are to unauthorized individuals.

Next, identify potential security threats by examining both internal and external factors that could jeopardize safety. Look for blind spots in surveillance coverage or entry points that lack adequate locks or alarms. Real-life incidents often reveal these vulnerabilities; for instance, an employee at a marketing agency discovered an unmonitored side entrance that allowed unauthorized access after hours.

Incorporating technology into your audit process can enhance both efficiency and accuracy. Tools like surveillance systems and access control software provide valuable data on visitor patterns and access attempts. For example, a financial institution utilized smart surveillance cameras with AI capabilities to analyze foot traffic trends, improving security while directing personnel to areas needing attention.

Conducting interviews with employees can yield additional insights during audits. Employees often possess firsthand knowledge of potential security issues in their work areas. Take this example, an IT manager at a small software firm reported repeated instances of equipment theft in common areas, leading to a reassessment of their equipment storage protocols. Engaging staff fosters a culture of security awareness, empowering them to actively contribute to the organization's safety.

After gathering data through observations and interviews, analyze your findings thoroughly. Identify patterns that indicate systemic weaknesses—such as inadequate lighting in parking lots or insufficient signage for emergency exits —and prioritize these vulnerabilities based on risk levels. Not all threats carry the same weight; understanding which require immediate attention allows for more effective resource allocation.

With risks assessed, develop actionable recommendations based on your analysis. These may involve physical improvements like installing motion-activated lights or reinforcing door locks, as well as policy changes such as implementing stricter access controls for sensitive areas or updating employee training on emergency procedures.

Documentation is crucial throughout this process. Maintain detailed records of audit findings, recommendations made, and actions taken. This documentation serves multiple purposes: it holds you accountable for follow-up actions and can be invaluable for compliance with regulations like HIPAA or PCI DSS.

Finally, establish a routine for conducting these audits regularly—at least annually or bi-annually—to ensure that your physical security measures evolve alongside emerging threats and organizational changes. After each audit cycle, review the effectiveness of implemented changes to determine if they adequately address previously identified vulnerabilities.

Thorough physical security audits are essential not only for safeguarding tangible assets but also for protecting sensitive data within those spaces. By proactively addressing identified risks through systematic evaluations and ongoing improvements, small businesses can strengthen their resilience against both physical intrusions and cyber threats. This commitment fosters an environment where security is woven into the fabric of organizational culture, instilling confidence among employees and clients alike. Each step taken fortifies defenses against potential breaches while promoting a pervasive ethos of vigilance throughout the organization.

Integration with Cybersecurity Measures

Integrating physical security measures with cybersecurity strategies is essential for small business owners; it's not just an operational necessity, but a strategic imperative. As the boundaries between physical and digital spaces continue to blur, understanding how these two aspects of security work together can significantly enhance an organization's resilience against threats. This holistic approach not only defends against intrusions but also fosters trust with clients and stakeholders.

The first step in this integration process is to conduct a comprehensive inventory of all assets, both physical and digital. For example, consider a small medical practice that handles sensitive patient data. A thorough assessment reveals electronic records stored on servers as well as paper files kept in locked cabinets. If the physical storage lacks adequate protection, the risk of unauthorized access increases dramatically. Addressing vulnerabilities in both areas ensures that robust protection measures are in place.

Once assets are identified, it's crucial to assess potential threats that could impact both domains. A familiar scenario involves a cyberattack facilitated by physical breaches—such as when attackers gain access to a facility to steal credentials or install malware on network devices. Take this example, a retail store's security breach might occur simply because someone tailgated an employee into the building. Similarly, some data breaches have originated from compromised employee devices left unattended in public spaces. By cross-referencing these potential threats, businesses can develop integrated strategies that encompass both realms.

Next, establishing uniform access control measures for both physical and digital environments is essential. The principle of least privilege should govern user permissions—only those who need access to specific areas or data should have it. For example, if a warehouse manager requires access to inventory management software, they should also have restricted physical access to storage areas containing high-value items. Implementing technologies like biometric scanners for both entry points and digital systems can streamline this process and reinforce security protocols.

Ongoing monitoring is also critical for effective integration. Surveillance systems should not only track movements within business premises but also monitor network traffic for unusual activity. A small tech startup might employ video analytics alongside network intrusion detection systems to flag suspicious behavior—whether it's an unauthorized individual accessing server rooms or abnormal data transmissions occurring after hours. These dual monitoring strategies ensure that anomalies are quickly addressed before they escalate into significant issues.

Training employees on security awareness further solidifies this integration. Regular workshops can highlight scenarios where lax physical security leads to cyber vulnerabilities. Encouraging staff members to report suspicious activities —whether they observe someone attempting unauthorized access or notice unusual system alerts—helps cultivate a culture of vigilance where everyone takes responsibility for maintaining security across all fronts.

Documentation plays a vital role in effectively integrating these measures. Keeping detailed records of audits performed on both physical locations and cybersecurity frameworks is essential, noting any changes made or new vulnerabilities identified. Take this example, after implementing additional locking mechanisms on server rooms following an incident report from staff, it's important to document these enhancements alongside any related updates to the digital access controls governing server usage.

Finally, regularly reviewing and adapting your integrated security strategy based on emerging threats and technological advancements is key. Creating a timeline for periodic assessments that includes both physical audits and cybersecurity evaluations ensures that your approach remains relevant and effective as your business evolves.

Integration isn't merely about merging processes; it involves cultivating a mindset where security is inherent across all operational aspects. By combining physical security measures with cybersecurity frameworks, small businesses can establish a fortified environment that significantly minimizes the risk of breaches while enhancing overall operational integrity. Each proactive step toward integration empowers organizations to navigate the complex landscape of modern threats more effectively, transforming vulnerability into strength within their operational DNA.

CHAPTER 11:
LEVERAGING
CYBERSECURITY
TECHNOLOGIES

Types of Cybersecurity Technologies

F or small business owners, grasping the various types of cybersecurity technologies is essential for protecting assets and sensitive data. The cybersecurity landscape is diverse, with each category designed to tackle specific threats and vulnerabilities. As we delve into these technologies, it's important to consider how they can be integrated into your organization's existing framework.

At the forefront of cybersecurity are firewalls, which act as the first line of defense against unauthorized network access. By monitoring incoming and outgoing traffic based on predetermined security rules, firewalls create a barrier between trusted internal networks and untrusted external ones. Small businesses should explore both hardware and software firewalls; for instance, a cloud-based company may benefit from software firewalls that are easily updated and managed remotely. Implementing a robust firewall not only thwarts external threats but also generates logs that can prove invaluable during security audits.

Following firewalls are intrusion detection systems (IDS) and intrusion prevention systems (IPS). Both technologies monitor network traffic for suspicious activities, but they serve different purposes. An IDS alerts administrators to potential threats, enabling proactive responses before a breach occurs. Conversely, an IPS actively blocks malicious traffic in real time. For example, a small e-commerce site might utilize an IPS to prevent credit card fraud by automatically blocking any transactions flagged as suspicious based on set criteria.

Encryption technologies are vital for protecting sensitive data, whether it is at rest or in transit. By converting information into unreadable code, encryption ensures that even if data is intercepted, it remains secure from unauthorized access. Small businesses should prioritize strong encryption protocols like AES (Advanced Encryption Standard) for data storage and TLS (Transport Layer Security) for online transactions. Take this example, a law firm storing client files can implement end-to-end encryption to safeguard confidential communications and comply with regulations regarding client privacy.

Another essential aspect of cybersecurity is endpoint security solutions that protect individual devices connected to the network. With remote work becoming increasingly common, securing endpoints—such as laptops and smartphones—has become vital. Endpoint detection and response (EDR) tools monitor these devices for signs of malicious activity or policy violations. For example, if an employee inadvertently downloads malware while accessing company resources remotely, an EDR solution can detect this behavior and quarantine the device until the threat is neutralized.

Despite being one of the oldest forms of digital protection, antivirus software remains crucial; however, its role has evolved significantly. Modern antivirus solutions now leverage artificial intelligence (AI) to learn adaptively from malware behavior patterns rather than relying solely on traditional signature-based detection methods. A small tech startup might employ AI-driven antivirus tools that continuously update their threat databases without requiring manual intervention, ensuring robust protection against emerging threats.

Data loss prevention (DLP) tools add another layer of security by preventing sensitive information from leaving the organization—whether unintentionally or maliciously. These solutions monitor data transfers across networks and endpoints to identify potential leaks or breaches based on established policies. Take this example, if an employee attempts to email confidential client information outside the organization's domain without proper authorization, DLP software will flag or block this action.

As more businesses migrate their operations online, cloud security technologies have become increasingly vital. Solutions such as cloud access security brokers (CASBs) help organizations enforce security policies while accessing cloud services by providing visibility into user activity across various platforms and ensuring compliance with organizational standards. A small business utilizing multiple SaaS applications can benefit from CASBs by centralizing monitoring efforts, streamlining management without sacrificing security.

Integrating these cybersecurity technologies requires careful planning and execution. Aligning them with your overall business strategy is crucial for success. When selecting technology solutions, consider how they fit within your organization's risk profile and operational needs. Regular assessments can help identify gaps in coverage or opportunities for improvement while ensuring your defenses remain adaptable to evolving threats.

By incorporating multiple layers of cybersecurity measures, you not only strengthen your defenses but also foster resilience throughout your organization's operations. Investing time in understanding these technologies and implementing them strategically empowers your business to navigate today's complex threat landscape with confidence —turning cybersecurity into a competitive advantage rather than merely a compliance obligation.

Automation in Cybersecurity

Automation in cybersecurity marks a significant evolution in how businesses safeguard themselves against increasingly sophisticated threats. For small business owners, grasping and utilizing automation can be crucial in effectively managing risks and avoiding the pitfalls of cyberattacks. By automating essential processes, organizations can alleviate the burden on human resources while ensuring robust security measures remain intact.

Central to cybersecurity automation are tools designed for real-time monitoring and threat detection. Security Information and Event Management (SIEM) systems, for instance, gather logs from various sources across a network and analyze them for anomalies that could indicate a breach. A small retail business could implement a SIEM to automatically flag suspicious transaction patterns or unauthorized access attempts. This approach not only enhances response times but also reduces the likelihood of human error in monitoring activities.

Automated incident response represents another vital area where efficiency can be greatly improved. By establishing predefined responses to common threats, businesses can act swiftly without waiting for manual intervention. For example, when a phishing email is detected, automation allows the system to isolate the affected account, notify the user of the potential threat, and initiate a password reset—all without human oversight. This rapid response mitigates potential damage while simultaneously educating employees about security protocols.

The integration of machine learning into cybersecurity tools further amplifies these advantages. Machine learning algorithms can analyze vast amounts of data to identify patterns and predict potential threats based on past incidents. Take this example, an insurance firm might leverage machine learning to detect anomalies in claims submissions that suggest fraudulent activity. As these algorithms learn from ongoing data, their predictive accuracy improves, making them increasingly effective at thwarting attacks before they escalate.

Additionally, automation enhances compliance efforts for small businesses navigating complex regulations governing data protection and privacy. Automated compliance tools continuously monitor processes to track adherence to standards like GDPR or HIPAA, flagging potential violations as they arise. Picture a healthcare practice employing automated compliance software to systematically audit patient records; discrepancies can be addressed proactively rather than during infrequent manual audits.

However, successful automation relies on collaboration. Small business owners should engage their teams in the implementation process to ensure everyone understands how to effectively use these new automated systems while maintaining security awareness. Involving employees in discussions about which tasks should be automated can lead to more tailored solutions, as those on the front lines often possess valuable insights into daily challenges and vulnerabilities that technology alone cannot resolve.

As organizations adopt increasingly sophisticated automation solutions, it's essential to regularly evaluate their effectiveness and adaptability to evolving threats. Periodically reassessing automated processes allows businesses to adjust based on emerging risks or changes in operations. For example, as a small business moves towards greater cloud integration or remote work, its automated systems should evolve accordingly to provide consistent protection across diverse environments.

embracing automation goes beyond enhancing security; it fosters a proactive cybersecurity culture within an organization. This shift empowers employees to focus on strategic initiatives rather than getting bogged down by routine tasks—creating a win-win scenario for both productivity and protection.

In today's digital landscape, where cyber threats are ever-present, automation emerges as an indispensable ally for small businesses seeking effective asset protection. By investing in automated technologies and thoughtfully integrating them into operations, you not only establish a robust defense against attacks but also cultivate an agile organization prepared to face future challenges head-on.

Artificial Intelligence and Machine Learning

Artificial intelligence (AI) and machine learning (ML) are revolutionizing cybersecurity strategies, particularly for small business owners who face a constant barrage of cyber threats. These advanced technologies not only enhance existing security measures but also automate response processes and provide valuable insights into potential vulnerabilities that may otherwise go unnoticed. As cyberattacks become increasingly sophisticated, the integration of AI and ML into cybersecurity is no longer just a trend; it is essential for businesses aiming to stay one step ahead.

Take, for example, AI-driven analytics that help small

businesses analyze vast amounts of data to identify anomalies that could indicate security breaches. An online retailer could utilize AI algorithms to monitor customer behavior in real time. If the system detects unusual spikes in transaction volumes or geographic access points that deviate from established patterns, it can automatically alert security teams for further investigation. This proactive strategy not only reduces response times but also strengthens the overall security posture.

Machine learning further enhances these capabilities by continuously refining its algorithms based on new data inputs. Consider a law firm that employs ML to scrutinize email traffic for potential phishing attempts. As the algorithm learns from past incidents—such as which emails led to successful breaches—it becomes increasingly skilled at recognizing subtle indicators of phishing in incoming communications. This adaptive ability improves over time, resulting in fewer false positives and higher detection rates.

And, AI can significantly streamline threat intelligence processes, a crucial need for small businesses that often lack the resources to actively monitor the threat landscape. By aggregating data from various sources—such as security blogs, forums, and real-time threat feeds—AI provides critical insights that guide decision-making. Take this example, a small financial services firm could use AI-driven threat intelligence platforms to receive alerts about vulnerabilities related to commonly used software within their environment, enabling them to take preventive measures before an attacker exploits these weaknesses.

Automation is another area where AI excels in cybersecurity practices. Tasks such as log analysis, user behavior monitoring, and vulnerability scanning can be automated using machine learning models that not only perform these functions but also learn from new data inputs to improve efficiency and accuracy over time. Picture a small manufacturing company implementing an automated vulnerability scanning tool; this tool runs periodically to identify outdated software versions or misconfigurations and generates reports for IT staff without requiring manual intervention. This automation frees up valuable human resources for more strategic initiatives while ensuring continuous monitoring.

However, integrating AI and ML into cybersecurity practices necessitates careful planning and consideration. Small business owners must invest time in understanding how these technologies work and what they require for successful implementation. Initiating pilot programs allows organizations to test specific AI solutions before fully committing, ensuring alignment with existing processes and readiness for adoption across their teams.

Education is equally important; employees must be trained not only on how these technologies operate but also on how they contribute to overall cybersecurity strategies. Enhancing employee awareness of the capabilities and limitations of AI systems fosters trust in automated responses and cultivates a culture of vigilance against cyber threats.

As the cyber landscape evolves with new challenges emerging daily, small businesses that leverage AI and ML will gain a distinct advantage. Regularly reviewing the effectiveness of implemented solutions ensures adaptability as technology and threats evolve over time. Take this example, as cybercriminals refine their tactics, small businesses should be prepared to adjust their machine learning models accordingly.

Investing in AI-driven cybersecurity is not just about keeping pace with technological advancements; it is about creating resilient organizations equipped to handle current and future challenges with agility and confidence. By thoughtfully embracing these innovations and aligning them with specific business needs, small business owners can protect their assets more effectively while unlocking new opportunities for growth amidst uncertainty.

In an age where every interaction carries potential risk, integrating artificial intelligence and machine learning into cybersecurity is not merely advantageous; it is becoming essential for maintaining operational integrity and trust within your business ecosystem.

Threat Intelligence Platforms

Threat Intelligence Platforms (TIPs) are vital tools for small businesses seeking to enhance their cybersecurity efforts. These platforms enable organizations to anticipate, prepare for, and respond to potential threats with greater effectiveness. By aggregating and analyzing vast amounts of threat data from diverse sources, TIPs provide actionable insights that empower decision-makers to strengthen their defenses. For small business owners grappling with the complexities of cybersecurity, leveraging a TIP can fundamentally change how they manage risk and address evolving threats.

Take, for example, a small healthcare provider that handles sensitive patient information. By utilizing a threat intelligence platform, this organization can gather intelligence specifically targeting threats in the healthcare sector. TIPs can identify known vulnerabilities in widely used software systems or alert the business about ongoing phishing campaigns aimed at healthcare professionals. With this timely information, the organization can implement necessary patches or conduct training sessions before a breach occurs, thereby safeguarding patient data and ensuring compliance with regulatory standards.

The integration of TIPs not only enhances situational awareness but also encourages collaboration both within the organization and across its network. Take this example, a small business operating within a larger supply chain can significantly benefit from shared threat intelligence among partners. If one entity experiences a cyber incident, it can share relevant details through the TIP, allowing all partners to collectively strengthen their defenses and mitigate risks. This collaborative approach helps identify trends that may be applicable across the industry, further enhancing overall cybersecurity.

However, implementing a TIP requires careful planning. Small business owners must first assess their current cybersecurity posture and identify gaps where enhanced intelligence could be beneficial. Choosing the right platform involves evaluating features such as integration capabilities with existing security tools, data enrichment options, and user-friendliness. Many platforms offer trial periods, enabling organizations to test compatibility before making significant financial commitments.

Once a TIP is in place, regular engagement with the platform is crucial for maximizing its potential. Business owners should ensure that relevant teams—such as IT, compliance, and management—are trained on how to effectively interpret the data provided by these systems. This training cultivates an informed workforce that understands not only how to react to threats but also how to anticipate them based on real-time information.

As businesses begin to utilize TIPs, they can expect various outputs that enhance their overall security strategy. Automated alerts regarding vulnerabilities allow for proactive remediation efforts rather than reactive responses after incidents occur. Also, regular reports generated by these platforms can guide strategic discussions around resource allocation for cybersecurity measures.

It's important to acknowledge the limitations of threat intelligence platforms as well. While they offer valuable insights, they cannot replace comprehensive security measures or human judgment. A well-rounded approach involves integrating insights gained from TIPs into broader security policies and practices. Continuous evaluation of the effectiveness of threat intelligence is essential as cybercriminals adapt their tactics; being nimble in response is crucial.

Consider a poignant example from a retail business that suffered a data breach due to outdated software exploited by attackers. After adopting a threat intelligence platform, they not only received alerts about vulnerabilities but also incorporated those insights into their regular patch management process. This proactive approach significantly reduced their exposure to similar threats moving forward.

In today's rapidly evolving digital landscape, small businesses must harness every available resource to defend against cyber threats effectively. By incorporating Threat Intelligence Platforms into their cybersecurity strategies, owners empower themselves with knowledge that informs decisions about risk management. This proactive stance not only protects against potential breaches but also builds trust with customers who expect robust safeguards around their sensitive information.

in an age where information is power, utilizing Threat Intelligence Platforms allows small business owners to remain vigilant and prepared against adversaries lurking in cyberspace. Embracing this technology is not merely about enhancing security; it is about cultivating resilience and fostering an environment where businesses can thrive amidst uncertainty and change.

Security Information and Event Management (SIEM)

Security Information and Event Management (SIEM) systems are essential for bolstering an organization's cybersecurity, particularly for small businesses navigating a landscape filled with threats. These systems allow organizations to gather, analyze, and correlate security data from various parts of their networks, offering a comprehensive view of potential incidents. For small business owners, implementing a SIEM can revolutionize their approach to cyber threats by delivering real-time insights that are vital for informed decision-making.

The primary function of SIEM lies in its ability to aggregate logs and event data from diverse sources such as firewalls, intrusion detection systems, and servers. This aggregation enables businesses to monitor security events as they happen, moving beyond a reliance on retrospective analysis. Take this example, imagine a small online retail store that recently adopted a SIEM solution. One evening, the system flagged unusual login attempts from multiple locations within a brief time span—a pattern suggestive of a possible brute-force attack. Thanks to this real-time alert, the business could swiftly activate its incident response plan, blocking malicious IP addresses before any damage occurred.

To fully leverage the capabilities of a SIEM system, small business owners should start with clear objectives. By identifying their goals—whether it's achieving regulatory compliance, improving incident response times, or gaining better visibility into network activity—they can tailor their implementation strategy accordingly. Selecting the right SIEM solution is also crucial; options range from comprehensive enterprise solutions to budget-friendly cloud-based services designed for smaller operations. Many providers offer scalable solutions that can adapt to the evolving needs of a business without straining financial resources.

Once a SIEM system is in place, regular tuning is necessary to maximize its effectiveness. This involves configuring alerts and refining log sources to ensure that only relevant information is processed. A common pitfall occurs when businesses set overly broad alerts, leading to alert fatigue among security personnel. This condition can result in genuine threats being overlooked amid the noise generated by false positives. For example, if every minor event triggers an alert, teams may become desensitized and less responsive to significant issues.

Also, integrating your SIEM solution with other security tools can enhance its capabilities even further. Pairing SIEM data with endpoint detection and response (EDR) systems, for instance, can yield deeper insights into potential incidents. When these technologies work together, they provide a richer context for understanding anomalies detected by either system independently.

Training staff to effectively interpret SIEM outputs is another critical aspect of successful implementation. Security analysts should be adept at using the platform's dashboard and reporting features while also understanding how to thoroughly investigate alerts. Regular training sessions that include scenario-based exercises can help build this competency; simulating incidents where employees must respond based on alerts generated by the SIEM cultivates an environment where practical skills are honed.

Ongoing evaluations of your SIEM's performance are essential to ensure it continues meeting your evolving cybersecurity needs. Reviewing incident reports and response times helps identify trends over time—perhaps you notice that phishing attempts peak during specific months or correlate with marketing campaigns. Armed with this knowledge, you could proactively increase training efforts during high-risk periods.

A practical example of effective SIEM implementation can be seen in a small financial advisory firm that adopted such a system after experiencing minor breaches due to unmonitored user behavior on their network. By effectively utilizing their SIEM platform—setting precise alerts and providing thorough training—they were able not only to detect unauthorized access attempts but also to mitigate risks before they escalated into larger issues.

As cyber threats continue to grow in sophistication

and prevalence, investing in Security Information and Event Management becomes increasingly imperative for small businesses seeking long-term resilience against cyber adversaries. The benefits gained through timely insights and strategic responses empower organizations not just to survive but to thrive amidst escalating challenges. By fostering an environment of proactive awareness and preparedness through SIEM integration, small business owners position themselves as resilient players ready to adapt in an uncertain digital landscape.

Deception Technology

Deception technology is transforming the way organizations defend themselves against cyber threats. Unlike traditional security measures that primarily aim to block attacks, deception technologies actively draw cybercriminals into controlled traps. This helps businesses to detect intrusions before they escalate into serious incidents. For small businesses, this proactive approach not only enhances their security posture but also turns potential vulnerabilities into valuable opportunities for intelligence gathering.

At the heart of deception technology lies the strategy of mimicking genuine assets within a network. These deceptive assets can take the form of fake servers, databases, or entire environments that resemble real systems. When attackers target these decoys, their actions are recorded and analyzed, providing insights into their methods and tactics. Take this example, consider a small business that has adopted a deception platform. If a hacker breaches its network, they might find themselves ensnared in a honeypot—an enticing but fake database filled with fictitious customer records. This scenario not only alerts the security team in real time but also offers invaluable data on the attacker's approach and tools.

To successfully implement deception technology, small business owners should begin with a comprehensive assessment of their environment. Identifying critical assets and understanding normal user behavior are essential first steps in crafting effective decoys that will lure would-be attackers. For example, if a business heavily relies on customer data, it might create fake databases brimming with sensitive-looking information. The objective is to make these decoys attractive enough to draw intruders while ensuring they remain undetectable by legitimate users.

Once the deception framework is in place, ongoing management becomes crucial. Regular updates to the decoy environments help keep them relevant and engaging for attackers. An e-commerce site, for instance, could periodically alter the types of products showcased in its honeypots or refresh inventory levels within deceptive databases. This strategy not only maintains attacker interest but also allows businesses to stay ahead of evolving threats.

Integrating deception technology with existing security infrastructure amplifies its effectiveness. Pairing deception systems with Security Information and Event Management (SIEM) tools enhances an organization's ability to respond promptly to detected incidents. When an attacker interacts with a honeypot and triggers an alert in the SIEM system, security personnel can swiftly initiate containment procedures based on actionable intelligence gathered from the incident.

Training staff to leverage insights gained from deception technologies is essential for maximizing their benefits. For example, security analysts should be equipped to distinguish between interactions with genuine assets and deceptive ones. Regular workshops focused on analyzing data harvested from traps can build these skills; team members can review instances where attackers were lured in and discuss subsequent measures.

And, deception technology cultivates a culture of

cybersecurity awareness within organizations. When employees witness firsthand how deceptions thwart cyber threats, they become more vigilant in recognizing suspicious activities within their daily roles. This cultural shift can have lasting effects across various departments as everyone contributes to maintaining the organization's security posture.

As cyberattacks become increasingly sophisticated and widespread, adopting deception technology offers small businesses not just a defensive tool but also a proactive strategy for gaining insight into their adversaries. By creating realistic bait environments and analyzing attacker behavior through this lens, businesses can transform vulnerabilities into strengths—turning potential chaos into structured learning experiences.

While investing in deception technology may initially seem daunting, such strategies are becoming indispensable as threats grow more complex and targeted towards smaller organizations with limited resources. With well-designed implementation plans and ongoing evaluation efforts—like testing trap effectiveness against various attack scenarios —businesses can effectively position themselves against emerging threats while building robust defenses over time.

At its core, embracing deception technology enhances immediate detection capabilities while empowering small businesses with knowledge about their adversaries' methods. This not only enables them to protect their assets but also illuminates a path forward in an increasingly treacherous digital landscape. By prioritizing this innovative approach today, small business owners can lay the groundwork for a secure tomorrow based on proactive rather than reactive measures.

Implementing New Technologies

As businesses seek to stay ahead of rapidly evolving cyber

threats, integrating new technologies has become essential. Implementing cutting-edge solutions not only enhances security but also allows organizations to operate more efficiently. The right technology can streamline processes, improve visibility, and strengthen defenses against malicious actors.

Artificial Intelligence (AI) has emerged as a cornerstone of cybersecurity, enabling systems to detect anomalies and respond to threats in real time. For small businesses, leveraging AI-driven tools can offer a significant competitive advantage. These systems analyze vast amounts of data at incredible speeds, identifying patterns that might elude human oversight. For example, an AI system can flag unusual login attempts from unknown IP addresses, prompting immediate investigation or automatic countermeasures.

To begin implementing AI-based security measures, small business owners should first evaluate their current data infrastructure. It's crucial to ensure that existing systems can seamlessly integrate AI tools. This assessment involves checking software compatibility and scalability. For businesses utilizing cloud services, platforms like AWS or Azure offer integrated AI capabilities specifically designed for security applications.

Once the infrastructure is prepared, selecting the right AI tool becomes critical. Numerous options are available, from machine learning-based threat detection solutions to identity verification tools that use biometric recognition. It is advisable for businesses to pilot these technologies on a smaller scale before full deployment. This phased approach allows for adjustments based on initial feedback and minimizes disruptions.

Another key technology in modern cybersecurity strategies is Security Information and Event Management (SIEM) systems. These platforms aggregate and analyze security data across an organization's IT environment in real time. Take this example, a small retail business could implement a SIEM solution to monitor transactions and system logs simultaneously. If an irregular transaction triggers an alert, security personnel can respond swiftly—investigating potential fraud before it escalates.

Successful SIEM implementation requires establishing defined use cases based on specific business needs. Companies should develop scenarios where alerts would be triggered by particular behaviors, such as multiple failed login attempts from different locations within a short timeframe. By tailoring these parameters to reflect genuine risks in their industry, businesses can minimize false positives while maximizing response efficiency.

In addition to AI and SIEM technologies, investing in multi-factor authentication (MFA) solutions significantly strengthens access controls across systems. MFA requires users to present two or more verification factors when logging in—such as something they know (password), something they have (a mobile device), or something they are (biometric). Implementing MFA adds a crucial layer of security that makes unauthorized access considerably more challenging for cybercriminals.

Education plays a pivotal role alongside technology adoption. Training employees on new security protocols ensures they understand how to use these tools effectively and recognize potential threats, such as phishing attacks that might bypass technical defenses. Regular training sessions not only reinforce awareness but also cultivate a culture of vigilance throughout the organization.

And, maintaining flexibility within technological implementations allows businesses to adapt as their needs evolve or as new threats emerge. Cybersecurity is not static; therefore, having processes in place for ongoing assessments of tool effectiveness is vital. Take this example, conducting quarterly reviews of incident response metrics can highlight areas needing improvement or indicate if additional resources are required.

Investing in emerging technologies positions small businesses strategically within their industries. By harnessing advanced capabilities like AI and comprehensive SIEM solutions alongside robust access controls like MFA, organizations enhance their resilience against cyber threats while also increasing operational efficiency.

With careful planning and execution—coupled with continuous employee education on cybersecurity awareness —a holistic approach emerges that not only addresses immediate concerns but also builds long-term organizational strength against digital adversaries.

In this landscape where innovation intersects with vigilance, small businesses have the opportunity to transform potential weaknesses into fortified strengths through smart technology adoption and proactive strategies aimed at fostering a secure environment today—and well into the future.

Vendor Management

Vendor management is a vital aspect of your cybersecurity strategy. The relationships you develop with external partners can greatly influence your overall security posture, especially as third-party services become more integrated into your operations. A single misstep in this area can lead to vulnerabilities that expose your business to potential threats. Therefore, understanding how to manage these vendor relationships effectively is not merely advantageous —it is essential for protecting sensitive data and ensuring compliance with regulations.

Start by identifying the vendors that have access to your sensitive data or systems. This may include cloud service providers, payment processors, and IT support companies.

Take this example, if you use a third-party payment processing service, their security protocols will directly impact the safety of your customer data. Assess the significance of each vendor's role in your operations; high-risk vendors will require a more stringent oversight process.

Once you've identified these vendors, create a comprehensive framework for managing them. Begin with a Vendor Risk Assessment (VRA), which should evaluate their security measures, adherence to relevant regulations, and the potential repercussions for your business in the event of a breach. Many organizations utilize questionnaires during the onboarding process to ensure that vendors meet fundamental cybersecurity standards. For example, you might inquire about their data encryption methods for both transit and storage or whether they conduct regular security audits.

After conducting this initial assessment, it's crucial to engage in ongoing monitoring of vendor performance and security practices. This continuous oversight helps ensure that vendors maintain the security standards they initially claimed. Establish periodic reviews—quarterly or annually, depending on the service nature—where you analyze their security updates and any reported incidents. Keep thorough records of these evaluations, as they will be invaluable in the event of a breach or regulatory scrutiny.

Effective communication is another essential element of successful vendor management. Set clear expectations regarding cybersecurity practices not only at the outset but also in establishing protocols for incident response should any issues arise. Define what steps are taken if a data breach occurs involving a vendor and clarify who is responsible for communicating with affected parties. Clearly outlining roles within both your organization and that of your vendor will streamline response efforts and minimize potential damage.

Incorporating cybersecurity provisions into vendor contracts is also critical. Specific clauses should outline expected security standards and responsibilities in case of a breach, such as how quickly vendors must notify you upon detecting incidents involving your data. A well-structured contract not only protects both parties but also clarifies the path forward during challenging situations.

Training vendors on your cybersecurity policies and expectations enhances accountability and collaboration. Consider hosting periodic training sessions or workshops to help key vendor representatives familiarize themselves with your protocols. If you regularly update your data handling policies, ensure they receive the latest information so they can adjust their processes accordingly. View vendors as extensions of your team; their adherence to your guidelines will strengthen your overall defense mechanisms.

Lastly, prioritize building strong relationships with these partners. A solid partnership encourages open dialogue, making it easier to address concerns promptly when issues arise. Invest time in regular check-ins—these interactions help foster trust and promote proactive communication regarding potential threats or weaknesses observed on either side.

Effective vendor management goes beyond simply monitoring access and compliance; it involves creating an ecosystem that prioritizes security collaboration and continuous improvement. By taking an active role in managing vendor relationships, small business owners can establish a more resilient defense against cyber threats while nurturing partnerships that drive mutual growth and success.

Future Trends in Cybersecurity Technology

As we explore future trends in cybersecurity technology, it's important to recognize that the digital landscape is anything but static. The rapid evolution of technology brings forth new innovations and threats that constantly reshape how businesses operate. For small business owners, staying informed about these trends is vital—not just for knowledge's sake, but for leveraging advancements to strengthen their defenses against increasingly sophisticated cyber threats.

At the forefront of this transformation is Artificial Intelligence (AI). Security solutions now increasingly integrate AI technologies to enhance threat detection and response capabilities. Traditional methods often struggle to keep pace with the speed and complexity of cyberattacks; however, AI can analyze vast amounts of data in real-time. Take this example, AI algorithms can monitor network traffic, identifying anomalies such as unusual login patterns or spikes in data transfers that could indicate a breach. By implementing AI-powered security tools that learn from previous attacks, businesses can adapt their defenses more effectively.

Complementing AI is machine learning (ML), which plays a crucial role in modern cybersecurity. Unlike static rule-based systems, ML models evolve based on experience, enabling them to identify patterns that may go unnoticed by human analysts. A small business using ML-enhanced security software could receive automated alerts when suspicious behavior is detected, allowing for swift intervention before damage occurs. This proactive strategy helps organizations stay ahead of potential threats rather than merely reacting after an incident.

Another significant trend gaining traction is the expansion of Zero Trust architecture. The core principle of Zero Trust is simple: never trust, always verify. In an environment where employees may work remotely and access company resources from various devices, relying solely on traditional perimeter defenses is insufficient. Adopting a Zero Trust model involves continuously validating users and devices before granting access to sensitive data, effectively treating every request as potentially malicious. Small businesses can embrace this approach through Multi-Factor Authentication (MFA), which adds an extra layer of security by requiring more than just a password for access.

The rise of remote work has also heightened the focus on endpoint security solutions. As employees use personal devices to connect to corporate networks, safeguarding these endpoints becomes essential. Investing in comprehensive endpoint protection tools—such as antivirus software, firewalls, and intrusion detection systems—ensures that every device linked to your network is fortified against vulnerabilities.

Integrating cybersecurity with business continuity planning is another trend gaining momentum. Cyber incidents can significantly disrupt operations; thus, having a well-defined plan with immediate response strategies is critical for minimizing downtime and financial losses. Small business owners should regularly review their incident response plans to ensure they align with evolving threats while providing clear communication guidelines during a crisis.

Blockchain technology represents another exciting frontier in cybersecurity innovation. While often associated with cryptocurrencies, blockchain's decentralized nature offers unique benefits for securing data transactions. For example, smart contracts can automate compliance checks within supply chains by ensuring all transactions are transparently recorded and verified among all parties involved—reducing opportunities for fraud or data manipulation.

In conjunction with these technological advancements, there is a growing need for robust training programs focused on cybersecurity awareness among employees. Since human error remains one of the leading causes of breaches, fostering a culture of security mindfulness is crucial moving forward. Regular training sessions can equip staff to recognize phishing attempts and social engineering tactics effectively— empowering them to act as the first line of defense against cyber threats.

Additionally, the evolving regulatory landscape demands vigilance from small businesses regarding compliance requirements relevant to their industries. Regulations like GDPR and CCPA are constantly adapting alongside emerging technologies; understanding how these changes impact operations will be essential in maintaining legal compliance while building customer trust through transparent data handling practices.

Finally, as you assess these trends, consider collaborating with third-party vendors specializing in cybersecurity services —known as Managed Security Service Providers (MSSPs). Engaging MSSPs allows small businesses to access advanced technologies and expert insights without needing extensive in-house resources or expertise.

By embracing these future trends, you position your business not only for success but also for resilience against emerging threats in our increasingly digital world. Proactively leveraging new technologies and strategies tailored to contemporary challenges will help cultivate a robust cybersecurity posture that protects your organization today and safeguards its growth potential tomorrow.

CHAPTER 12:
REGULATORY
AND COMPLIANCE
REQUIREMENTS

Overview of Cybersecurity
Regulations

C ybersecurity regulations are designed to protect sensitive data and provide a framework for organizations to address cybersecurity challenges. For small businesses, grasping these regulations is essential—not only do they help safeguard your company, but they also foster trust with clients and partners. Neglecting compliance can result in severe penalties, reputational damage, and a loss of customer confidence.

Key regulations, such as the General Data Protection Regulation (GDPR) in Europe and the California Consumer Privacy Act (CCPA) in the United States, signify a move towards stricter data privacy protections. These laws mandate that businesses actively implement measures to protect consumer data. Take this example, GDPR requires companies to obtain explicit consent from users before collecting personal data and grants individuals the right to access and delete their information. Small business owners need to understand these requirements; failure to comply can lead to fines of up to 4% of annual global turnover.

Navigating these regulations involves more than just legal compliance; it requires practical applications in daily operations. Businesses should evaluate their data collection and storage practices to ensure alignment with regulatory standards. For example, a small retail business that collects customer email addresses for newsletters must properly secure those records and provide customers with easy options to unsubscribe or delete their information upon request.

Another important regulation for many small businesses is the Payment Card Industry Data Security Standard (PCI DSS). If your business processes credit card transactions, adherence to PCI DSS is non-negotiable. Compliance involves implementing security measures such as data encryption during transmission, regular security testing, and maintaining a secure network infrastructure. A small online store can enhance customer confidence by prominently displaying PCI compliance certificates on its checkout page, assuring shoppers that their payment details are secure.

In addition to specific regulations, broader frameworks like the National Institute of Standards and Technology (NIST) Cybersecurity Framework offer guidelines that apply across various industries. NIST advocates for a risk-based approach to managing cybersecurity risks by identifying assets, assessing vulnerabilities, protecting against threats, effectively responding to incidents, and recovering from disruptions. Implementing this framework might involve conducting regular risk assessments to identify weaknesses in your system and developing strategies for mitigation.

Local laws and industry-specific regulations further influence your cybersecurity strategy. For example, healthcare providers must comply with the Health Insurance Portability and Accountability Act (HIPAA), which enforces strict privacy and security requirements for medical information. Non-compliance with HIPAA can lead to hefty fines and erode patient trust.

Adhering to cybersecurity regulations is not just about avoiding penalties; it also presents an opportunity to improve overall business practices. Cultivating a culture of compliance can drive organizational accountability and enhance operational efficiency. As your business grows, you may need to establish an internal compliance team or appoint a dedicated compliance officer.

Equally important is training employees on regulatory requirements. Regular workshops or online training sessions can keep your team informed about best practices related to data privacy laws relevant to your industry. This proactive approach nurtures a security-minded workforce that understands its role in protecting sensitive information.

The relationship between cybersecurity regulations and overall business strategy is critical; organizations that prioritize compliance not only meet legal obligations but also gain competitive advantages through enhanced customer trust and loyalty. By integrating regulatory understanding into daily operations, businesses foster transparency—customers are increasingly aware of how their data is managed and prefer companies that prioritize their protection.

To wrap things up, navigating the intricate landscape of cybersecurity regulations requires diligence but offers substantial rewards. As threats evolve alongside regulatory changes, continuously updating your knowledge will be essential for maintaining compliance while strengthening your organization against cyber risks. The proactive measures you take today will not only help mitigate potential damages but also position your business as a leader in cybersecurity excellence within your industry.

Industry-Specific Regulations

Understanding industry-specific regulations is essential for small businesses, especially since different sectors have unique compliance requirements. Each industry faces distinct cybersecurity challenges that influence the regulations governing them. Take this example, the healthcare sector operates under stringent rules due to the sensitivity of patient data, while the financial services industry must adhere to strict guidelines designed to protect consumer financial information.

Let's explore some of these industry-specific regulations, beginning with healthcare. The Health Insurance Portability and Accountability Act (HIPAA) establishes rigorous standards for safeguarding medical information. Small healthcare providers need to implement adequate security measures to protect electronic health records (EHRs). This can involve setting up access controls, conducting regular risk assessments, and ensuring data encryption both at rest and during transmission. For example, a small clinic might adopt a secure patient management system that meets HIPAA requirements, helping to streamline operations while ensuring compliance.

In contrast, companies within the financial sector face their own regulatory landscape. The Gramm-Leach-Bliley Act (GLBA) mandates that financial institutions safeguard customers' sensitive information. Compliance requires clear privacy notices and giving customers the option to opt out of sharing personal data with non-affiliated third parties. A small credit union could strengthen its position by developing a transparent privacy policy that not only adheres to GLBA but also fosters customer trust through open communication.

Retail businesses also contend with specific regulations when handling payment card transactions. Adhering to the Payment Card Industry Data Security Standard (PCI DSS) is crucial for any business processing credit card payments. Take this example, an online retailer should ensure that its website uses SSL encryption for all transactions and conducts regular vulnerability scans of its network systems. Displaying PCI compliance badges on their website can further reassure customers about their security practices.

Beyond these well-known regulations, there are additional mandates like the Federal Information Security Management Act (FISMA), which applies to federal agencies and contractors. This act emphasizes the need for comprehensive security programs that include risk assessments and continuous IT system monitoring. While FISMA primarily targets government entities, its principles can serve as a model for small businesses striving for high security standards.

Educational institutions also face compliance requirements under the Family Educational Rights and Privacy Act (FERPA), which protects student education records. Given the vast amount of sensitive data they handle, educational organizations must understand FERPA's implications by implementing proper data management systems and training staff on appropriate handling practices.

Navigating these complex regulations often necessitates that small business owners engage actively with legal counsel or compliance experts who understand their specific industry landscapes. This approach not only ensures compliance but also helps identify gaps in current practices that could expose them to risks or liabilities. Additionally, organizations should regularly review and update their policies in response to evolving laws and technologies.

Creating a culture of compliance within your organization extends beyond understanding regulatory requirements; it involves integrating those insights into everyday operations.

Regular training sessions can help employees stay informed about relevant laws and their impacts on business processes. For example, role-playing scenarios related to data breaches or misuse can prepare teams for real-world challenges they may face.

To strengthen compliance efforts, consider forming partnerships with cybersecurity firms specializing in your industry's regulatory landscape. Such collaborations can provide critical insights into emerging threats and develop strategies tailored to meet specific regulatory needs effectively.

 recognizing that compliance is an ongoing process rather than a one-time task is vital for small business owners. By proactively auditing processes against regulatory standards, organizations not only protect themselves from potential penalties but also build a reputation as trustworthy entities in their markets.

General Data Protection Regulation (GDPR)

The General Data Protection Regulation (GDPR) marks a pivotal change in how businesses manage and safeguard personal data. Enforced in May 2018, the GDPR aims to enhance individual control over personal information while imposing stringent requirements on organizations that handle such data. Small businesses, regardless of their size, must understand that compliance with GDPR is not merely a choice; it is crucial for maintaining customer trust and avoiding significant penalties.

At the heart of GDPR is the requirement for businesses to obtain clear consent from individuals before processing their personal data. This means small business owners should only collect information essential for their operations. Take this example, if an e-commerce site collects email addresses for order confirmations, those emails cannot be used for marketing purposes without explicit consent. Implementing double opt-in processes can effectively secure this consent while fostering customer confidence.

Transparency plays a vital role in GDPR compliance. Businesses are required to inform individuals about how their data will be used, stored, and shared. Having a clear privacy policy that outlines these aspects should be easily accessible on your website. This policy not only fulfills legal obligations but also strengthens customer relationships. For example, a small online boutique might clarify that customer information is solely used for order fulfillment and is never sold to third parties.

Another fundamental principle of GDPR is the concept of data protection by design and by default. This principle encourages small businesses to incorporate data protection measures into their daily operations rather than treating compliance as an afterthought. By implementing security measures such as encryption and access controls from the beginning, businesses can effectively safeguard sensitive information. A local coffee shop offering an app for ordering ahead, for instance, should ensure that user accounts are secured with strong passwords and that payment information is encrypted.

In addition, if your business engages in large-scale processing of sensitive data or regularly monitors individuals on a large scale, appointing a Data Protection Officer (DPO) may be necessary. While budget constraints may make this challenging for many small businesses, designating someone internally to oversee compliance efforts can be beneficial. This individual can stay updated on regulatory changes and ensure adherence to best practices.

Data breach notification is another critical requirement under GDPR; businesses must report any breaches involving personal data within 72 hours of becoming aware of them. Failing to notify authorities can lead to substantial fines. Establishing an incident response plan enables your team to respond swiftly in the event of a breach, minimizing damage and ensuring compliance with notification requirements. For example, a small tech startup could develop a protocol detailing steps for investigating breaches, notifying affected individuals, and documenting incidents for regulatory purposes.

Regular audits of your data processing activities are essential for demonstrating compliance with GDPR standards. These audits should evaluate the personal data you hold, the reasons for holding it, how it is processed, and whether adequate security measures are in place. A checklist approach may facilitate this process:

1. Identify all personal data collected.

2. Review consent mechanisms.

3. Evaluate security measures like encryption or anonymization.

4. Document all processing activities.

Engaging employees through training programs focused on GDPR principles further cultivates a culture of compliance within your organization. It is important that everyone, from front-line staff handling customer interactions to management, understands the significance of data protection laws and their roles in ensuring compliance.

The consequences of failing to comply with GDPR extend beyond financial penalties; they can severely damage your reputation and erode consumer trust—a crucial asset for any small business seeking growth in today's digital landscape. By proactively embedding these practices into your operations, rather than addressing issues reactively as they arise, you position your business not only as compliant but also as a leader in ethical data management.

While the journey toward full GDPR compliance may initially seem daunting, breaking it down into manageable steps empowers small business owners to take charge confidently.

This approach fosters stronger relationships with customers built on transparency and respect for their privacy rights.

Payment Card Industry Data Security Standard (PCI DSS)

The Payment Card Industry Data Security Standard (PCI DSS) is a vital framework established to protect cardholder data and ensure secure transactions worldwide. Compliance with these standards goes beyond mere regulatory obligations; it reflects a commitment to maintaining customer trust and integrity within the payment processing ecosystem. For small business owners, understanding and implementing PCI DSS can initially seem daunting, but breaking it down into manageable steps can simplify the process.

Take this example, one requirement under the goal of building and maintaining a secure network is the installation and maintenance of a firewall configuration to protect cardholder data. This entails assessing existing firewall settings to ensure they effectively shield sensitive information from unauthorized access. A practical approach would be to regularly document firewall rules and configurations, ensuring they align with PCI DSS requirements while accommodating your business's unique needs.

Another critical aspect is the protection of cardholder data itself. Businesses are required to encrypt the transmission of this data across open networks. By implementing encryption protocols such as TLS (Transport Layer Security) during online payment processing, you can significantly reduce the risk of data breaches. For example, if you operate an online retail store, ensuring that all checkout pages utilize HTTPS encryption is essential for safeguarding customer payment information.

Maintaining a vulnerability management program is equally important. This involves routinely updating software and systems to address known vulnerabilities. A straightforward way to manage this requirement is through regular software updates for both operating systems and applications used in payment processing. If you partner with third-party payment processors or platforms, it's crucial to verify their compliance with PCI DSS standards by periodically reviewing their certifications.

Access control measures also play a vital role in compliance. Ensuring that only employees who need access to cardholder data can obtain it is essential. Implementing role-based access controls (RBAC) allows small business owners to efficiently manage who can view or handle sensitive payment information. For example, if only your accounting team requires access to transaction records for reconciliation, you can configure user permissions accordingly within your financial software.

Regularly monitoring and testing your networks is another critical requirement. This involves conducting vulnerability scans at least quarterly and following any significant changes in your network infrastructure. Engaging external security professionals or using automated scanning tools can help identify potential weaknesses before they are exploited by malicious actors. Tools like Qualys or Nessus enable businesses to automate vulnerability assessments effectively while providing detailed reports on necessary remediations.

Finally, establishing an information security policy fosters a culture of security awareness within your organization. This policy should outline how your business protects cardholder data and include procedures for reporting security incidents or breaches. Training employees on this policy ensures that everyone understands their responsibilities regarding payment security.

Non-compliance with PCI DSS not only exposes businesses to potential financial penalties but also risks significant reputational damage if customer data is compromised. The consequences extend beyond immediate losses; even a single breach can irreparably harm the trust customers place in your brand.

For small businesses striving for PCI DSS compliance, prioritizing these requirements not only ensures adherence but also positions them as trustworthy entities in the marketplace. Proactive steps—such as regular training sessions for staff on payment security best practices—can further enhance employee awareness and emphasize the importance of protecting customer information.

While navigating PCI DSS may seem overwhelming at first glance, adopting a systematic approach can simplify the journey toward compliance and bolster your overall cybersecurity posture. Every effort made to secure cardholder data not only protects transactions but also fosters lasting relationships with customers who value their privacy and security in today's digital landscape.

Health Insurance Portability and Accountability Act (HIPAA)

The Health Insurance Portability and Accountability Act (HIPAA) serves as a fundamental pillar of data protection in the healthcare sector, ensuring that personal health information (PHI) remains secure in our increasingly digital world. For small business owners in healthcare, the implications of HIPAA compliance are significant. By adhering to these regulations, not only do they safeguard patient data, but they also bolster the credibility and trustworthiness of their practices.

HIPAA's requirements hinge on two main rules: the Privacy Rule and the Security Rule. The Privacy Rule establishes standards for protecting individuals' medical records and personal health information, ensuring that patients can access their own data. Complementing this, the Security Rule outlines specific safeguards designed to protect electronic PHI (ePHI). A solid understanding of both rules is essential for small businesses, particularly those managing sensitive patient information.

Take this example, the Privacy Rule grants patients the right to obtain copies of their health records and request corrections. Small practices can take practical steps by establishing clear protocols for managing these requests. A systematic process not only ensures compliance but also enhances patient satisfaction. Implementing software that facilitates easy retrieval and modification of health records—while keeping logs of access and changes—can streamline operations and promote transparency.

The Security Rule introduces three categories of safeguards: administrative, physical, and technical. Administrative safeguards encompass policies and procedures that guide the selection, development, implementation, and maintenance of security measures. Conducting regular risk assessments is a vital practice for small business owners; a straightforward checklist can help identify potential vulnerabilities in their systems. This might include questions about access controls, employee training on data security, and incident response plans.

Physical safeguards focus on protecting facilities and equipment that house ePHI. Simple yet effective strategies —such as ensuring that offices are locked after hours or using secure cabinets for sensitive paper files—can make a significant difference. Additionally, maintaining visitor logs can help track who accesses physical locations where health information is stored.

Technical safeguards are critical as well; encrypting ePHI is one of the most effective strategies for preventing unauthorized access during transmission or storage. Utilizing encryption protocols like AES (Advanced Encryption Standard) not only secures data but also facilitates compliance with HIPAA requirements. It is essential that business associates who handle or transmit patient data adhere to these encryption standards as well.

And, ongoing workforce training on HIPAA compliance is crucial for small business owners. Regular training sessions ensure that employees understand their responsibilities under HIPAA while emphasizing the importance of protecting patient information. Incorporating real-life scenarios into training sessions allows employees to role-play common situations—like accidental disclosures or phishing attempts—preparing them for real-world challenges.

Another key aspect of HIPAA compliance is establishing clear policies for breach notification procedures. In the event of a data breach involving ePHI, organizations are required to notify affected individuals within 60 days and report incidents to the Department of Health and Human Services (HHS). Developing an incident response plan that outlines how breaches will be managed can significantly reduce response times and mitigate potential damage.

Failure to comply with HIPAA can result in substantial fines and irreparable harm to a small business's reputation within its community. A breach affecting patient data carries extensive consequences; beyond financial repercussions, it can erode trust that takes years to build but can be lost in moments when security is compromised.

By prioritizing HIPAA compliance, healthcare providers not only protect patient privacy but also position themselves as trustworthy entities in a competitive market. To maintain ongoing compliance efforts, conducting regular audits is vital —they help identify gaps in practices and highlight areas needing improvement while ensuring adherence to evolving regulations.

Although HIPAA may seem daunting at first glance, adopting a structured approach brings clarity amid complexity. By breaking down regulations into actionable steps—such as effectively training staff, implementing robust security measures, and safeguarding sensitive data—organizations can foster a culture that values confidentiality at every level.

 creating an environment where patients feel confident their health information is protected builds loyalty and enhances a practice's standing in an increasingly security-conscious landscape. Through diligent efforts toward achieving HIPAA compliance, small business owners not only shield themselves from penalties but also cultivate meaningful relationships with those they serve—a cornerstone of any thriving healthcare enterprise.

National Institute of Standards and Technology (NIST) Framework

The National Institute of Standards and Technology (NIST) Framework for Improving Critical Infrastructure Cybersecurity serves as a vital resource for businesses looking to enhance their cybersecurity practices. This framework provides a structured approach to managing and mitigating cybersecurity risks, promoting a proactive stance that can be customized to meet the diverse needs of organizations.

Essentially, the NIST Framework consists of five essential functions: Identify, Protect, Detect, Respond, and Recover. Together, these functions create a cohesive strategy tailored to address the unique challenges faced by small business owners. In the Identify phase, for instance, businesses take stock of their assets and resources—a crucial step in understanding what requires protection. Utilizing asset management tools to catalog hardware and software can simplify this process, ensuring that all critical components are accounted for.

Moving to the Protect function, small businesses can implement safeguards designed not only to secure data but also to enhance operational efficiency. This may involve establishing access controls through role-based permissions or deploying firewalls to guard against external threats. A practical exercise is developing a straightforward security policy document that outlines acceptable use of company resources. By distributing this document during onboarding sessions and revisiting it regularly, organizations foster an informed workforce that understands its security responsibilities.

As cyber threats continue to evolve at an alarming rate, detection becomes increasingly important. In the Detect phase, organizations need capabilities to promptly identify anomalies or breaches. Small business owners might consider solutions like intrusion detection systems (IDS), which monitor network traffic for suspicious activity. The focus here is not solely on prevention; it's about creating a robust monitoring system that alerts teams when potential incidents arise—much like having a security camera system with real-time notifications.

When an incident occurs, the Respond function is crucial in minimizing damage. An effective response plan should detail clear procedures for how employees should act in various scenarios—whether dealing with data theft or ransomware attacks. A recent case study highlights this importance: when a mid-sized retailer faced a ransomware attack, their pre-established incident response protocols enabled them to quickly isolate affected systems and restore operations with minimal downtime.

Once an incident has been addressed, recovery becomes the next priority. The Recover function focuses on restoring disrupted services and enhancing resilience against future incidents. Small business owners can implement regular backup procedures—both onsite and offsite—to ensure that critical data remains retrievable after an attack. Take this example, utilizing cloud services for backups not only provides redundancy but also allows for faster recovery compared to traditional storage methods.

Integrating the NIST Framework into daily operations fosters continuous improvement in cybersecurity practices. Regular training sessions are essential; they help staff stay updated on policy changes and emerging threats relevant to their roles within the organization. Engaging workshops that simulate real-world scenarios—such as phishing attempts or data breaches—enable employees to recognize potential threats before they escalate into actual incidents.

Also, fostering collaboration among teams nurtures a culture of security awareness throughout the organization. Encouraging open communication about cybersecurity concerns empowers every employee—not just IT staff—to play an active role in safeguarding company assets.

As small businesses navigate an increasingly complex landscape of cyber threats, leveraging established frameworks like NIST provides clarity amid intricate regulations and guidelines. This approach equips them with essential tools while fostering resilience—a key characteristic for sustainability in today's digital world.

adopting the NIST Framework transcends mere compliance; it embodies a commitment to proactive risk management and continuous enhancement of cybersecurity measures. By embedding these principles into their operations, small business owners position themselves not only as defenders against cyber threats but also as leaders dedicated to building trust with clients and stakeholders—a significant competitive advantage in an ever-evolving marketplace where security assurance is paramount.

Preparing for Regulatory Audits

Preparing for regulatory audits requires a strategic and thorough approach, particularly for small business owners navigating a complex landscape of compliance requirements. The journey begins with a clear understanding of the specific regulations relevant to your industry, which may include data privacy, financial transactions, or cybersecurity practices. Each regulation introduces its own expectations and standards, making it essential to tailor your compliance efforts accordingly.

A practical first step is conducting a comprehensive gap analysis. This process involves reviewing your existing policies and procedures against the requirements set forth by relevant regulations. Take this example, if your business must comply with the General Data Protection Regulation (GDPR), you would assess how you collect, store, and process personal data in relation to GDPR's stringent guidelines. Documenting these findings not only highlights areas for improvement but also helps create a roadmap for achieving compliance.

After identifying gaps, it's crucial to develop a clear compliance plan that outlines specific steps your organization will take to address deficiencies and meet regulatory standards. For example, if you find that your data retention policies do not align with GDPR mandates, consider implementing a robust data lifecycle management strategy. This could involve automated systems for data deletion or archiving to ensure personal information is not retained longer than necessary.

Training employees on compliance requirements is another essential aspect of preparation. By engaging team members in understanding their roles within the framework of regulatory audits, you foster accountability and promote a culture of compliance throughout the organization. Tailoring regular training sessions to different departments can enhance effectiveness; marketing teams might focus on privacy implications when handling customer data, while IT staff could concentrate on security protocols mandated by various regulations.

Simulating audit scenarios can serve as an effective training tool as well. Conduct mock audits where employees must demonstrate their knowledge of compliance processes and show adherence to established protocols. These exercises not only prepare staff for real audits but also help identify potential weaknesses in understanding or execution before they escalate into critical issues.

Documentation is pivotal to audit readiness. Ensure that all processes are well-documented and that clear records are available for review during an audit. This encompasses everything from policies governing data access to logs detailing how information is used and shared within the organization. A well-organized documentation system facilitates auditors' assessments of your compliance efforts without unnecessary delays.

Engaging legal counsel or compliance experts can provide additional insights into the regulatory nuances specific to your industry. Their expertise can clarify ambiguous requirements and suggest best practices tailored to your business model. Regular consultations with these professionals help ensure that your compliance strategies remain current as regulations evolve.

When an audit occurs, maintaining transparency is key. Open communication with auditors fosters trust and demonstrates your organization's commitment to compliance rather than treating it as a mere checkbox exercise. Be prepared not only to discuss what has been accomplished but also how you plan to address any findings that arise during the audit process.

Once an audit concludes, take time for critical reflection on the feedback received. Evaluate what went well and where improvements can be made. This evaluation process can drive continuous enhancement of your compliance posture, ensuring you are better prepared for future audits.

Navigating regulatory audits doesn't have to be daunting; instead, it can present an opportunity for growth and refinement within your organization. By taking proactive measures—such as conducting thorough analyses, developing comprehensive plans, investing in employee training, maintaining meticulous documentation, and fostering open communication—you can transform the audit process into a strategic advantage rather than a burden.

preparation for regulatory audits represents more than mere adherence; it reflects a culture committed to ethical practices and operational excellence in an ever-evolving landscape of compliance requirements. As small business owners embrace this mindset, they position themselves not only as compliant entities but as trusted leaders in their industries—an invaluable asset in building customer loyalty and enhancing reputation amidst increasing scrutiny on data protection and privacy standards.

Penalties for Non-Compliance

Non-compliance with regulatory standards can result in substantial penalties that vary based on the nature of the violation and the jurisdiction in which a business operates. For small business owners, understanding these consequences is crucial, as they can jeopardize not only financial stability but also the organization's reputation. Cultivating a culture of compliance and accountability begins with grasping these potential ramifications.

Take, for instance, the General Data Protection Regulation (GDPR) implemented in the European Union. Businesses that fail to comply with GDPR face fines of up to 20 million euros or 4% of their annual global revenue—whichever amount is greater. Such staggering penalties underscore the financial risks tied to inadequate data protection practices. A small business processing personal data without adhering to GDPR guidelines could quickly find itself in a vulnerable position, struggling to recover from the impact of a significant fine.

In addition to financial penalties, businesses may encounter legal repercussions. This includes lawsuits initiated by affected customers or regulatory agencies seeking redress for violations. If a company's failure to protect customer data leads to a breach, impacted individuals might pursue legal action for damages related to identity theft or other losses. The costs of defending against such claims can escalate swiftly, depleting resources that could otherwise be invested in growth and development.

Reputational damage is another serious consequence of non-compliance that is often overlooked. When businesses fail to meet regulatory requirements, they risk losing customer trust—a critical asset in today's market. As consumers grow increasingly concerned about data privacy and security, negative publicity from compliance failures can tarnish a brand's image for years. Retaining customers becomes challenging when clients feel their personal information is mishandled.

And, operational disruptions frequently follow compliance violations. Regulatory bodies may require organizations to cease specific operations until non-compliance issues are resolved. This interruption can lead to lost revenue, diminished productivity, and even layoffs as companies scramble to adjust their practices to meet regulatory standards.

To mitigate these risks, proactive measures are essential. Establishing a robust compliance program tailored to your industry serves as a foundation for preventing costly violations. Regular audits of internal processes can help identify vulnerabilities before they escalate into significant problems. For example, if your business is subject to the Health Insurance Portability and Accountability Act (HIPAA), periodic assessments of patient data management and security can ensure alignment with established guidelines.

Fostering an organizational culture that prioritizes compliance enhances employee awareness regarding their roles and responsibilities in maintaining regulatory standards. When staff members understand the implications of non-compliance, they are more likely to adhere strictly to protocols designed to protect sensitive information.

Additionally, staying informed about changing regulations is crucial in today's dynamic landscape. Laws governing data protection and cybersecurity are continually updated; what was compliant last year may not hold up under new scrutiny today. Subscribing to industry newsletters or participating in forums can provide valuable insights into emerging trends and regulatory changes.

Implementing training programs focused on compliance also plays a vital role in reducing risks associated with non-compliance. Regular workshops tailored toward specific compliance topics equip employees with the knowledge and tools needed to navigate complex regulations effectively. Take this example, sessions dedicated to understanding PCI DSS requirements for handling credit card transactions ensure that payment processing practices align with industry standards.

recognizing the serious consequences associated with non-compliance empowers small business owners to prioritize cybersecurity and regulatory adherence effectively. By taking proactive steps—such as developing comprehensive compliance strategies, fostering a culture of awareness, investing in employee education, and staying informed about industry changes—businesses not only position themselves to avoid penalties but also build trust with customers and partners alike.

As you reflect on these implications, consider this: embracing compliance is not just an obligation; it represents an opportunity for growth, trust-building, and sustained success in an increasingly competitive marketplace where safeguarding data is paramount.

CHAPTER 13: WORKING WITH CYBERSECURITY PARTNERS

Identifying Cybersecurity Needs

I dentifying your cybersecurity needs is the crucial first step in strengthening your small business against a growing array of digital threats. Without a clear understanding of what you need to protect, you leave yourself vulnerable to exploitation by malicious actors. This process begins with a thorough assessment of your business assets, including data, systems, and personnel.

Start by considering the types of data your business collects and processes. Customer information, financial records, and intellectual property are just a few examples of valuable assets that require diligent protection. Take this example, a local e-commerce store must safeguard not only customer payment information but also personal details such as addresses and order histories. Recognizing the sensitivity of this data is essential; for many customers, their trust hinges on knowing that their personal information is secure.

Once you have identified the types of data at stake, it's important to map out the systems that house this information. This includes your primary databases as well as any third-party services you rely on, such as cloud storage or payment processing solutions. If your business uses a cloud-based CRM system like Salesforce or HubSpot to manage customer relationships, you need to understand both the security measures they implement and your responsibilities for protecting any data stored there.

Human resources also play a critical role in identifying cybersecurity needs. Your employees can be both your greatest asset and your biggest vulnerability. Training staff on best practices for data handling and security can significantly reduce risks associated with human error. This involves implementing robust onboarding programs to educate new hires about security protocols, along with ongoing training sessions to keep all team members informed about evolving threats and defenses.

As you evaluate these elements, engage stakeholders across your organization. A collaborative approach encourages diverse perspectives that may reveal needs you might overlook as a leader focused on daily operations. Involving team members from different departments provides a holistic view of cybersecurity requirements; IT personnel may highlight technical vulnerabilities while marketing staff can identify risks associated with social media engagement.

After gathering this information, conduct a risk assessment to prioritize these needs based on their potential impact and likelihood of occurrence. Utilizing tools like the FAIR (Factor Analysis of Information Risk) framework can help quantify risks in financial terms. This approach allows you to make informed decisions grounded in measurable metrics rather than relying on guesswork.

For example, if your assessment reveals that customer data breaches could cost your business thousands in fines and damage to your reputation while phishing attacks pose a lower financial risk but could disrupt daily operations significantly, this insight will help guide your strategic focus and resource allocation.

Implementing cybersecurity measures tailored to your identified needs involves developing specific policies and practices aligned with your organizational goals. If protecting customer data is paramount due to regulatory requirements such as GDPR or HIPAA, adopting stringent data encryption methods becomes essential. Conversely, if minimizing operational downtime is critical for your service-oriented business, prioritizing comprehensive incident response protocols should be a key focus.

And, regularly reviewing and updating your cybersecurity strategy is vital as technology and threat landscapes evolve rapidly. What worked six months ago may not suffice today; therefore, establishing a routine for reassessing needs ensures you remain agile in addressing new vulnerabilities.

recognizing these needs lays the groundwork for building a resilient cybersecurity posture within your organization. As you embark on this journey, remember that it's about creating an environment where security is integrated into the fabric of daily operations rather than treated as an afterthought or mere compliance checkbox.

With the right understanding and proactive measures in place, you will not only safeguard essential assets against cyber threats but also foster a culture of vigilance and accountability among all team members. Each step taken now prepares your business for future challenges—enabling sustainable growth even amidst uncertainty in the digital realm.

Selecting the Right Partner or Vendor

Choosing the right cybersecurity partner is a strategic decision that can greatly enhance your small business's defenses against cyber threats. Just as you would meticulously select an accountant or supplier, this choice demands careful thought and thorough research. A cybersecurity partner brings not only essential tools and services but also invaluable expertise to help your organization navigate complex security challenges.

Start by identifying the specific services you need from a cybersecurity partner. Your requirements may include managed security services, incident response capabilities, vulnerability assessments, or compliance support with regulations like GDPR or HIPAA. For example, if your business handles sensitive healthcare data, it's crucial to work with a vendor experienced in health-related compliance. They will be familiar with the intricacies of safeguarding patient information and ensuring adherence to relevant laws.

With a clear understanding of your needs in place, move on to evaluating potential partners. Focus on vendors with a proven track record in the industry. One effective way to gauge their capabilities is by reviewing case studies or client testimonials that highlight their experience with businesses similar to yours. If you operate a retail business that processes online payments, seek out vendors who have successfully implemented security measures for other e-commerce operations. Their sector-specific knowledge can provide valuable insights into the unique threats you may face.

Another critical aspect to consider is the vendor's approach to customer service and support. Cybersecurity incidents can strike at any moment, often without warning, making a responsive support team essential. Investigate how quickly they respond to inquiries and whether they offer 24/7 support. Engaging with their customer service representatives during the evaluation phase can give you an idea of their responsiveness and willingness to address your concerns.

Additionally, technology compatibility is a key factor that should not be overlooked. Your chosen partner must seamlessly integrate with your existing systems and infrastructure without causing disruptions. If you rely on specific software platforms—such as Office 365 for productivity or QuickBooks for accounting—confirm that the vendor's solutions are compatible with these tools. Also, inquire about their capabilities regarding updates and scalability, particularly if you anticipate future growth.

Cost is an important consideration for small businesses operating on tight budgets. While finding an affordable solution is essential, it's equally important not to compromise on quality. Be cautious of vendors offering significantly lower prices than competitors; such pricing often sacrifices security effectiveness or service quality. Request detailed proposals from potential partners that outline costs associated with setup, ongoing services, and any additional fees you might encounter.

Also, explore each vendor's approach to compliance and regulatory requirements. A responsible cybersecurity partner should prioritize these aspects and demonstrate an understanding of how they relate to your business's unique context. During discussions, ask them to explain their strategies for maintaining compliance and how they adapt to changing regulations.

Don't overlook the importance of incident response planning either; every business is susceptible to cyberattacks, so having a well-defined plan can minimize damage when incidents occur. Inquire about how potential partners handle security breaches: What protocols do they follow? What steps do they take to recover data? A robust incident response plan not only protects your assets but also instills confidence among your stakeholders.

As you narrow down your list of candidates, schedule meetings or demonstrations where they present their solutions in action. This gives you an opportunity not only to see their tools but also to understand their methodologies and philosophies toward tackling cybersecurity challenges. Observing them in real-time can clarify whether their offerings genuinely align with your operational goals.

Lastly, consider the value of long-term relationships when making this choice. Establishing a partnership goes beyond signing a contract; it involves ongoing collaboration as both technology and threats evolve over time. Look for vendors who prioritize partnership over transactional relationships—those willing to adapt their strategies alongside your business growth while providing continuous training and insights for your team.

By taking the time to carefully evaluate these considerations, you'll be better positioned to select a cybersecurity partner who meets both your immediate needs and contributes meaningfully to your long-term security strategy. This informed decision lays a solid foundation for building resilience against cyber threats, ensuring that when challenges arise, you have capable allies equipped with the expertise necessary to navigate them effectively.

Managed Security Service Providers (MSSPs)

Selecting a Managed Security Service Provider (MSSP) can be overwhelming, particularly for small business owners who may lack extensive experience in cybersecurity. However, partnering with an MSSP can significantly enhance your security posture while allowing your team to focus on core business functions. These specialized firms provide a comprehensive suite of services designed to monitor, manage, and respond to cybersecurity threats—an invaluable resource for organizations that may not have the capacity for a dedicated in-house security team.

To begin your search for an MSSP, assess your specific needs and determine which services align with your risk profile. Take this example, if your organization deals with sensitive customer data or financial information, you might prioritize services such as threat detection and response, data protection, or compliance management. Conversely, if you operate in a less regulated environment, you may opt for basic monitoring and incident response capabilities.

A successful partnership with an MSSP starts with a thorough evaluation of your current security landscape. This assessment typically involves reviewing existing systems, identifying vulnerabilities, and understanding the unique threats facing your business. An MSSP might conduct risk assessments that include penetration testing or vulnerability scans—tools that help uncover weaknesses in your network before they can be exploited by malicious actors. As cybersecurity expert Bruce Schneier aptly puts it, "Security is not a product but a process." Therefore, it's essential to understand how an MSSP integrates continuous monitoring into its service offerings.

Once you have identified potential MSSPs, take the time to explore their specific service offerings. Look for providers that offer managed firewall services alongside intrusion detection systems (IDS). Firewalls serve as the first line of defense against unauthorized access, while IDS monitors network traffic for suspicious activity. A well-rounded MSSP should also provide endpoint protection solutions to safeguard individual devices from malware and other threats.

Another critical factor in selecting an MSSP is their incident response capabilities. You need reassurance that they will act swiftly if a breach occurs. Inquire about their incident response plan: How quickly can they identify a breach? What protocols do they follow for containment? Additionally, ask about their familiarity with compliance standards relevant to your industry; for example, adherence to regulations like HIPAA or PCI DSS is essential if you're in healthcare or finance.

Effective communication is vital for successful collaboration with your MSSP. Establish clear lines of communication from the beginning to ensure timely updates about potential threats or incidents. Schedule regular meetings to discuss ongoing security efforts and review reports detailing detected incidents and vulnerabilities over time.

Cost considerations will also influence your decision-making process. While many small businesses may hesitate at the expense associated with hiring an MSSP, it's important to view this as an investment rather than just a cost. Take this example, recovering from a data breach can often be far more expensive than implementing preventive measures through an MSSP. A 2023 report by IBM Security estimated the average cost of a data breach at)4 million—this staggering figure highlights the value of proactive cybersecurity measures.

As you engage with potential partners, don't hesitate to request case studies or references from similar-sized businesses within your sector. Real-world examples can provide valuable insights into how effectively they handle various scenarios and reassure you of their expertise.

integrating an MSSP into your cybersecurity strategy should not only strengthen your technical defenses but also promote a culture of security awareness throughout your organization. The right provider will help you build resilience against evolving cyber threats while allowing you to focus on growth opportunities.

Consider this: choosing an MSSP isn't merely about outsourcing security functions; it's about forming a partnership that evolves alongside changing cyber threats. By investing wisely in such partnerships today, you'll not only protect your assets but also pave the way for sustainable success tomorrow.

Third-Party Risk Management

Third-party risk management is a crucial aspect of your overall cybersecurity strategy, especially for small business owners who often depend on external vendors for various services. While these partnerships can provide essential functions—such as cloud storage and payment processing—they also introduce vulnerabilities that could jeopardize your organization's security. Effectively managing these risks is vital for maintaining a strong cybersecurity posture.

To begin, identify all third-party vendors and service providers that interact with your systems or data. This includes not only obvious choices like software suppliers and cloud services but also less direct relationships, such as contractors or partners with network access. Once you compile a comprehensive list, categorize these vendors based on the sensitivity of the data they handle and their importance to your operations. Take this example, a payment processor that manages credit card transactions warrants more scrutiny than a non-essential supplier providing office supplies.

Next, evaluate the security practices of each vendor. This assessment should include a review of their compliance with relevant standards and regulations specific to your industry. If you operate in healthcare, for example, verify that any vendor handling patient data complies with HIPAA regulations. Request documentation regarding their security protocols, incident response plans, and disaster recovery strategies. Conducting this due diligence allows you to determine whether the third party maintains adequate security measures aligned with your business requirements.

Regular assessments are another key element of effective third-party risk management. Vendors may change their policies, technologies, and personnel over time, so it's important to periodically revisit and evaluate their security practices. Implementing a standardized assessment framework can streamline this process. Consider using tools like questionnaires or audits that cover critical areas such as data encryption practices, access controls, and vulnerability management programs. In 2022 alone, nearly 80% of organizations faced breaches due to supply chain or third-party relationship issues—underscoring the necessity of consistent evaluations.

In addition to assessments, establishing clear contractual obligations regarding cybersecurity with your vendors is essential. These contracts should explicitly outline security requirements and expectations for incident reporting timelines. Take this example, if a vendor experiences a breach affecting your data, it's crucial to know how quickly they must inform you and what steps they will take in response. Such agreements promote accountability and ensure both parties understand their responsibilities in protecting sensitive information.

Consider developing a third-party risk management program that encompasses all these elements within an organized framework. This program could involve ongoing monitoring of vendor performance through metrics like service level agreements (SLAs), periodic reviews of compliance certifications, and incident response drills involving third parties.

And, creating strong lines of communication is vital for effective collaboration with your vendors. Regular discussions about potential threats or changes in their operations can help you address risks proactively before they escalate into larger issues.

Finally, it's important to educate your internal team about the significance of third-party risk management as part of your broader cybersecurity culture. Encourage vigilance regarding vendor interactions and establish protocols for escalating concerns related to vendor security practices.

The reality is straightforward: while third-party vendors can enhance efficiency and productivity in your business operations, they also present inherent risks that must be actively managed. By implementing structured processes around vendor evaluations, contractual obligations, ongoing monitoring, and communication strategies, you'll not only strengthen your defenses but also build trust among stakeholders in an increasingly interconnected digital landscape.

With these proactive measures in place, you will create a resilient network where risks are systematically identified and mitigated—allowing you to focus on advancing your business without compromising security integrity.

Building Long-Term Partnerships

Building long-term partnerships in cybersecurity is crucial for small businesses aiming to develop a robust security framework. These relationships not only enhance your overall security posture but also foster collaboration that can lead to innovative, tailored solutions. Establishing and maintaining these partnerships requires a strategic approach that prioritizes mutual benefits, transparency, and shared objectives.

Begin by selecting partners who resonate with your business values and align with your security goals. This might include managed security service providers (MSSPs), software vendors, or compliance consultants. It's essential that these partners understand the unique challenges of your industry and can provide customized solutions. Take the time to engage in discussions that clarify your expectations and the specific outcomes you wish to achieve; this initial dialogue lays the groundwork for a collaborative relationship where both parties feel invested.

Once the partnership is established, ongoing communication becomes critical. Regular check-ins allow both sides to stay informed about new threats, regulatory changes, and emerging technologies that may affect your cybersecurity strategy. Consider scheduling meetings—perhaps quarterly or biannually—where you can review performance metrics, address any concerns, and brainstorm potential improvements together. Such proactive communication not only strengthens the partnership but also fosters a culture of shared accountability.

Another effective way to solidify these partnerships is through joint training initiatives. Collaborate with your vendors to create workshops or training sessions focused on cybersecurity best practices tailored specifically for your team. Take this example, if you utilize a particular software solution, work with the vendor to provide training that not only covers how to use the software but also emphasizes the associated security measures and each employee's role in safeguarding data. This investment in employee education ensures everyone understands security protocols while reinforcing the commitment both parties share towards maintaining high standards.

Sharing insights and resources with your partners is equally important. If you discover an effective threat mitigation strategy or a new tool that enhances data protection, communicate this knowledge with your partners. This reciprocal exchange not only strengthens relationships but positions both parties as thought leaders within their respective fields. A collaborative environment encourages innovation and responsiveness to emerging threats.

When evaluating partner performance, utilize clear metrics that measure success against agreed-upon objectives. Metrics could range from incident response times to compliance with specific regulations or even customer satisfaction regarding service delivery. Regular evaluations based on concrete data create opportunities for constructive feedback while allowing both parties to celebrate achievements together.

Finally, cultivate an atmosphere of trust where open discussions about potential issues are encouraged. If a partner faces challenges that may impact their ability to deliver services securely, it's better for them to communicate these concerns early rather than waiting for them to escalate into significant problems. Foster transparency by establishing clear channels for reporting issues and encourage discussions focused on solutions rather than blame.

As you work towards building enduring partnerships in cybersecurity, remember that these alliances are not merely transactional—they represent a commitment to shared success and resilience against evolving threats. By prioritizing communication, joint initiatives, resource sharing, performance assessments, and trust-building measures, you lay the foundation for lasting relationships that will significantly enhance your organization's security capabilities while paving the way for future growth and innovation.

Contractual Considerations

When partnering with cybersecurity providers, the nuances of your contracts can significantly influence the success of the relationship. These contractual elements go beyond mere administrative tasks; they are vital in establishing clear expectations, responsibilities, and deliverables that will ultimately shape your security landscape. A well-structured contract lays the groundwork for collaboration, ensuring that both parties understand the scope of services, timelines, and the nature of the partnership.

Begin by explicitly outlining the services to be provided. This could encompass a range of offerings, from specific security solutions like firewalls and intrusion detection systems to ongoing support and incident response capabilities. For example, if you're engaging with a managed security service provider (MSSP), it's important to detail their responsibilities regarding network monitoring and incident response. Be clear about expected response times for alerts or breaches and include provisions for regular updates on system performance and threat assessments. This level of clarity helps reduce misunderstandings and establishes accountability between both parties.

Next, it's essential to incorporate confidentiality agreements that protect sensitive information exchanged between your business and your partners. In cybersecurity, where data protection is critical, both parties must agree to keep confidential any proprietary technologies, client data, and vulnerabilities discovered during assessments. Take this example, if an MSSP identifies a potential weakness in your system during an audit, they must manage this information discreetly to prevent leaks that could undermine your business's integrity.

Another important aspect to address is liability in the event of a breach or failure to meet contractual obligations. It's crucial to define who is responsible if a data leak occurs due to negligence on your partner's part. Clearly articulated liability clauses can help mitigate risk and ensure that all parties are aware of their legal exposure. Consulting with legal professionals specializing in cybersecurity law can aid in effectively drafting these clauses.

Also, outlining compliance requirements based on relevant industry regulations is critical. Whether your business is subject to GDPR, HIPAA, or PCI DSS standards, your partners should be held accountable for adhering to these regulations in their operations related to your organization. This not only offers legal protection but also reinforces a shared commitment to compliance that benefits both parties.

Including service level agreements (SLAs) in your contracts is also vital. SLAs set performance benchmarks that partners are expected to consistently meet—think of them as guarantees of quality service delivery. Specify key performance indicators

(KPIs) such as uptime percentages or incident response times; these metrics provide a tangible way to assess how well your partner meets established standards.

Termination clauses are equally significant; they clarify how either party can exit the agreement if necessary. Conditions might include non-performance or changes in business strategy that affect the partnership's viability. A well-defined exit strategy ensures that both parties know what actions need to be taken if the partnership no longer meets its intended goals.

Lastly, it's essential not to overlook the need for flexibility within contracts. Given the rapid evolution of cybersecurity threats, having provisions that allow for adjustments based on changing needs is crucial. Consider including clauses that enable modifications to service levels or scopes in response to emerging technologies or shifts in regulatory landscapes. Such adaptability allows both partners to remain responsive and relevant amid evolving threats.

In summary, crafting effective contractual considerations demands careful thought and collaboration between both parties involved. By prioritizing clear definitions of services, confidentiality protections, liability limits, compliance requirements, SLAs, termination processes, and flexibility clauses within contracts, you create a robust framework for successful partnerships in cybersecurity—one built on trust, accountability, and mutual benefit. This approach not only strengthens your immediate security posture but also establishes a foundation for long-term resilience against future challenges in an ever-evolving digital landscape.

Evaluating Partner Performance

For partnerships in cybersecurity, evaluating the performance of your providers is just as crucial as the initial selection process. By establishing metrics for success early on, you set the foundation for ongoing assessments and foster a culture of accountability. Without a clear framework to measure effectiveness, even the most robust cybersecurity strategies can struggle.

To start, identify key performance indicators (KPIs) that align with your business objectives. These KPIs should encompass various aspects of service delivery, including incident response times, system uptime, and user satisfaction. For example, if you've engaged a managed security service provider (MSSP), a critical KPI could be the average time taken to detect and respond to incidents. Monitoring these metrics not only sheds light on operational efficiency but also provides valuable data for performance discussions.

Conducting regular performance reviews is another essential element of this evaluation process. Aim to schedule these assessments at least quarterly to ensure both you and your partner remain aligned on goals and can adjust strategies as needed. During these reviews, analyze the collected data against your agreed-upon KPIs and investigate any discrepancies. If an MSSP consistently misses response time targets, it's important to discuss potential underlying causes—such as staffing issues or resource limitations—and collaboratively develop solutions.

Feedback from your internal team is also vital in assessing partner performance. Gather insights from those who interact directly with the cybersecurity provider, such as IT staff or security personnel. Their experiences can highlight strengths and weaknesses that may not be immediately evident in raw data alone. Take this example, if team members report challenges in communication with your MSSP during incident response, this feedback could lead to improvements in both protocols and relationships.

Next, evaluate adherence to compliance standards relevant to your industry. Assess whether your partners consistently meet necessary regulatory requirements like GDPR or HIPAA.

Non-compliance can result not only in legal consequences but also harm your business's reputation. Regular audits—whether conducted internally or by third-party services—can help uncover gaps in compliance efforts and prompt corrective actions before issues escalate.

Additionally, consider the innovation and responsiveness of your partners. The cybersecurity landscape is ever-evolving; therefore, it's essential for providers to not only keep pace but also anticipate emerging threats. Ask probing questions about how they stay updated on trends and new technologies: Are they participating in industry forums? Do they invest in continuous education for their teams? This evaluation should focus not only on current capabilities but also on their commitment to adapting alongside evolving threats.

Client satisfaction surveys can also serve as a valuable tool for evaluating partner performance. Create structured surveys that capture qualitative insights from various stakeholders within your organization who regularly interact with the partner. These surveys can provide essential context regarding perceived value versus actual outcomes—an often overlooked aspect in purely numerical assessments.

establishing an effective evaluation process is a continuous journey rather than a one-time event. As you refine this approach over time—drawing on lessons learned and adapting to changes within both your business environment and the cybersecurity landscape—you'll cultivate stronger partnerships rooted in trust and transparency.

In summary, consistently reviewing partner performance through well-defined KPIs, regular feedback loops from internal teams, compliance checks, assessments of innovative capacity, and client satisfaction surveys creates a comprehensive strategy that fosters robust relationships with cybersecurity providers while ensuring they deliver optimal value aligned with your business goals.

Collaborative Incident Response

In today's cybersecurity landscape, adopting a collaborative approach to incident response is not just advantageous; it's essential. The speed and effectiveness of your response during a cyber incident can significantly influence the extent of damage incurred. By working closely with your cybersecurity partners, your organization can be better prepared to act swiftly when threats arise.

At the heart of effective collaboration lies the establishment of clear communication channels between internal teams and external partners. Designating specific points of contact within both your organization and the cybersecurity provider streamlines communication during incidents, reducing confusion and ensuring that critical information flows efficiently. Utilizing secure messaging platforms or dedicated incident response portals can facilitate real-time updates and documentation sharing. For example, during an incident involving data breach attempts, a well-defined communication strategy can drastically reduce response time by allowing immediate alerts and coordinated actions.

Regular joint exercises are also vital for enhancing collaborative incident response capabilities. By simulating various cyber incidents—from ransomware attacks to phishing attempts—your team and the provider can practice their roles and refine their strategies. Conducting tabletop exercises, where all stakeholders engage in discussions about hypothetical scenarios, encourages proactive thinking and strengthens relationships. If one of your security providers specializes in threat intelligence, incorporating their expertise into these drills can yield invaluable insights into emerging attack vectors, thereby improving overall readiness.

After managing an incident, debriefing sessions become crucial for refining future responses. Gathering all relevant stakeholders—including internal teams and external partners

—to analyze what transpired helps identify successes and areas for improvement. This is also the ideal time to discuss any tools or processes that may not have met expectations during the incident. Take this example, if detection software failed to recognize a specific threat type, engaging your provider in discussions about upgrading or adapting technology can bolster preparedness for future incidents.

Thorough documentation plays an essential role in fostering collaboration during incident response as well. Keeping detailed records of incidents—tracking actions taken, timelines, and outcomes—promotes transparency and accountability among all parties involved. This documentation not only serves as a valuable reference for future incidents but also builds trust between your organization and its partners. Consider using shared document repositories where both teams can access real-time data on ongoing incidents and previous cases.

Aligning objectives between your business goals and those of your cybersecurity partner is key to creating a cohesive response strategy. Understanding their protocols for handling incidents—ensuring they align with the needs of businesses like yours—means that everyone is working toward common goals rather than operating under different assumptions or timelines. For example, if rapid restoration of services post-attack is a priority for your organization, it's crucial that your cybersecurity partner understands this urgency so they can allocate resources accordingly.

Creating an environment of mutual trust encourages open dialogue about challenges faced during incident management. If a partner encounters resource allocation issues during an attack, knowing they can communicate these difficulties openly will lead to improved performance in critical moments. Establishing regular check-ins to discuss ongoing challenges and successes not only strengthens partnerships but reinforces a commitment to collective growth.

To effectively encapsulate this collaborative ethos, leverage tools such as project management software or shared dashboards that track the progress of ongoing incidents and provide real-time updates on resolution strategies. This approach ensures visibility into the status of incidents while promoting accountability across teams.

By embracing collaboration at every stage—from preparedness through recovery—you cultivate an adaptive incident response capability that stands resilient against evolving threats. The combined strengths of your internal resources paired with those of your cybersecurity partners create a formidable defense against potential cyber threats, ensuring that when incidents do occur, you are ready to respond cohesively and effectively.

CHAPTER 14: NAVIGATING CYBERSECURITY INSURANCE

Understanding Cyber Insurance

I n today's landscape of increasing cyber threats, grasping the intricacies of cyber insurance is essential for small businesses looking to enhance their risk management strategies. Cyber insurance serves not just as a safety net but as a strategic asset that can help mitigate financial losses resulting from incidents such as data breaches, ransomware attacks, and business interruptions.

cyber insurance offers coverage for the expenses associated with managing and responding to an incident. This includes costs related to data recovery, notifying affected individuals, legal fees, public relations efforts to address reputation damage, and even regulatory fines. Take this example, if your small retail business experiences a data breach that exposes customer credit card information, the expenses involved in notifying customers and potentially facing penalties from regulatory bodies can mount quickly. A well-crafted cyber insurance policy can help absorb some of these financial shocks.

Before exploring policies and providers, it's crucial to assess your specific needs. Consider the type of data your business handles and whether you are subject to industry regulations that could lead to significant fines for non-compliance. Analyzing your digital footprint will help you identify vulnerabilities within your operations. For example, if you store sensitive client information on cloud servers without sufficient security measures, comprehensive coverage may be warranted.

When searching for a cyber insurance policy, it's important to examine the types of incidents covered by various plans. Not all policies are created equal; they can differ significantly in terms of coverage limits and exclusions. Some may provide strong support for first-party losses—those directly incurred by your business—while others focus more on third-party liabilities resulting from breaches affecting customers or partners. Ensure that the policy you choose aligns with both your potential risks and your business objectives.

An often-overlooked aspect of cyber insurance is the inclusion of incident response services. Many insurers now partner with cybersecurity firms to offer immediate assistance when incidents occur. That means when you report a breach or attack, expert resources may be just a phone call away. Access to these services not only speeds up recovery times but also strengthens your overall resilience against future threats.

Navigating the fine print of cyber insurance is another crucial step in understanding what you're getting into. Terms like "sub-limits," which indicate maximum payouts for specific incidents such as data breaches or system downtime, can greatly affect the effectiveness of your coverage. Take this example, if a policy has a low sub-limit for data recovery while offering more generous coverage for other incidents, this mismatch could leave you vulnerable when protection is most needed.

To deepen your understanding and utilization of cyber insurance, consider working with an experienced broker. Brokers bring specialized knowledge of the market and can help tailor a policy that suits your operational risks and industry standards. They can assist in comparing various options and clarifying differences between providers, guiding you through this complex terrain.

As part of a proactive risk management approach, regularly reassess whether your existing coverage remains adequate as threats evolve or as your business grows. This review should take place at least annually or whenever significant changes occur—such as adopting new technologies or entering new markets.

By understanding the fundamentals of cyber insurance, small business owners can become informed decision-makers who actively shape their organization's risk profile. Aligning cyber insurance with broader cybersecurity strategies—such as implementing strong access controls and training employees on security awareness—creates multiple layers of defense against cyber risks while ensuring financial stability during crises.

The exploration of cyber insurance is just the beginning; it paves the way for building a resilient enterprise capable of navigating unpredictable challenges while thriving amid them. The real power lies in effectively integrating these strategies into your overall risk management framework— ultimately fostering not only an insured future but one fortified against potential threats through proactive planning and collaboration.

Types of Cyber Insurance Policies

Understanding the different types of cyber insurance policies is essential for tailoring coverage to your business's unique needs. Not all cyber incidents are the same, and neither are the policies designed to address them. As a small business owner, recognizing these distinctions is vital to ensuring adequate protection against potential threats.

The first major category of cyber insurance is first-party coverage, which directly addresses the losses your business may incur from a cyber incident. This includes costs associated with data breaches, business interruptions, and even cyber extortion. For example, if your company falls victim to a ransomware attack that locks you out of critical systems, first-party coverage can help cover the expenses involved in regaining access—whether through ransom payments or hiring cybersecurity experts for recovery efforts.

In contrast, third-party coverage deals with liabilities that arise when clients or partners file claims against your business due to a data breach. If sensitive customer information is compromised because of inadequate security measures, third-party coverage can help manage legal costs, settlements, and regulatory fines resulting from the breach. Take this example, if you operate an e-commerce site and customer credit card data is leaked, this type of insurance can assist with legal defense fees and the necessary notifications to affected customers.

Within these broad categories, policies can be tailored to address specific risks associated with various incidents. Data breach insurance is one such tailored policy that provides financial support for managing the aftermath of a data breach. This often includes legal fees incurred while complying with notification laws and costs for public relations efforts aimed at restoring your reputation after an incident.

Another key type of policy is business interruption insurance, which covers lost income when a cyber event disrupts operations. For example, if your systems go down due to an attack and you cannot conduct business as usual, this policy helps mitigate financial losses during the downtime. Consider a scenario where an online retailer's website becomes inaccessible due to a denial-of-service attack; this coverage would compensate for the revenue lost during that period.

You should also consider cyber extortion insurance, which specifically addresses threats like ransomware. This policy not only covers ransom payments but may also include expenses related to system restoration and forensic investigation services post-incident. For example, if you receive a ransomware demand after an attack on your network infrastructure, this type of insurance ensures you have the necessary resources available without straining your cash flow.

Emerging risks have led to newer categories such as social engineering fraud insurance, which protects against losses resulting from deceptive practices that manipulate employees into revealing sensitive information or transferring funds. This coverage has become increasingly relevant due to the rise in phishing scams and other tactics that exploit human behavior rather than technical vulnerabilities.

Choosing the right mix of these policies requires a thorough understanding of your unique business operations and risk profile. Conducting a comprehensive risk assessment can reveal vulnerabilities that impact which types of coverage will be most beneficial. Take this example, businesses that handle large amounts of customer data may find it necessary to prioritize third-party liability insurance more heavily than those whose operations rely less on data.

It's also crucial to consider how these various policies interact within your overall risk management strategy. Having multiple layers of protection—such as both first-party and third-party coverages—can enhance resilience against diverse threats while ensuring comprehensive support during incidents.

Reviewing potential exclusions in each policy is equally important; some plans may not cover specific types of cyber incidents or may impose sub-limits on aspects like data recovery or crisis management expenses. Small business owners should carefully examine these details before making decisions to ensure their chosen policy aligns well with their operational needs and risk exposure.

navigating the landscape of cyber insurance requires diligence and foresight. By understanding these various types of policies, small business owners can safeguard their interests and build confidence in their preparedness against evolving cyber threats. The right combination serves not just as a financial safety net but also empowers businesses to act decisively when facing the unpredictable challenges posed by today's digital world.

Coverage and Exclusions

When selecting cyber insurance policies, it is essential to thoroughly understand the scope of coverage and any potential exclusions. The specifics of your coverage can greatly impact the level of protection your business receives, making it crucial to dissect these details to know what to expect in the event of a cyber incident.

Policies can vary significantly in their coverage, affecting both small businesses and larger enterprises. For example, first-party coverage may include expenses related to data recovery, forensic investigations, and notification costs associated with data breaches. However, some policies may exclude costs related to reputational damage or loss of market share after a breach—an important consideration for businesses that rely heavily on customer trust.

As you explore your options, pay close attention to any exclusions that could impact your operations. Many policies specifically exclude coverage for acts of negligence or intentional misconduct. If an incident stems from failing to follow basic security practices—such as neglecting software updates or ignoring security patches—your claim could be denied due to these exclusions. This shows the necessity of establishing strong cybersecurity protocols within your organization, not just to protect your assets but also to ensure the effectiveness of your insurance coverage.

Another critical area to consider is business interruption coverage. While many policies provide compensation for lost income during system downtime due to cyberattacks, specific criteria often must be met before compensation is activated. Take this example, your policy might require physical damage to your systems or infrastructure as a prerequisite for business interruption claims. Understanding these stipulations is vital to ensure you are not left vulnerable when operational continuity is at stake.

Regulatory fines and penalties resulting from data breaches also represent a common exclusion. Although some policies cover defense costs associated with legal proceedings, fines imposed by regulatory bodies may not be included in standard coverage provisions. This can pose a significant risk for businesses operating in heavily regulated industries— such as healthcare or finance—where a breach could lead to substantial penalties.

Additionally, potential sub-limits within policies can further complicate matters by capping the amount an insurer will pay for certain types of claims. These limits may apply to specific incidents like data breaches or losses stemming from phishing scams. For example, if your policy has a sub-limit of (100,000 for data breach-related costs but your actual expenses total)150,000, you would need to cover the 50,000 difference out-of-pocket. Small businesses should carefully scrutinize these sub-limits to ensure they have adequate protection without unexpected gaps.

While these exclusions and limitations may seem daunting, they also present opportunities for proactive planning. Being aware of potential gaps in coverage allows business owners to seek additional endorsements or riders that enhance their policy's reach. Consulting with an insurance broker knowledgeable about cybersecurity issues can facilitate discussions on customizing policies that address your unique vulnerabilities while maximizing coverage.

cultivating a comprehensive understanding of what is covered —and what is not—empowers small business owners to make informed decisions regarding their cyber insurance policies. This clarity helps align insurance choices with overall risk management strategies and fosters greater resilience against evolving cyber threats.

By navigating these complexities, you will gain insights essential not only for selecting appropriate policies but also for ensuring that your organization remains fortified against digital vulnerabilities in an ever-changing landscape. Your dedication to understanding the intricacies of coverage positions you as a leader in cybersecurity preparedness within your industry and enables you to foster a culture that values security at every level of operation.

Determining Coverage Needs

Understanding your coverage needs is a crucial step in developing a strong cybersecurity insurance plan. This process goes beyond merely selecting a policy; it requires a thorough examination of the unique risks your business faces and their potential impact on your operations and financial health. To accurately determine these needs, it's essential to evaluate both the assets at stake and the specific threats that could compromise them.

Start by taking inventory of your business's digital assets. This includes customer databases, proprietary software, intellectual property, and physical equipment like servers.

Each asset carries its own value, which will guide you in determining the necessary coverage. For example, if your customer database contains sensitive information, the financial repercussions of a data breach could be significantly greater than those from other incidents. When assessing value, consider not only the replacement costs but also the potential liabilities associated with data breaches, such as legal fees, notification costs, and possible fines.

Next, focus on the cyber threats that are most pertinent to your industry. Retail businesses may be particularly vulnerable to payment data breaches, while healthcare organizations must be on high alert for ransomware attacks targeting patient information. Conducting a comprehensive risk assessment can help identify these vulnerabilities. Utilizing cybersecurity frameworks from organizations like NIST or ISO can provide valuable insights into common threats in your sector.

As you evaluate risks, also consider operational factors that might influence your coverage needs. If your business relies heavily on third-party vendors for services such as cloud storage or payment processing, it's important to understand their security practices. A breach at one of these vendors can have significant repercussions for your operations. Many policies require you to account for third-party exposures when determining coverage limits.

Compliance with industry regulations is another critical aspect to consider. Regulations often impose stringent requirements for data protection and breach response. Take this example, businesses handling healthcare data must comply with HIPAA regulations, which outline how personal health information should be managed and safeguarded. These regulations not only define compliance necessities but also inform how much coverage you should secure to protect against regulatory fines resulting from non-compliance after a breach.

Anticipating future growth and changes in your business model is equally important when assessing coverage needs. If you plan to expand into new markets or introduce products that rely heavily on customer data, you may require higher coverage limits than you currently possess. Growth often introduces additional risks, making it essential to regularly reassess your insurance requirements.

As you compile this information, consult with an insurance advisor who specializes in cyber insurance to further refine your analysis. They can offer insights into common pitfalls that small businesses encounter when selecting coverage and assist in tailoring a policy that closely aligns with your operational realities.

In crafting an effective cyber insurance strategy, remember that it's not just about meeting minimum requirements or adhering to industry standards; it's about ensuring comprehensive protection specifically tailored to your business's needs. By taking these proactive steps to assess what you truly need—considering both current risks and future aspirations—you position yourself not merely as a passive participant but as an informed leader ready to navigate the complexities of cybersecurity.

Your efforts in this regard will build a solid foundation for safeguarding your assets and fostering resilience within your organization as threats continue to evolve rapidly. The clarity gained through this process empowers you to make informed decisions that significantly enhance both your security posture and peace of mind in an increasingly digital landscape.

Working with Insurers

Navigating the landscape of cybersecurity insurance involves more than simply assessing your own needs; it requires establishing a strategic partnership with insurers who can effectively protect your business. To foster this relationship, open communication and a clear understanding of expectations on both sides are essential. This collaborative approach is vital for minimizing coverage gaps and ensuring you receive the tailored protection your business requires.

Start by identifying potential insurers that specialize in cybersecurity coverage. Research their industry reputation by looking into reviews, ratings, and case studies. Seek out providers with a proven track record of assisting businesses similar to yours. Many insurers offer resources or case studies that highlight how they have helped other organizations manage breaches or respond to threats, which can provide valuable insights into their capabilities as partners.

Once you've narrowed down your options, initiate discussions about your specific risks and coverage requirements. Share insights from your risk assessment to highlight the unique vulnerabilities your business faces. For example, if you operate in healthcare and handle sensitive patient data, it's important to explain the regulatory landscape you navigate daily. Insurers appreciate businesses that come prepared with knowledge, as this fosters a collaborative environment where they can offer more targeted solutions.

Thoroughly discussing policy terms is equally crucial. Clarify what each policy option covers and identify any exclusions or limitations that may apply. Some policies may provide extensive coverage but exclude certain events—such as acts of cyber terrorism or third-party breaches—unless specifically included. Pay close attention to how "incident" and "data breach" are defined within the policy framework to ensure they align with your operational realities.

Take this example, consider a policy that covers ransomware attacks but excludes social engineering fraud. If your employees are susceptible to phishing scams—common across many industries—you could be left vulnerable if such an attack were to exploit that weakness. Therefore, it's important to ask critical questions that reveal potential blind spots: What triggers coverage? Are there sub-limits for different types of incidents? How does the insurer define a "cyber incident," and does this align with your cybersecurity approach?

Additionally, establish clear communication protocols for incident reporting. Insurers typically require prompt notification following a breach to process claims efficiently; understanding these timelines will help facilitate smoother interactions when issues arise. Request detailed information about their claims process so you're not caught off guard during a crisis.

Building relationships with multiple insurers can enhance your negotiating power. This strategy not only provides options during renewal periods but also allows you to compare offerings, ensuring you receive the best value for your investment. Engage in conversations about potential discounts or bundled services—for example, some insurers may offer reduced rates for purchasing both cybersecurity insurance and general liability coverage together.

It's advisable to review your policy annually or bi-annually with your insurance advisor—especially after significant business changes such as mergers, expansions, or technological shifts. These changes can significantly impact risk exposure and may necessitate adjustments in coverage amounts or types.

Consider leveraging emerging technologies that insurers might offer as part of their services—such as advanced threat intelligence tools or incident response teams—to bolster your overall security posture while meeting policy requirements for proactive risk management.

Finally, cultivate an ongoing relationship beyond just annual reviews; maintain regular communication with your insurer regarding updates in cyber threats and industry standards. This dialogue fosters mutual understanding and encourages anticipatory measures from both parties moving forward.

As you collaborate with insurers, remember that this partnership is not merely transactional; it aims to fortify your business against unforeseen cyber threats while enabling growth and resilience through proactive measures tailored specifically for you. Embracing this collaborative approach allows you to harness the full potential of cybersecurity insurance—not just as a safety net but as a strategic ally in navigating today's digital landscape effectively.

Claims Process

Navigating the claims process for cybersecurity insurance is essential for ensuring your business recovers quickly and effectively from a cyber incident. The journey begins with a thorough understanding of your policy, particularly the conditions under which claims can be made. While each insurer has its own claims process, there are common elements that can help you manage this experience more smoothly.

When a cyber incident occurs, prompt communication with your insurer is crucial. Most policies require that you report breaches or incidents within a specific timeframe—often between 24 to 72 hours. This urgency highlights the importance of having an internal incident response plan in place beforehand. Make sure your team knows exactly who to contact at your insurance provider right after a breach, as this can significantly influence the handling and resolution of your claim.

Once you've initiated the claims process, you'll typically need to provide detailed documentation regarding the incident. This may include timelines of events, descriptions of the breach, and any evidence gathered during the initial response. For example, if a ransomware attack encrypted critical business files, gather logs that show when the breach occurred and how it was detected. Clear and comprehensive information not only expedites processing but also demonstrates your professionalism.

Insurers often require proof of loss as well. This could involve financial statements that illustrate how the breach impacted revenue or any additional costs incurred during recovery efforts. If possible, quantify these impacts—whether through lost sales due to downtime or expenses related to IT consultations and recovery services. Detailed financial reporting not only supports your claim but also underscores how proactive measures can mitigate losses in future incidents.

It's also important to understand what resources your insurer provides throughout this process. Many companies assign dedicated claims adjusters who will work with you from start to finish. Building a rapport with this individual can lead to smoother interactions and a better understanding of what is needed from both sides. They can assist you in collecting necessary information and clarifying policy terms relevant to your claim.

Be prepared for potential disagreements that may arise during the evaluation process. Insurers might contest aspects of your claim based on their interpretation of policy terms —this could involve coverage limits or exclusions related to specific incidents like phishing attacks versus hacking intrusions. Having thorough documentation readily available will empower you to negotiate effectively; well-prepared businesses often find they have stronger leverage when discussing coverage interpretations.

After submitting your claim along with all requested documentation, there will usually be a waiting period while the insurer investigates and assesses it. Patience is important during this time; however, regular follow-ups can ensure that your claim remains a priority without appearing overly demanding.

If your claim is approved, you'll receive compensation

according to the policy terms—understanding how payout calculations are derived is essential at this stage. Some policies cover specific damages up to predetermined limits while excluding others altogether; knowing where you stand allows for more accurate expectations regarding reimbursements.

Unfortunately, there may be instances where claims are denied or undervalued due to misunderstandings about coverage details or inadequate documentation. If this happens, don't hesitate to appeal the decision by presenting additional evidence or clarifying any misinterpretations.

Finally, integrate lessons learned from each claims experience into your ongoing risk management strategy. After navigating through an incident, take time to review what went well and identify areas for improvement in both your cybersecurity practices and engagement with insurers. These reflections are vital for strengthening not only your defense mechanisms but also your relationship with insurance providers moving forward.

In summary, understanding the claims process empowers small business owners not only to recover from incidents but also to enhance their overall approach to cybersecurity resilience—transforming potential setbacks into strategic opportunities for growth and improvement.

Reducing Insurance Premiums

Reducing insurance premiums is a vital part of managing cybersecurity expenses, especially for small business owners who often operate with limited budgets. While cyber insurance is essential for protecting against potential financial losses from data breaches and cyber incidents, the costs can escalate quickly. Fortunately, a proactive approach can help you lower these premiums without sacrificing your security measures.

A key strategy for reducing insurance costs is to demonstrate your commitment to cybersecurity through effective risk management practices. Insurers favor businesses that actively implement security measures, as this reduces the likelihood of claims. Take this example, adopting industry-standard frameworks like NIST or ISO 27001 not only strengthens your security but also signals to insurers that you take cybersecurity seriously. Regular audits and assessments can help identify vulnerabilities; addressing them promptly provides documentation to share with insurers, showcasing your commitment to maintaining a secure environment.

In addition to establishing strong cybersecurity protocols, investing in employee training programs focused on security awareness can be highly beneficial. Educating your staff on best practices—such as recognizing phishing attempts and using strong passwords—can significantly reduce human error, which accounts for approximately 95% of cybersecurity incidents according to a study by IBM. By cultivating a culture of security awareness and documenting these training sessions, you further enhance your credibility with insurers when it comes to preventing incidents.

Exploring technology solutions that bolster your cybersecurity defenses is another effective way to lower premiums. Implementing tools like multi-factor authentication (MFA), endpoint detection and response (EDR), and firewalls can significantly mitigate risks associated with unauthorized access and malware attacks. Many insurers offer discounts for businesses that use advanced technologies, as these solutions decrease the potential impact of cyber incidents.

Proactive incident response planning is equally important. Having a well-documented incident response plan not only prepares your team for potential breaches but also reassures insurers of your readiness to act swiftly in the event of an incident. This preparedness often leads to lower premiums because it minimizes both the duration and extent of disruptions related to cyber threats.

Regularly reviewing and updating your coverage is another crucial step in reducing premiums. As your business evolves, so do its associated risks. Ensure that your insurance policy reflects current operations by discussing any changes with your insurer. They may recommend adjustments based on emerging threats in the digital landscape.

Building strong relationships with underwriters can also lead to more favorable terms during policy renewals. If you have made significant improvements in your cybersecurity posture since last year's renewal, make sure to communicate these changes effectively during discussions with insurers. Transparency is appreciated, and underwriters are often willing to negotiate better rates when they see active engagement from clients regarding their security strategies.

For small businesses seeking cost-effective options, bundling policies can yield significant savings as well. Many insurers provide discounts if multiple types of coverage—such as general liability or property insurance—are purchased alongside cyber insurance. It's worth exploring this option, as it could lead to substantial overall savings while ensuring comprehensive protection across various risks.

Lastly, remain vigilant about understanding the specific factors that influence premium costs within your industry sector. Engaging directly with an insurance broker who specializes in cyber risk can provide tailored insights and help identify potential areas for cost reduction based on emerging trends and common challenges faced by similar businesses.

By implementing these strategies, small business owners can effectively manage their cyber insurance costs while strengthening their overall security posture. The objective extends beyond merely cutting expenses; it's about building resilience against evolving threats and ensuring that when incidents occur, you are well-prepared both financially and operationally to respond effectively.

Case Studies on Insurance Payouts

Case studies on insurance payouts shed light on the practical implications of cyber insurance, highlighting its critical role in protecting small businesses from significant financial losses. By exploring real-world examples, we can better grasp how effective risk management strategies facilitate successful claims, providing valuable lessons for other business owners facing similar challenges.

Take, for instance, a mid-sized retail company that fell victim to a ransomware attack. This incident disrupted their operations for several days, resulting in substantial revenue loss and damage to customer trust. Fortunately, the company had invested in a comprehensive cyber insurance policy that covered ransomware incidents. As part of their incident response plan, they quickly contacted their insurer, and within hours, a claims adjuster was assigned to assist with the recovery process. The insurance provider not only covered the ransom payment but also reimbursed lost income during the downtime and offered access to forensic experts who helped uncover how the breach occurred.

This proactive approach underscores the significance of having a well-defined incident response plan in place before an attack strikes. Businesses that prepare for such events often recover more effectively, as demonstrated by the retail company's swift action and thorough documentation of their losses.

Another pertinent example involves a healthcare organization that faced a data breach due to insufficient security measures. This breach exposed sensitive patient information and led to hefty fines from regulatory bodies, as well as legal costs from lawsuits filed by affected individuals. Thankfully, the healthcare provider had enrolled in an insurance policy specifically designed for cybersecurity risks in the healthcare sector. When they filed their claim, they were able to recover a significant portion of the expenses incurred, including legal fees and regulatory fines.

This scenario serves as a cautionary tale about the importance of aligning cyber insurance policies with specific industry needs. Organizations must carefully evaluate their coverage options to ensure they address risks unique to their operations. It emphasizes that not all cyber policies are created equal; those tailored to industry standards often yield better outcomes when crises arise.

In yet another case involving a small law firm, an employee inadvertently clicked on a phishing email link, compromising client data stored on their servers. Fortunately, the firm had implemented multi-factor authentication (MFA) and conducted regular training programs focused on recognizing such threats. While the incident caused some disruption, the firm's quick containment efforts minimized damage and significantly aided recovery. Their cyber insurance provider acknowledged these proactive measures during claims processing, enabling them to cover costs associated with data restoration and client notifications without protracted disputes.

These examples illustrate recurring themes: preparation and investment in cybersecurity best practices directly influence claims outcomes. Small business owners should prioritize establishing comprehensive training programs for employees while ensuring that technological defenses remain robust and current.

A case involving a manufacturing company further reinforces these insights. The company experienced operational disruptions following an insider threat when an employee misused credentials to access sensitive data and subsequently leaked proprietary information online. Although this incident stemmed from internal issues rather than external attacks, having appropriate coverage allowed them to file for damages related to lost contracts and legal ramifications affecting stakeholders impacted by the breach.

The lesson here is clear: effective cybersecurity goes beyond technology alone; fostering an organizational culture that prioritizes security can significantly shape insurers' responses when claims arise due to employee misconduct or negligence.

Collectively, these case studies illuminate the nuanced interplay between preparedness, cybersecurity practices, and insurance policy effectiveness in real-world scenarios. By closely examining these experiences, small business owners can extract actionable insights that reinforce their commitment to both preventive measures and recovery strategies—ensuring they not only protect themselves financially but also bolster their reputations against future threats.

CHAPTER 15: FUTURE PROOFING AGAINST EMERGING THREATS

The Evolution of Cyber Threats

The landscape of cyber threats has undergone a profound evolution over the past few decades, shifting from rudimentary hacking attempts to sophisticated attacks that target the very backbone of our digital infrastructure. This evolution is crucial for small business owners to understand as they navigate the complexities of cybersecurity in an era where threats are not only increasing in frequency but also in complexity.

In the early days of the internet, cyber threats were often driven by curiosity or mischief. Hackers exploited simple vulnerabilities primarily for personal bragging rights, gaining unauthorized access to systems without malicious intent. These so-called "script kiddies" utilized basic tools to target unsecured servers and systems. At that time, the repercussions for businesses were generally minimal; security measures were less stringent, and data breaches had not yet become a mainstream concern. However, as businesses began to recognize the value of their digital assets, the stakes grew significantly.

The late 1990s and early 2000s marked a shift in motivation as more organized cybercriminal networks emerged. Attacks became increasingly focused on financial gain rather than mere exploration. Cybercriminals began deploying malware —such as viruses and worms—that could spread across networks with alarming ease. Ransomware also emerged as a particularly insidious form of attack during this period; a notorious example is the Melissa virus, which affected millions of computers in 1999 and showcased how even simple code could disrupt operations on a massive scale, foreshadowing the more complex ransomware attacks we face today.

As technology advanced, so too did the sophistication of cyber threats. With businesses increasingly relying on cloud computing and remote work solutions, attackers adapted their tactics to exploit new vulnerabilities introduced by these technologies. Phishing scams gained prominence, tricking employees into revealing sensitive information through seemingly legitimate communications. The infamous Target data breach in 2013 exemplifies this shift; hackers gained access through a third-party vendor, underscoring the critical need for robust supply chain security.

Today, cyber threats have become alarmingly advanced and varied. Attackers utilize artificial intelligence (AI) and machine learning to create smarter malware capable of adapting and evading traditional security measures. Social engineering techniques have also evolved; today's attackers often target individuals within organizations rather than just their networks. Spear phishing attacks, for instance, are meticulously tailored to high-ranking officials within companies, making them incredibly effective.

Additionally, state-sponsored attacks introduce another layer of complexity to the threat landscape. Nation-states now engage in cyber warfare to disrupt economies, steal intellectual property, or undermine political stability in rival nations. The SolarWinds breach of 2020 serves as a stark reminder that even well-established companies can be vulnerable to attacks orchestrated at a national level, resulting in massive ramifications for numerous organizations across various sectors.

As we navigate this evolving terrain, it is clear that small business owners must remain vigilant and proactive. The threats they face today are not merely technical challenges but existential risks that can jeopardize their entire operations. By recognizing how these threats have evolved—from mischievous hackers seeking notoriety to organized criminals exploiting sophisticated technologies—business leaders can better prepare their defenses.

This understanding allows for a more nuanced approach to cybersecurity strategy development. Take this example, investing in employee training programs that emphasize recognizing phishing attempts is crucial given the rise of social engineering tactics. Also, integrating advanced threat detection systems that leverage AI can help identify suspicious activities before they escalate into full-blown crises.

Understanding this evolution does more than inform preparedness; it fosters resilience against future threats as well. Cybersecurity is no longer a one-time setup but an ongoing commitment requiring constant vigilance and adaptation to counteract ever-evolving adversaries. Cultivating an organizational culture centered around cybersecurity best practices will be paramount for small business owners looking to safeguard their enterprises effectively.

This comprehensive view of how cyber threats have transformed provides valuable insights into crafting strategies that not only protect but empower businesses in a digital world filled with challenges yet rich with opportunity.

Emerging Technologies and Their Risks

Emerging technologies are rapidly transforming the business landscape, presenting small business owners with innovative tools and opportunities for growth. However, these advancements also bring a range of cybersecurity risks that must be addressed. For small businesses aiming to harness these technologies effectively, understanding potential vulnerabilities is essential to maintaining a strong security posture.

Consider cloud computing as an example. The shift to cloud services allows businesses to store large amounts of data remotely and access it from anywhere. This flexibility is advantageous but also introduces new threats. Without proper security measures, data breaches can occur in cloud environments. A notable incident involved a major financial services company that faced a breach due to misconfigured cloud storage settings, exposing sensitive customer information. This case highlights the need for stringent access controls and regular audits when utilizing cloud platforms.

Another significant concern lies with the Internet of Things (IoT). Devices such as smart sensors and security cameras can enhance operational efficiency, but many IoT devices are designed with minimal security features, making them vulnerable targets for cybercriminals. A prime example is the Mirai botnet attack in 2016, where compromised IoT devices were used to execute one of the largest DDoS attacks in history, disrupting major websites. To mitigate these risks, small businesses should prioritize strong authentication protocols and ensure regular firmware updates for any deployed IoT devices.

Artificial intelligence (AI) and machine learning present their own unique challenges alongside their benefits. These technologies can significantly improve threat detection by analyzing vast amounts of data in real time and identifying anomalies that signal cyber threats. However, they can also be exploited by attackers who use AI to automate phishing campaigns or create sophisticated malware that adapts to existing security measures. A balanced approach for businesses involves leveraging AI-driven solutions while remaining alert to potential adversarial tactics that could compromise these systems.

Blockchain technology offers promising opportunities, especially for industries that require secure transactions or data integrity verification. While blockchain's decentralized nature provides built-in security against tampering and fraud, vulnerabilities may still exist within blockchain applications themselves. For example, poorly designed smart contracts can lead to substantial financial losses if targeted by malicious actors. Small business owners should conduct thorough evaluations of any blockchain implementations to ensure robust coding practices and continuous monitoring.

As businesses increasingly integrate emerging technologies into their operations, there's also a growing reliance on mobile devices—an evolution accelerated by the COVID-19 pandemic's shift toward remote work. While mobile devices facilitate productivity from virtually anywhere, they often lack the comprehensive security measures found in traditional computing environments. Numerous instances demonstrate how unsecured mobile applications have led to data leaks or unauthorized access; thus, implementing Mobile Device Management (MDM) solutions becomes critical for controlling access and securing sensitive information on employee devices.

And, social media platforms have become essential marketing tools for small businesses but come with their own set of risks related to data privacy and brand reputation management. Cybercriminals may exploit social media accounts through phishing attacks or impersonation tactics aimed at both consumers and organizations. Businesses should proactively communicate with customers about potential threats while implementing two-factor authentication across their social media accounts.

In summary, while emerging technologies offer significant advantages for small business growth and efficiency, they also introduce new complexities into the cybersecurity landscape that cannot be ignored. Adopting a proactive approach that includes risk assessments focused on these technologies is vital—not only from a technical perspective but as part of a broader strategy that aligns technological adoption with robust cybersecurity practices.

To navigate this intricate landscape effectively requires ongoing education about both technological advancements and evolving threats. Empowering your team through training that emphasizes recognizing potential vulnerabilities associated with emerging tools fosters a culture where everyone contributes to safeguarding the organization's digital assets.

As we embrace these innovations, it is crucial to remember that every advancement comes with responsibilities— responsibilities that demand our utmost attention if we are truly committed to protecting our enterprises from today's sophisticated cyber threats.

Developing Proactive Defense Strategies

Proactive defense strategies are crucial for small businesses facing the constantly evolving cyber threat landscape. Rather than simply reacting to incidents, organizations should adopt a mindset focused on prevention. This shift requires not only the implementation of technological solutions but also the cultivation of a culture of vigilance and readiness among employees.

At the heart of a proactive defense is a robust cybersecurity policy that clearly outlines expectations, processes, and protocols. This policy serves as a foundational document, detailing how to respond to various types of threats while providing clear guidelines for employee behavior. For example, it can include sections that define acceptable use of company devices and outline procedures for reporting suspicious activities. A well-crafted policy empowers employees with knowledge, positioning them as key players in your security framework.

Integrating threat intelligence into your strategy further enhances your ability to anticipate potential risks. Threat intelligence involves gathering information about current and emerging threats specific to your industry and business environment. Subscribing to threat intelligence feeds can provide valuable insights into recent attacks on similar organizations, enabling you to strengthen your defenses in response to these trends. Take this example, a healthcare provider successfully utilized threat intelligence to address vulnerabilities that had been exploited in a series of ransomware attacks targeting health data systems.

Regular training sessions are also vital for fostering an awareness-oriented culture. Employees should be equipped not only with basic cybersecurity knowledge but also with scenario-based training that simulates real-life phishing attempts or social engineering tactics. Such immersive experiences prepare staff to recognize and react appropriately when confronted with actual threats. A local bakery implemented monthly security briefings, during which employees learned about current scams affecting small businesses; this initiative helped them identify attempted phishing attacks before they could lead to significant losses.

Vulnerability management is another essential component of a proactive defense strategy. This ongoing process involves identifying, assessing, and remediating vulnerabilities within your systems. Conducting regular vulnerability scans can help reveal weaknesses before attackers can exploit them. Small business owners should establish a routine schedule for these scans—ideally quarterly or bi-monthly—depending on how quickly technology evolves within their operations. For example, a retail chain discovered previously unpatched software vulnerabilities through regular scanning; addressing these issues before they could be exploited saved the company from potential financial harm.

In conjunction with vulnerability management, consider integrating advanced security technologies such as intrusion detection systems (IDS) and security information and event management (SIEM) solutions into your defense strategy. An IDS monitors network traffic for suspicious activity and sends alerts when anomalies are detected, while SIEM systems aggregate data from various sources within your infrastructure for real-time analysis and rapid response. Take this example, an IDS identified unusual login attempts from unknown IP addresses at a manufacturing firm; prompt action prevented unauthorized access before it escalated into a breach.

Creating layered defenses—a concept known as "defense in depth"—further strengthens your cybersecurity posture by employing multiple security measures across different levels of your organization's infrastructure. This approach ensures that if one layer fails, others remain intact to protect against intrusions. Firewalls, antivirus software, secure configurations, and data encryption should all work together to create robust barriers against threats.

Finally, proactive incident response planning prepares businesses for the possibility of a breach despite their best efforts at prevention. Develop an incident response plan that includes clearly defined roles and responsibilities during an incident, along with communication strategies for both internal teams and external stakeholders. Conducting tabletop exercises that simulate potential cyber incidents allows teams to practice their responses without the pressure of real-world chaos—ensuring they're ready when it counts.

By embracing proactive defense strategies, small businesses not only enhance their immediate security posture but also cultivate resilience against future threats. Each layer implemented—from policies and employee training to advanced technology—contributes cohesively towards creating an environment where cybersecurity is integral rather than ancillary. adopting this proactive stance positions businesses favorably amid ongoing digital transformations while reinforcing trust among clients who prioritize their privacy and security above all else.

Continuous Improvement in Cybersecurity

Continuous improvement in cybersecurity is vital for small businesses navigating the ever-evolving landscape of digital threats. Cyber threats are not static; they change and adapt just as rapidly as the technologies created to combat them. Embracing a mindset of continuous improvement helps ensure that your defenses are effective against both current and emerging risks.

At the heart of continuous improvement is the principle of regular assessment. This means systematically evaluating your cybersecurity policies, practices, and technologies to identify areas that require enhancement. For example, conducting annual audits can uncover gaps in security measures or reveal outdated protocols that need updating. Consider a small law firm that discovered during an audit that its data encryption methods no longer met industry standards. By addressing this issue promptly, the firm not only strengthened its data protection strategy but also bolstered client trust.

Feedback loops are essential for refining your cybersecurity strategy. After any incident—whether a minor phishing attempt or a significant breach—it's important to conduct a thorough review to analyze what went wrong and how responses could be improved. This post-incident evaluation should involve relevant team members, as their insights can highlight overlooked vulnerabilities or weaknesses in communication during the event. Take this example, after a ransomware attack, a small retail company held a debriefing session where employees shared their experiences and suggested improvements to incident response protocols. These discussions led to more streamlined communication channels and increased employee awareness.

Incorporating metrics into your cybersecurity practices also quantifies the effectiveness of the measures you implement. Establishing key performance indicators (KPIs) related to threat detection, incident response times, and employee training completion rates is crucial. Tracking the number of phishing emails reported by staff, for example, can reveal how well your training programs resonate with employees. A local nonprofit organization adopted this approach and observed a significant increase in reported phishing attempts following enhanced training sessions; this indicated that employees were becoming more vigilant and engaged with security practices.

Technology plays a vital role in facilitating continuous improvement as well. Utilizing automated tools for threat monitoring and vulnerability assessments can provide real-time insights into your security posture. Integrating solutions like Security Information and Event Management (SIEM) systems allows businesses to collect data from multiple sources and analyze it for unusual patterns indicative of potential threats. For example, a manufacturing firm that implemented a SIEM solution was able to detect suspicious behavior within its network before it escalated into a breach, illustrating the value of proactive technology use.

Also, fostering a culture of learning within your organization encourages ongoing development in cybersecurity practices.

Encourage employees to stay informed about the latest threats and trends by providing access to resources such as webinars or industry conferences. Creating incentives for participation can enhance staff engagement; one marketing agency incentivized attendance at cybersecurity workshops by offering bonuses to employees who completed advanced training courses. This investment not only empowered employees but also strengthened the organization's overall security awareness.

Collaboration with external partners can further enhance your continuous improvement efforts. Engaging with cybersecurity consultants or participating in industry groups allows businesses to share knowledge and learn from others' experiences. A small financial services firm benefited from joining an industry consortium where members exchanged insights on recent threats and effective mitigation strategies. Such collaborations promote a culture of shared responsibility for security across the broader community.

Finally, it's essential to remember that continuous improvement is not just a one-time initiative but an ongoing commitment. Regularly revisiting your cybersecurity framework ensures it evolves alongside new challenges posed by cybercriminals and technological advancements. By embedding this principle into your organizational culture, you cultivate resilience against future threats while reinforcing trust among clients who expect their sensitive information to be protected diligently.

embracing continuous improvement in cybersecurity empowers small business owners to not only fortify their defenses but also navigate an unpredictable digital world with confidence. Every enhancement—whether through technological upgrades or cultural shifts—contributes to creating a robust security environment where proactive measures take precedence over reactive responses.

Adapting to the Changing Threat Landscape

Adapting to the evolving threat landscape is crucial for small businesses aiming to maintain strong cybersecurity. The digital environment is not static; it constantly shifts, with threats evolving and new vulnerabilities arising almost daily. To navigate this landscape effectively, small business owners must remain vigilant, ensuring that their strategies not only address current threats but also anticipate future risks.

A fundamental part of this adaptation involves understanding the nature of emerging threats. Cybercriminals are becoming increasingly sophisticated, often using advanced tactics such as social engineering or zero-day exploits. For example, a small healthcare provider might find itself targeted by ransomware that exploits human error—such as an employee inadvertently clicking on a malicious link in an email. By staying informed about these tactics, businesses can implement targeted training and awareness programs, equipping employees to recognize and respond to real-world scenarios they might face.

In addition to training, leveraging technology is essential. Automation tools can significantly enhance threat detection and incident response. Consider a retail business that integrates machine learning algorithms into its cybersecurity framework; these systems can analyze user behavior patterns and flag anomalies that may indicate a potential breach. By adopting such technologies, businesses not only streamline their security processes but also improve their ability to respond swiftly to incidents, thereby minimizing potential damage.

Regularly updating software and security protocols is another vital adaptation strategy. Cybersecurity tools can quickly become outdated as new vulnerabilities are discovered and patched in software applications. Take this example, a small accounting firm might find its outdated antivirus solution unable to recognize a new variant of malware targeting specific financial software. By committing to regular updates for both security tools and underlying systems, businesses can safeguard themselves against known vulnerabilities and close gaps that cybercriminals might exploit.

And, incorporating threat intelligence feeds into cybersecurity strategies provides actionable insights into the evolving threat landscape. These feeds offer real-time data about emerging risks, enabling businesses to proactively adjust their defenses. A local e-commerce company, for example, might subscribe to threat intelligence services that alert them about phishing campaigns targeting similar businesses in their sector. This information allows them to strengthen their email filtering systems and educate employees on identifying suspicious communications before they lead to breaches.

Collaboration with industry peers also plays a critical role in adaptation. Sharing knowledge about recent threats fosters a community-focused approach to cybersecurity resilience. For example, a group of small financial institutions collaborating through an information-sharing consortium can pool resources and insights to collectively strengthen defenses against common threats. This collaboration not only enhances individual security measures but also contributes to a more secure overall environment within the industry.

Additionally, maintaining flexibility within cybersecurity policies greatly influences an organization's ability to adapt effectively. Small businesses should develop policies that allow for swift changes in response to the current threat landscape, avoiding bureaucratic delays that could hinder critical updates or responses. An agile policy framework facilitates quicker decision-making when faced with new types of attacks or significant regulatory changes impacting cybersecurity practices.

Regular scenario planning exercises can further prepare organizations for potential crises stemming from cyberattacks. Small teams can simulate various attack vectors —such as phishing schemes or distributed denial-of-service (DDoS) attacks—to evaluate existing response protocols and identify weaknesses in real-time decision-making processes. Take this example, during one such exercise, a small tech startup discovered that its incident response communication plan lacked clarity, prompting revisions before an actual breach occurred.

Lastly, fostering an adaptive mindset throughout the organization is essential for long-term resilience against evolving threats. Employees should feel empowered to voice concerns related to cybersecurity and contribute ideas for improvement without fear of repercussions. A culture of openness leads to greater awareness and vigilance; when every team member understands their role in protecting sensitive data, organizations become more resilient as a whole.

As the digital landscape continues to shift—a perpetual game of cat and mouse between cyber defenders and attackers— small business owners who embrace adaptability will not only protect their enterprises but also cultivate trust among clients who rely on them for secure transactions and data handling. In this ever-changing world, agility isn't just an advantage; it's imperative for survival and success.

Building a Resilient Organization

Central to this organizational resilience is a well-defined cybersecurity framework. This framework should clearly outline not only the specific security measures in place but also the reasoning behind them. Take this example, a small business might implement multi-factor authentication (MFA) across all user accounts to reduce the risk of unauthorized access. Communicating the importance of such measures encourages employee buy-in, which in turn leads to stronger compliance and engagement. Each layer of security must be interconnected, forming a protective shield that evolves as new threats emerge.

Training is equally essential in cultivating a resilient workforce. Cybersecurity awareness programs should extend beyond traditional training sessions; they must engage employees through interactive methods that simulate real-life scenarios. Regular phishing simulations, for example, can help employees identify potential threats in their inboxes. When team members learn to spot red flags—such as unexpected attachments or suspicious links—they become the first line of defense against breaches. This knowledge empowers employees to actively participate in safeguarding sensitive information, fostering a collective sense of responsibility toward cybersecurity.

Clear communication channels regarding security practices and incidents are also critical. Organizations should establish protocols for promptly reporting suspicious activities or potential breaches. When employees feel empowered to voice their concerns without fear of repercussions, issues can be addressed before they escalate into significant threats. Take this example, if an employee notices unusual activity on their computer, knowing how and when to report it can prevent further compromise of systems or data.

Additionally, building relationships with external partners can bolster organizational resilience. Collaborating with cybersecurity experts or managed service providers grants small businesses access to resources and insights that may otherwise be out of reach. These partnerships offer not only advanced technology solutions but also valuable perspectives on emerging threats tailored to specific industries. For example, a local restaurant chain working with a cybersecurity firm to enhance point-of-sale (POS) system protection can safeguard customer payment information while ensuring compliance with industry standards.

Incorporating feedback loops into cybersecurity practices is another effective strategy for resilience. Regular audits and assessments enable organizations to continuously identify weaknesses within their existing frameworks. By acting on feedback from these evaluations, businesses can refine processes and proactively address vulnerabilities. A tech startup might discover through an audit that certain software updates have been overlooked; addressing these gaps swiftly strengthens overall defenses against exploitation by cybercriminals.

To maintain organizational resilience over time, it's vital to foster a culture that embraces continuous learning and adaptation. Given the dynamic nature of cybersecurity—with evolving tactics employed by attackers—ongoing education for all employees—from management to new hires—is essential. Emphasizing learning helps organizations remain agile in the face of rapid technological changes and new threat vectors. Hosting monthly workshops or inviting guest speakers to share insights on cybersecurity trends cultivates an environment where knowledge sharing becomes ingrained in the company's culture.

And, integrating cybersecurity objectives into broader business goals solidifies its importance within organizational priorities. Aligning security measures with growth strategies ensures that as businesses expand—whether through digital transformation or entry into new markets—security remains at the forefront rather than being an afterthought. A small e-commerce startup looking to scale its operations must consider how each new platform or service impacts its security posture, avoiding pitfalls that could jeopardize customer trust.

Finally, resilience involves preparing for worst-case scenarios through incident response planning and tabletop exercises that simulate potential crises. Regularly revisiting these plans ensures clarity among team members about their roles during an incident while identifying any gaps in response strategies beforehand. For example, a small accounting firm may develop an incident response plan specifically addressing data breaches, ensuring that every employee understands how to act swiftly and effectively if a breach occurs.

building a resilient organization requires commitment from every level—from leadership down to individual contributors —to cultivate an environment where cybersecurity is embedded in everyday operations rather than merely treated as a compliance obligation or box-checking exercise. In doing so, businesses don't just react to cyber threats; they construct defenses robust enough to withstand potential attacks while fostering trust among clients who increasingly value transparency and reliability in their service providers. Resilience is not just about surviving; it's about thriving in an era defined by change and unpredictability.

The Role of Cybersecurity in Digital Transformation

The role of cybersecurity in digital transformation is crucial as businesses increasingly harness technology to improve operations, enhance customer engagement, and boost overall efficiency. As organizations embark on their digital journeys, they face new risks that could jeopardize their efforts if not adequately addressed. Thus, integrating robust cybersecurity measures into this transformation is not just a technical necessity; it's a strategic imperative that significantly impacts a company's capacity to innovate and adapt in a rapidly evolving landscape.

This integration begins with the understanding that digital transformation extends beyond merely adopting new technologies. It requires reimagining business processes and developing new value propositions for customers. For example, a retail business transitioning to an online sales model may find that while expanding its digital presence can foster growth, it also introduces vulnerabilities—such as the risk of customer data breaches if appropriate security measures are not implemented from the start. Therefore, cybersecurity must be an integral part of this transformation; without it, businesses risk facing serious consequences, including reputational harm and financial loss.

Aligning cybersecurity with digital transformation initiatives starts with a clear understanding of the organization's specific goals and the associated risks. Take a healthcare provider moving towards electronic health records (EHR) systems: protecting patient information against breaches while ensuring compliance with regulations like HIPAA is paramount. Conducting thorough risk assessments allows organizations to pinpoint vulnerable areas during the transition and implement tailored security controls that align with their strategic objectives.

And, security considerations should be embedded in the planning and execution of technology adoption. Take this example, when implementing cloud solutions, organizations must evaluate the security features provided by service vendors alongside their own data management and access control policies. A small business utilizing cloud services might choose providers that offer encryption and continuous monitoring capabilities, thereby adding essential layers of protection for sensitive data during transmission and storage.

Equally important is fostering a culture of security awareness throughout the digital transformation process. Employees need to understand their role in maintaining cybersecurity as they adapt to new tools and workflows. This entails providing training sessions focused on specific risks associated with new technologies while highlighting best practices for data handling and protection. For example, a software company introducing collaborative platforms can organize workshops on recognizing phishing attempts or securely sharing sensitive information within teams.

The relationship between agility and security becomes

particularly evident when organizations adopt agile methodologies during their transformation efforts. Agile frameworks allow teams to respond swiftly to changing market demands but can inadvertently lead to security oversights if not managed carefully. By incorporating security reviews into agile sprints, organizations ensure that every iteration considers potential vulnerabilities before deploying updates or features. Take this example, an app development team might allocate time during each sprint to assess whether new functionalities expose user data or introduce other risks, enabling proactive adjustments prior to launch.

Another critical aspect is leveraging data analytics within cybersecurity strategies as part of digital transformation. By utilizing analytics, organizations can gain valuable insights into user behavior and emerging threat patterns, allowing them to address vulnerabilities proactively before they are exploited. For example, a financial services firm employing advanced analytics could detect unusual transaction patterns indicative of fraudulent activity, facilitating swift interventions that safeguard both customer assets and organizational integrity.

Additionally, collaborating with external cybersecurity experts can significantly enhance resilience during digital transformations. Engaging managed service providers (MSSPs) not only brings specialized expertise but also helps businesses stay ahead of evolving threats without overstretching internal resources. Take this example, a manufacturing company transitioning to smart factory technologies might partner with an MSSP for comprehensive risk assessments tailored to IoT devices deployed on the shop floor, ensuring that these innovations do not compromise operational safety or intellectual property.

 embedding cybersecurity within digital transformation initiatives lays the groundwork for sustainable growth and innovation. By recognizing that robust security measures are foundational—integral to strategy rather than merely compliance—organizations position themselves as trustworthy leaders in their industries. As businesses navigate this complex intersection of technology and strategy, those who prioritize cybersecurity will not only survive but thrive amidst rapid change.

To wrap things up, effectively integrating cybersecurity into digital transformation requires a multi-faceted approach that emphasizes strategic alignment, employee engagement, continuous improvement, and collaboration with external partners. By adopting this comprehensive strategy, organizations can build a resilient foundation capable of adapting to current challenges while seizing future opportunities in an increasingly interconnected world.

Long-Term Planning and Visioning

Long-term planning and visioning in cybersecurity are crucial for businesses aiming to remain resilient against evolving threats while effectively leveraging new technologies. This strategic foresight requires organizations to anticipate not only the technical landscape but also the regulatory and market dynamics that could impact their security posture over time. Small business owners, in particular, must adopt a proactive mindset, aligning their cybersecurity strategies with broader organizational goals to foster sustainable growth.

At the heart of effective long-term planning is a thorough understanding of the cybersecurity landscape. This includes staying informed about emerging trends, threat vectors, and vulnerabilities that are unique to specific sectors. For example, consider a small financial firm looking to implement blockchain technology for transaction processing. While this innovation offers enhanced security features, it also presents new challenges, such as smart contract vulnerabilities and potential regulatory scrutiny. By keeping abreast of both advancements and pitfalls within their sector, business leaders can make informed decisions that strengthen their cybersecurity frameworks.

A practical approach to long-term planning is establishing a multi-year roadmap that integrates cybersecurity into overall business objectives. This roadmap should delineate key milestones—such as implementing new security technologies, conducting regular risk assessments, or achieving compliance with relevant regulations like GDPR or PCI DSS. Take this example, a healthcare provider might create a timeline for transitioning to electronic health records, detailing the necessary security enhancements to protect patient data. Specific measures like encryption protocols and staff training sessions can be outlined at each implementation stage.

In addition to immediate operational goals, long-term planning should incorporate scenario modeling, which involves analyzing how various internal and external factors might affect the business in the coming years. By developing scenarios around potential cyber incidents or data breaches, organizations can better prepare for responses that mitigate impact. A small retail business expecting increased online transactions during peak shopping seasons might devise contingency plans addressing potential e-commerce platform failures or customer data leaks from third-party vendors.

Fostering a culture of continuous improvement within the organization is another critical component of long-term planning. This goes beyond mere compliance checklists; it necessitates regularly revisiting and updating policies based on lessons learned from incidents and industry developments. For example, after experiencing a phishing attack that compromised employee credentials, a company should respond by tightening access controls and incorporating insights gained into ongoing training programs to enhance employees' ability to recognize similar threats in the future.

Engagement across all organizational levels is paramount.

Leadership must clearly and consistently communicate its vision for cybersecurity throughout the company, fostering buy-in from employees who play vital roles in maintaining daily security measures—whether by adhering to password policies or participating in incident response drills. Involving teams from different departments in strategic discussions allows for diverse perspectives on risk assessment and mitigation strategies, enriching the overall approach.

Partnerships with external cybersecurity experts can further bolster long-term planning efforts. Engaging consultants or managed service providers brings specialized knowledge and capabilities that may not be available internally. Take this example, when considering an overhaul of network infrastructure to effectively support remote work while maintaining robust security measures, collaborating with an expert can offer valuable insights into best practices tailored specifically for remote workforce challenges.

Finally, monitoring technological advancements is essential as organizations adapt their strategies over time. With innovations like artificial intelligence (AI) increasingly integrated into cyber defense systems—performing tasks from threat detection to automated response—businesses must remain agile enough to incorporate these developments without compromising existing protocols or training efforts.

Long-term planning and visioning are not merely reactive measures; they are strategic imperatives necessary for navigating an increasingly complex digital environment. When small businesses proactively integrate comprehensive cybersecurity strategies into their organizational visions— ensuring alignment with broader objectives—they position themselves not only as survivors in an unpredictable landscape but also as leaders capable of harnessing opportunities while effectively managing risks for sustainable success over time.

CONCLUSION

Navigating the complexities of cybersecurity for small businesses has revealed essential strategies, practical steps, and valuable insights designed to empower you as an owner. You've gained not only theoretical knowledge but also actionable methodologies that can be directly applied to strengthen your organization against a constantly evolving threat landscape. Each chapter has provided a perspective that encompasses not just the technical aspects of cybersecurity but also the human elements, emphasizing the importance of fostering a culture of security awareness among employees and stakeholders.

As we reflect on the diverse threats that small businesses face today, it becomes evident that cybersecurity transcends the realm of IT; it is now a fundamental component of your overall business strategy. By understanding the landscape —identifying vulnerabilities and implementing robust data protection measures—you are equipped to make informed decisions. Whether it's establishing effective incident response plans or utilizing advanced technologies like AI for threat detection, you have learned that a proactive stance is far more effective than merely reacting to breaches.

Engaging your team in this mission is essential. A culture that prioritizes cybersecurity at all levels transforms every employee into a guardian of sensitive information. Through regular training and clear communication, you can ensure that everyone understands their role in protecting the organization's assets. This shared responsibility is crucial; even the most sophisticated security systems can falter if users fall victim to social engineering tactics or overlook best practices.

Integrating cybersecurity into your overall business plan underscores its significance in achieving long-term goals. As you adapt to technological advancements and market changes, maintaining flexibility in your security strategy is vital. Embracing a mindset of continuous improvement will empower your business not only to survive but also to thrive amidst challenges. Conducting regular reviews of your security posture and staying informed about emerging threats will enable you to pivot as necessary, keeping your defenses robust.

And, cultivating partnerships with cybersecurity experts can offer invaluable insights and resources. Whether through consulting firms or managed service providers, these collaborations can enhance your organization's capabilities and provide peace of mind as you navigate complex regulatory environments. With their expertise at your disposal, you can implement best practices tailored specifically to your unique challenges.

Looking ahead, consider the role cybersecurity will play not only in protecting your business but also in shaping its future. The insights you've gained are stepping stones toward building resilience against emerging threats while also seizing new opportunities for growth and innovation. Your journey doesn't end here; it continues as you apply what you've learned, remaining vigilant and adaptable in a world where cyber threats are both inevitable and manageable.

To wrap things up, embrace the knowledge and strategies shared within these pages as integral components of your business ethos. As a small business owner, you are not merely navigating challenges—you are positioning yourself as a leader within your industry who prioritizes security and fosters trust among clients and partners alike. This proactive approach will not only safeguard your assets but also enhance your reputation as a forward-thinking organization capable of thriving in the digital age.

- **Recap of Key Points**

As we reflect on the key themes presented in this guide, it becomes evident that a comprehensive approach to cybersecurity is crucial for small business owners. You've explored the foundational concepts of cybersecurity, recognizing its importance not just as a technical requirement but as a vital component of your overall business strategy. By understanding the distinct yet interconnected realms of cybersecurity and information security, you've gained a framework to effectively assess risks and allocate resources.

A fundamental insight is the necessity of identifying your organization's valuable assets and data. Knowing what requires protection enables you to prioritize threats and vulnerabilities, ensuring your defenses are both relevant and focused. This strategic focus is further strengthened by conducting thorough vulnerability assessments, which allow you to pinpoint weaknesses before they can be exploited by adversaries.

Developing a robust cybersecurity strategy is another essential element of your security posture. By setting clear goals and establishing comprehensive policies, you ensure that every team member understands their role in protecting sensitive information. Regular training sessions engage employees and foster a culture of security awareness, transforming them into active participants in safeguarding the organization rather than passive observers.

Equally important is recognizing the critical role

technology plays in today's security landscape. The integration of advanced technologies such as artificial intelligence and machine learning facilitates real-time threat detection. Meanwhile, effective data protection measures—like encryption and secure backup solutions—help safeguard your information from breaches and data loss.

Incident response management also deserves attention. By developing a well-structured incident response plan, you prepare your organization to act swiftly when breaches occur—which they inevitably will. This proactive approach minimizes potential losses and builds trust with clients who expect you to prioritize their data privacy.

Collaborating with cybersecurity partners further enhances your strategy's resilience. Identifying trusted vendors or managed service providers can augment your capabilities by providing specialized expertise that complements your internal efforts. These partnerships are invaluable for navigating complex regulatory landscapes, allowing you to remain compliant while focusing on your core business operations.

Throughout this journey, you've gained insights into the evolving nature of cyber threats and how to adapt accordingly. Continuous improvement is essential; embracing flexibility within your cybersecurity practices ensures that you remain agile in responding to new challenges or opportunities arising from technological advancements.

The overarching message is clear: cybersecurity should no longer be perceived as an isolated function but as an integral part of your business operations. As you move forward, integrating these principles into your daily practices will not only protect against potential threats but also position you as a leader prioritizing security within your industry.

This guide serves as more than just a reference; it's a call to action for small business owners like yourself to proactively take charge of cybersecurity, fostering trust among stakeholders while driving innovation and growth within your organization. Your journey doesn't end here; it begins anew each day as you apply these insights and strategies, transforming challenges into opportunities for resilience in an ever-changing digital landscape.

- **Encouragement for Small Business Owners**

Cybersecurity may appear overwhelming, especially for small business owners who are already managing numerous responsibilities. However, facing this challenge can turn vulnerability into strength. Consider a local café that begins to implement security measures. At first, the process may seem burdensome, but as employees familiarize themselves with new protocols and technologies, their confidence grows. The owner soon observes not only a reduction in cybersecurity incidents but also an uplift in team morale. The staff takes pride in safeguarding their establishment and their customers' information, which fosters a stronger sense of community among the team.

Take Sarah, who runs a boutique marketing agency, as a case in point. Initially, she dismissed cybersecurity threats, believing her small size would protect her business—"We're too small to be targeted," she thought. However, after a minor incident involving compromised client emails, her outlook changed dramatically. Sarah came to understand that every business, regardless of size, can be a target for breaches or data leaks. By adopting fundamental cybersecurity practices—such as implementing strong password policies and conducting regular training sessions—she not only secured her business but also cultivated a culture of vigilance and awareness among her employees.

The economic implications of investing in cybersecurity are significant. Research shows that the average cost of a data breach for small businesses can soar into the hundreds of thousands when accounting for recovery efforts, loss of customer trust, and legal fees. This sobering reality underscores that proactive measures are not just expenses; they are vital investments in your business's long-term sustainability. Even simple steps can prevent catastrophic losses down the line.

Building a resilient cybersecurity culture doesn't have to be daunting. Start by fostering open discussions about security practices during team meetings or casual check-ins. Encouraging dialogue around these topics can demystify cybersecurity and promote participation across all levels of your organization. Invite feedback on current practices and suggestions for improvements; involving your team in the solution helps cultivate ownership of their responsibilities.

Additionally, as you strengthen your defenses against cyber threats, remember that collaboration with fellow small businesses is crucial. Sharing experiences and strategies at local networking events or participating in online industry forums can help address common challenges collectively, leading to innovative solutions and more robust security systems.

Approach these initiatives with patience and perseverance; transformation takes time. Celebrate small wins—like successfully training employees on phishing awareness or establishing routine security audits—as these achievements accumulate into significant advancements over months or years. Acknowledging these milestones reinforces commitment throughout your organization.

Finally, adopting a mindset of continuous improvement will keep you ahead in the rapidly evolving landscape of cyber threats. As technology advances, your strategies must adapt to meet new challenges. Staying informed through industry news and additional educational resources will empower you well beyond your initial efforts.

In this complex and uncertain landscape, remember that the goal is not perfection but rather fostering resilience and adaptability within your business framework. Each step you take not only protects your enterprise but also enhances its reputation as a trustworthy entity among clients and partners—a distinction that ultimately drives growth in our interconnected world.

- ### Next Steps on the Cybersecurity Journey

Bolstering cybersecurity measures in your business is not a one-time effort; it's an ongoing journey that demands continuous commitment and refinement. This next phase requires you to evaluate your current initiatives, assess their effectiveness, and actively seek opportunities to strengthen your security posture.

Begin by thoroughly reviewing the cybersecurity policies you've established. Are these policies actively enforced, or have they become mere documents collecting dust? Involving your team in this evaluation can yield invaluable insights. Organize feedback sessions where employees can share their experiences with existing protocols. Were the training sessions engaging? What obstacles hinder compliance? The answers to these questions will help shape your approach moving forward.

For example, if employees express confusion about password management practices, it highlights the need for clearer policies and possibly additional training. Implementing password management tools like LastPass or 1Password can simplify secure password usage throughout the organization, allowing employees to maintain strong, unique passwords without the burden of memorization.

Next, consider advancing your training options beyond basic awareness programs. Bringing in external experts for workshops on incident response or cyber threat intelligence can significantly enhance your team's understanding and preparedness. Hosting a simulated phishing attack, for instance, allows employees to experience firsthand how these scams operate while equipping them with practical skills to recognize potential threats.

Take advantage of technology to further strengthen your defenses. If you haven't already done so, consider implementing security software such as endpoint detection and response (EDR) systems or security information and event management (SIEM) tools. These solutions provide real-time monitoring and analysis capabilities, helping to identify unusual activity within your network before it escalates into a serious incident.

Regular audits are also critical in maintaining an effective cybersecurity stance. Establish a schedule for comprehensive assessments—quarterly or bi-annually—to ensure vulnerabilities are identified before they can be exploited by malicious actors. These audits should evaluate not only technical safeguards but also employee adherence to security policies and protocols.

Building relationships with cybersecurity professionals or consultants can provide tailored expert guidance for your business's specific needs. These partnerships foster knowledge sharing and keep you informed about emerging threats and best practices in the industry.

Don't underestimate the value of community engagement. Collaborating with other local businesses on joint training sessions or resource sharing can strengthen collective defenses against cyber threats. Informal networking groups may arise from these collaborations, allowing members to discuss cybersecurity challenges and share lessons learned—benefiting everyone involved.

Establishing a robust incident response plan is essential for preparedness in the event of a breach or attack. This plan should outline roles and responsibilities during an incident, as well as communication protocols for both internal stakeholders and affected clients.

Finally, remain agile in adapting to technological advancements and evolving threats. Cybersecurity is dynamic; it requires continuous learning and adaptation as new risks emerge. Subscribing to industry newsletters or participating in webinars can keep you updated on best practices while providing actionable insights for enhancing your overall strategy.

In summary, the next steps on your cybersecurity journey involve reinforcing existing measures while fostering a culture of proactive growth and improvement. By regularly assessing strategies, investing in ongoing education for yourself and your team, leveraging technology effectively, engaging with the community, building professional partnerships, developing strong incident response plans, and remaining adaptable to change, you will create a resilient organization ready to face whatever challenges may arise.

· Additional Resources for Continued Learning

Navigating the complexities of cybersecurity requires more than just initial training and implementation; it demands a commitment to lifelong learning and adaptation. To enhance your knowledge and skills in this critical area, a wealth of resources is available to support your ongoing education.

Begin with reputable online platforms that offer comprehensive courses on various aspects of cybersecurity. Websites like Coursera, Udemy, and LinkedIn Learning provide a wide range of classes tailored for small business owners and professionals at every level. For example, you can find courses focused on risk management, incident response strategies, and specific software tools such as SIEM systems or endpoint protection. Opting for courses that include hands-on projects allows you to apply what you've learned directly to your business context.

Books also serve as invaluable resources for gaining deeper insights into cybersecurity principles and practices. Titles such as "Cybersecurity for Dummies" by Joseph Steinberg and "The Art of Deception" by Kevin Mitnick introduce foundational concepts alongside real-world applications, enhancing your understanding of threats and defenses. Maintaining a dedicated library of these resources can provide a reliable reference point whenever you face challenges or need to refresh your knowledge.

In addition to formal education, industry forums and online communities play a vital role in fostering shared learning experiences. Platforms like Reddit's r/cybersecurity or specialized forums such as Spiceworks enable engagement with peers who share similar interests. By participating in discussions, asking questions, or sharing your own experiences, you gain diverse perspectives on current trends and challenges within the field. These interactions not only enhance your learning but also expand your professional network.

Attending cybersecurity conferences is another effective way to stay informed about emerging threats and best practices. Events like Black Hat, DEF CON, or regional security summits often feature sessions led by industry experts discussing the latest advancements in technology and strategy. Participating in these gatherings provides opportunities for networking with fellow business owners, security professionals, and vendors who can offer insights tailored to the needs of small businesses.

Podcasts have also surged in popularity as accessible avenues for learning on the go. Shows like "Darknet Diaries" explore real-life cyber incidents while providing expert commentary. Subscribing to relevant podcasts not only entertains but also educates you on developments in the field, fitting seamlessly into busy schedules.

And, governmental agencies and non-profit organizations frequently offer resources specifically designed for small businesses. The Cybersecurity & Infrastructure Security Agency (CISA), for instance, provides guidelines, toolkits, and checklists aimed at helping businesses strengthen their cybersecurity measures without overwhelming them with technical jargon. Utilizing these resources ensures alignment with national standards while tailoring strategies that fit your unique operational context.

Establishing relationships with local colleges or universities can also prove beneficial; many institutions have outreach programs focused on cybersecurity awareness and training. Engaging with students through internships or collaborative projects not only brings fresh ideas into your organization but also contributes to the educational growth of future professionals.

Finally, fostering a culture of continuous improvement within your organization is essential. Encourage team members to pursue their own learning paths related to cybersecurity by facilitating access to online courses or organizing group learning sessions. This approach builds collective expertise while promoting engagement among staff members.

By embracing these diverse resources for continued learning, you strengthen both individual capabilities and organizational resilience against cyber threats. Investing time in education —whether through formal courses, engaging literature, community involvement, or local partnerships—equips you with the necessary tools to adapt effectively in an ever-evolving landscape of cyber threats. This proactive approach not only protects your business but also empowers you as a leader within your industry, ready to share knowledge and foster security awareness beyond just your own operations.

APPENDICES

The appendices are an essential part of this guide, offering practical tools and resources that will enhance your cybersecurity practices. Here, you'll discover checklists, sample security policies, and recommended tools designed to help you establish robust cybersecurity measures for your business.

We begin with the Glossary of Cybersecurity Terms, which provides clear definitions of key concepts and jargon commonly encountered in the field. Understanding these terms is critical not only for your own knowledge but also for effective communication with your team and external partners. Each term is paired with examples or contextual applications, ensuring that even complex concepts are broken down into easily digestible insights.

Next, you will find a collection of Cybersecurity Checklists tailored to various aspects of your cybersecurity strategy. These actionable guides allow you to assess different components of your security framework. Take this example, the checklist for conducting a risk assessment outlines steps such as identifying assets, analyzing vulnerabilities, and prioritizing risks. By prompting you to consider critical factors that may impact your business, these checklists help ensure that nothing is overlooked in your planning.

Following the checklists, we present Sample Security Policies that provide a solid foundation for creating your own customized documents. These samples address essential policies including data protection, acceptable use, incident response, and remote work protocols. Each template offers suggestions for customization based on your organization's specific needs, enabling you to implement policies that not only comply with regulatory requirements but also reflect the unique culture and operational dynamics of your business.

The appendices also include a comprehensive List of Cybersecurity Tools and Resources. Here, you will find categorized lists of software solutions that enhance various aspects of cybersecurity—from antivirus programs and firewalls to encryption tools and data loss prevention systems. Each entry features brief descriptions of the tools' functionalities along with the potential benefits they could bring to your organization. This resource empowers you to make informed decisions about which tools best align with your security objectives.

Additionally, we have included case studies that showcase real-world applications of the strategies discussed throughout the book. These studies highlight small businesses similar to yours that faced cybersecurity challenges and successfully navigated them through practical implementations of various security measures. By examining these scenarios, you can glean valuable insights into what worked well—and what didn't—informing your own approach.

Finally, our Additional Resources for Continued Learning section encourages ongoing professional development. This compilation includes links to reputable online courses, relevant podcasts, industry publications, and notable conferences where you can deepen your understanding of cybersecurity trends and best practices. Engaging with these resources ensures that you're not just responding to current threats but also positioning yourself as a proactive leader in the ever-evolving landscape of cybersecurity.

By utilizing the appendices effectively, you will equip yourself with practical tools while reinforcing the core principles outlined in this guide. Together, these resources not only support immediate security measures but also foster long-term resilience against evolving cyber threats—empowering you as a small business owner in an increasingly digital world where staying informed is crucial to safeguarding your assets and operations.

- **Glossary of Cybersecurity Terms**

Understanding the language of cybersecurity is essential for small business owners aiming to navigate this complex landscape effectively. To aid in this endeavor, the following glossary offers definitions of key terms and concepts commonly encountered in discussions about cybersecurity. Each entry includes practical examples to enhance clarity and contextual relevance.

Access Control:** This refers to the methods used to determine who can view or use resources within a computing environment. Take this example, a business might employ role-based access control (RBAC) to ensure that only employees with specific job functions can access sensitive data.

Antivirus Software:** These programs are designed to detect, prevent, and remove malware from computers and networks. For example, installing antivirus software like Norton or McAfee can help safeguard against viruses and spyware that could compromise business data.

Data Breach:** An incident in which unauthorized individuals gain access to sensitive, protected, or confidential information. A small retail business, for instance, may experience a data breach if hackers exploit vulnerabilities in their payment processing system, resulting in compromised customer credit card information.

Encryption:** This is the process of converting information into a coded format that can only be read by someone with the correct decryption key. For example, an organization might encrypt email communications containing confidential client information, ensuring that even if these messages are intercepted, their contents remain unreadable without the appropriate key.

Firewall:** A network security device that monitors and controls incoming and outgoing traffic based on predetermined security rules. For example, a company might implement a firewall to block unauthorized access attempts while allowing legitimate traffic through.

Incident Response Plan (IRP):** This is a documented strategy outlining how an organization will respond to cybersecurity incidents. An effective IRP includes steps for identification, containment, eradication, recovery, and lessons learned. A small business might establish an IRP that details specific roles for staff members during a cyber incident.

Malware:** Malicious software designed to harm or exploit any programmable device or network. This category includes viruses, worms, trojan horses, and ransomware. For example, if a small business unknowingly downloads infected software via an email attachment, it may face significant operational disruptions as malware spreads through its systems.

Multi-Factor Authentication (MFA):** This security mechanism requires more than one form of verification before granting access to an account or system. Take this example, implementing MFA might involve requiring users to enter both their password and a code sent to their mobile device when logging into company systems.

Phishing:** A type of cyber attack where attackers attempt to deceive individuals into providing sensitive information by impersonating trustworthy entities in electronic communications. For example, an employee might receive an email that appears legitimate from their bank asking them to verify account details—this is a classic phishing attempt.

Ransomware:** A form of malware that encrypts files on a

victim's computer or network until a ransom is paid to the attacker. A small healthcare provider could be targeted by ransomware attackers demanding payment in exchange for unlocking critical patient records.

Risk Assessment:** This process involves identifying potential hazards and analyzing what could occur if these hazards materialize. Regular risk assessments help businesses pinpoint vulnerabilities in their systems—such as outdated software—and develop effective strategies to mitigate those risks.

Security Information and Event Management (SIEM):** This technology aggregates and analyzes security alerts generated by applications and network hardware in real-time. By utilizing SIEM tools, businesses can respond promptly to threats while gaining comprehensive visibility into their security posture.

Familiarity with these terms is fundamental to grasping the principles of cybersecurity. By integrating this vocabulary into your daily operations, you empower yourself and your team to make informed decisions about your organization's security strategy. As you explore this guide further, keep these definitions close at hand; they will serve as invaluable reference points in your journey toward establishing robust cybersecurity practices within your business.

- **Cybersecurity Checklists**

Cybersecurity checklists are essential tools for small business owners, providing structured guidance to systematically improve security measures. By using checklists, you can streamline the implementation of cybersecurity protocols, ensuring that no critical area is neglected. It's important to tailor each checklist to your specific needs, encompassing essential tasks that reflect your unique operational environment.

Begin with a Network Security Checklist. This should outline steps like verifying the use of strong passwords for all devices, ensuring firewalls are properly configured, and implementing virtual private networks (VPNs) for remote access. Regularly updating router firmware is equally vital, as many attacks target outdated software vulnerabilities. For example, a small retail business could conduct monthly checks on their point-of-sale systems to ensure they remain secure and compliant with industry standards.

Next, develop a Data Protection Checklist. Start by identifying sensitive data within your organization and categorizing it based on its importance and risk level. Make sure that data encryption protocols are in place for both stored and transmitted information, which may include using SSL certificates for web applications or employing BitLocker on Windows devices to encrypt hard drives. A case study from a small accounting firm highlighted that implementing encryption significantly reduced the risk of data breaches during client communications, thereby preserving client trust and safeguarding sensitive information.

An Incident Response Checklist is also crucial; it outlines the immediate actions required when a cyber incident occurs. This checklist should include steps such as detecting the breach, containing the threat, notifying affected parties, and documenting actions taken. Clearly defining roles within your team for incident response is vital—designate who will handle communication with stakeholders and who will investigate the breach itself. Take this example, after a malware incident at a local manufacturing company, having pre-defined roles allowed for a swift response that minimized downtime and maintained operational integrity.

A Compliance Checklist ensures that your business adheres to relevant regulations and standards such as GDPR or HIPAA. Start by reviewing the specific compliance requirements for your industry, then verify that necessary safeguards are in place. This may involve conducting regular audits of data handling practices or training employees on compliance protocols. A healthcare provider discovered that a thorough compliance checklist not only helped meet regulatory demands but also increased cybersecurity awareness among staff.

Don't forget an Employee Training Checklist, which is crucial for cultivating a security-conscious culture within your organization. Training sessions should cover topics like recognizing phishing attempts and understanding social engineering tactics. Incorporating interactive elements such as simulated phishing attacks can enhance engagement and prepare employees to identify real threats effectively. A tech startup reported that after initiating regular training programs, incidents of successful phishing attempts among staff decreased significantly.

Finally, implement an Equipment Maintenance Checklist to keep all hardware and software up-to-date and functioning securely. Regular updates to antivirus software and conducting vulnerability scans can help identify weaknesses before they are exploited by attackers. For example, a small law firm found that scheduling quarterly maintenance checks not only improved system performance but also uncovered vulnerabilities requiring immediate attention—reinforcing their cybersecurity measures.

By utilizing these checklists, you enhance accountability within your organization while fostering a proactive approach to cybersecurity management. Each item serves as both a reminder and an actionable step toward achieving robust security practices tailored to your specific business needs. Integrating these structured checklists into your routine simplifies complex tasks and empowers your team to actively engage in safeguarding organizational assets against cyber threats.

- **Sample Security Policies**

Establishing robust security policies is a crucial step for small businesses looking to protect their digital environments. Sample security policies can serve as customizable blueprints, tailored to meet the specific operational needs of your organization. These policies not only lay the foundation for effective cybersecurity practices but also foster a culture of security awareness among employees.

Begin with an Acceptable Use Policy (AUP), which sets clear boundaries around acceptable behavior when using company resources. This policy should address areas such as internet usage, email protocols, and the use of personal devices in the workplace. For example, an AUP may prohibit employees from accessing unauthorized websites or using personal email accounts for business communications, thereby reducing the risk of phishing attacks. By taking this proactive approach, you not only mitigate risks but also align employees with your organization's security objectives.

Following this, consider implementing a Data Protection Policy that outlines how sensitive information should be handled, stored, and shared. It is important to categorize data based on its sensitivity and define access levels accordingly. Take this example, a small healthcare provider may restrict access to patient records to authorized personnel only, employing encryption for data both at rest and in transit. Such measures not only ensure compliance with regulations like HIPAA but also instill confidence among clients regarding their privacy.

Another critical element is a Password Management Policy, which helps combat unauthorized access. This policy should establish requirements for creating strong passwords, detailing guidelines on length, complexity, and regular updates. Encouraging employees to use password managers can significantly enhance security by reducing the temptation to reuse passwords across multiple accounts. A financial consulting firm discovered that after implementing a password management policy, instances of account breaches declined notably as employees adopted stronger practices.

In addition, incorporating an Incident Response Policy is essential for equipping your business to respond effectively to cybersecurity incidents. This policy should define what constitutes an incident and outline the steps for detection, reporting, response, and recovery. For example, if an employee notices unusual activity on their computer, it's crucial they know whom to notify immediately and what actions to take prior to professional intervention. Clear documentation within this policy ensures that everyone understands their roles during an incident—an aspect that was vital for a local retail business that successfully contained a data breach thanks to its well-defined response protocol.

Given the rise of remote work, a Remote Work Policy has become increasingly relevant. This document should specify the security measures required when employees access company networks from outside the office. Guidelines might include using VPNs for all connections or requiring multi-factor authentication (MFA) for logging into critical systems remotely. A technology startup that implemented such a policy during the pandemic noted an improved security posture by minimizing vulnerabilities associated with unsecured home networks.

Finally, establishing a Mobile Device Policy is essential in an era where personal devices are often used for work tasks. This policy should clarify acceptable behaviors regarding mobile devices, such as installing antivirus software and avoiding public Wi-Fi networks when accessing company data. By clearly defining these parameters, you help mitigate risks associated with mobile access—an important lesson learned by a small law firm that lost client trust due to a breach stemming from inadequate mobile security practices.

These sample policies represent key components that can be tailored to your organization's specific context and regulatory requirements. By embedding these structured frameworks into your business operations, you not only create rules but also establish guidelines that enhance accountability and promote a culture committed to cybersecurity resilience.

In summary, developing comprehensive security policies goes beyond mere protection; it empowers your team with knowledge about their roles in maintaining cybersecurity hygiene—an invaluable investment as cyber threats continue to evolve at an alarming pace.

- ### List of Cybersecurity Tools and Resources

Let's begin with firewall solutions. Acting as the first line of defense, firewalls monitor and control incoming and outgoing network traffic based on predetermined security rules. For small businesses, affordable yet effective options like pfSense or Ubiquiti's EdgeRouter provide essential protection without overwhelming complexity. These solutions help block unauthorized access while facilitating legitimate communication—a critical balance for protecting sensitive data from external threats.

Next, it is vital to consider antivirus and anti-malware software. These programs play a crucial role in detecting, preventing, and removing malicious software from your systems. Leading options such as Bitdefender or Malwarebytes offer comprehensive scanning capabilities, real-time protection, and user-friendly interfaces suitable for non-technical users. Regular updates are essential; an antivirus solution is only as effective as its most recent update. Establishing a routine check—perhaps monthly—can help ensure all systems remain fortified against evolving threats.

Moving forward to data protection, encryption tools are indispensable for safeguarding sensitive information both at rest and in transit. Solutions like VeraCrypt for file encryption or NordVPN for secure internet connections are designed to prevent unauthorized access during data transmission. By employing these tools, businesses can secure client information from interception during online transactions—a critical necessity in today's digital landscape.

For organizations handling extensive data or utilizing cloud services, prioritizing data loss prevention (DLP) solutions is essential. DLP tools monitor user activities and identify potential data breaches by analyzing patterns in the use of sensitive information. Companies like Symantec offer DLP services that help prevent unauthorized sharing of confidential information, providing peace of mind—especially for those in industries with strict regulatory compliance requirements.

In the realm of identity management, implementing an identity and access management (IAM) system is key to controlling user identities and access rights. Tools such as Okta or Microsoft Azure Active Directory enable businesses to enforce strict authentication measures, ensuring that only authorized personnel have access to sensitive systems. Integrating multi-factor authentication (MFA) adds an additional layer of security that significantly reduces the risk of account breaches due to compromised passwords.

Additionally, monitoring network traffic is crucial for identifying anomalies that may indicate potential breaches or attacks. Investing in intrusion detection systems (IDS) like Snort or Security Onion allows businesses to analyze traffic patterns and detect suspicious activity early on. Implementing these systems enables prompt responses to potential threats —an approach that has proven invaluable for companies that identified ongoing attacks through diligent monitoring before any damage occurred.

It's equally important not to overlook employee training;

incorporating security awareness training platforms such as KnowBe4 equips staff with the knowledge necessary to recognize phishing attempts and social engineering tactics. Regular training sessions cultivate a culture of security awareness throughout your organization while helping mitigate human errors—the leading cause of security incidents in many businesses.

Finally, staying informed about the latest trends and vulnerabilities is crucial for maintaining an effective cybersecurity strategy. Subscribing to trusted cybersecurity blogs or platforms like Krebs on Security or Threatpost provides valuable insights into emerging threats and best practices tailored for small business owners. Keeping updated ensures your defenses evolve alongside the ever-changing threat landscape.

Together, these tools create a comprehensive cybersecurity toolkit capable of fortifying your business against various threats while facilitating compliance with regulatory requirements. Each component plays a pivotal role in developing a cohesive defense strategy tailored specifically for small businesses navigating an increasingly complex digital environment. By strategically adopting these resources, you are investing not only in technology but also in the long-term resilience and success of your enterprise against cyber threats.

REFERENCES

This guide has been developed with a diverse range of sources to provide small business owners with accurate and actionable information for navigating the complexities of cybersecurity. The references included encompass foundational texts, industry reports, and expert opinions that have shaped the strategies and insights presented throughout the book.

Books like "Cybersecurity Essentials" by Charles J. Brooks and "The Cybersecurity Playbook" by Allison Cerra serve as excellent starting points, offering comprehensive overviews of key cybersecurity concepts. These texts not only define critical terms but also explore practical applications, making them invaluable resources for small business owners aiming to establish or enhance their cybersecurity frameworks.

In addition to these foundational texts, industry reports from organizations such as the Ponemon Institute provide statistical insights into the financial ramifications of cyber incidents. Their annual reports reveal trends in data breaches and security spending, highlighting the urgent need for small businesses to invest in robust cybersecurity practices.

Regulatory guidelines from entities like the National Institute of Standards and Technology (NIST) further support this need by offering structured frameworks, such as the NIST Cybersecurity Framework. These guidelines are particularly useful for small businesses looking to manage cybersecurity risks effectively. By understanding these regulations, organizations can align their security strategies with compliance requirements, thereby reducing potential legal vulnerabilities.

To stay informed about the rapidly evolving cybersecurity landscape, online resources like Krebs on Security and Threatpost are invaluable. These platforms offer up-to-date information on emerging threats and best practices, enabling business owners to adapt their strategies proactively. Engaging with such content fosters a culture of continuous learning within an organization, essential for staying ahead of cyber threats.

Also, insights from experts like Bruce Schneier and Mikko Hypponen highlight the critical interplay between technology and human factors in cybersecurity. Their writings advocate for a holistic approach that integrates technical measures with employee training—an essential aspect for nurturing a security-aware culture within any business.

The collective knowledge drawn from these diverse sources provides a well-rounded perspective on cybersecurity that permeates this guide. By incorporating findings from respected publications, industry reports, regulatory frameworks, expert insights, and real-world examples, this book aims to equip small business owners with a solid foundation for building resilient cybersecurity practices tailored to their unique needs.

As you navigate through this material, reflect on how each reference relates to your specific context and challenges. Embracing insights from these varied sources can significantly enhance your understanding of cyber threats while empowering you to implement effective defenses against them.

- **Cited Works**

In crafting this guide, we have drawn upon a wealth of expertise and research to provide small business owners with accurate and actionable insights into the world of cybersecurity. This curated collection of cited works forms a foundational pillar for the strategies and methodologies presented here.

One significant reference is "Cybersecurity Essentials" by Charles J. Brooks, which explores the fundamental concepts of cybersecurity in depth. Brooks' work offers a comprehensive overview, making it an ideal starting point for anyone looking to build a solid understanding of the field. The book not only clarifies essential terminology but also emphasizes practical applications in real-world scenarios, helping small business owners develop effective security frameworks tailored to their unique needs.

Complementing Brooks' insights is "The Cybersecurity Playbook" by Allison Cerra, which provides actionable tactics organizations can implement to strengthen their defenses against cyber threats. Cerra's emphasis on strategic planning underscores the importance of aligning cybersecurity measures with business objectives—a principle that resonates throughout this guide.

Industry reports from respected organizations like the Ponemon Institute further illuminate the financial implications of cyber incidents. Their annual studies reveal alarming trends in data breaches, detailing not only the costs incurred but also highlighting the urgent need for investment in robust cybersecurity practices. By incorporating these statistics, small business owners can better grasp the necessity of establishing sound security measures and advocate for appropriate budget allocations.

Regulatory guidelines from bodies such as the National Institute of Standards and Technology (NIST) enrich our discussion on cybersecurity. The NIST Cybersecurity Framework provides a structured approach to managing risks effectively. Understanding these guidelines enables small businesses to align their security strategies with compliance requirements, minimizing potential legal vulnerabilities. This regulatory insight empowers business leaders to take proactive steps toward fortifying their organizations against ever-evolving threats.

To stay informed about emerging threats and best practices, engaging with online resources like Krebs on Security and Threatpost is invaluable. These platforms offer real-time updates that are essential for adapting strategies in an unpredictable digital landscape. By regularly engaging with this content, business owners foster a culture of continuous learning within their organizations—an indispensable aspect of maintaining vigilance against cyber risks.

Expert opinions from figures such as Bruce Schneier and Mikko Hypponen add depth to this conversation by emphasizing the interplay between technology and human factors in cybersecurity. Their advocacy for a holistic approach highlights the necessity of integrating technical measures with comprehensive employee training programs. This dual focus not only enhances defenses but also cultivates a security-aware culture that is crucial for long-term resilience.

The citations within this guide weave together a rich tapestry of knowledge drawn from diverse sources, each contributing valuable perspectives on effective cybersecurity practices tailored for small businesses. As readers engage with these works, they are encouraged to consider how each reference aligns with their specific challenges and contexts. Embracing insights from this array of resources can significantly deepen one's understanding of cyber threats while empowering business owners to implement effective defenses suited to their operational realities.

With this robust foundation established through scholarly works, industry reports, regulatory frameworks, expert insights, and real-world examples, small business owners are now well-equipped to embark on their journeys toward building resilient cybersecurity practices that address their unique needs in today's dynamic digital landscape.

- **Suggested Further Reading**

In your quest to deepen your understanding of cybersecurity, it's important to acknowledge that the landscape is constantly changing. The following selections provide valuable insights that enhance the information presented in this guide, each carefully chosen to bolster your knowledge and practical skills.

Starting with "Cybersecurity Essentials" by Charles J. Brooks, this book serves as an excellent introduction for newcomers. It presents fundamental concepts in a clear and accessible way, helping readers familiarize themselves with essential terminology while connecting theory to real-world applications. Brooks illustrates these concepts through relatable scenarios, enabling small business owners to apply what they learn directly to their operations.

If you're looking for a more tactical perspective, "The Cybersecurity Playbook" by Allison Cerra is worth exploring. This book focuses on strategic planning and actionable tactics that organizations can implement right away. Cerra's insights into aligning security measures with broader business objectives are particularly relevant for small businesses aiming to weave cybersecurity into their everyday practices.

Understanding the financial implications of cyber incidents is also vital for making a compelling case for investing in cybersecurity. Annual reports from the Ponemon Institute offer data-driven insights into the costs associated with data breaches and cyberattacks. Familiarity with these financial trends empowers business leaders to advocate effectively for stronger security investments and budget allocations.

Another key resource is the NIST Cybersecurity Framework, which provides a structured approach to managing cybersecurity risks. By familiarizing yourself with this framework, you can develop a robust security strategy while ensuring compliance with various regulatory requirements, thereby safeguarding your business from legal vulnerabilities.

To stay agile in an unpredictable digital environment, engaging with online platforms like Krebs on Security and Threatpost is invaluable. These websites offer ongoing updates about emerging threats and best practices, fostering a culture of continuous learning within your organization. Regularly reviewing articles from these sources keeps you informed about current cybersecurity issues and encourages proactive measures against potential vulnerabilities.

Enhancing your understanding further are insights from industry experts like Bruce Schneier and Mikko Hypponen. Their focus on integrating technology with human factors underscores the importance of a holistic approach to cybersecurity. By combining technical solutions with comprehensive employee training programs, you can nurture a security-aware culture that is essential for long-term resilience against cyber threats.

Beyond individual resources, engaging with professional organizations such as (ISC)² or ISACA can significantly expand your knowledge base. These organizations often offer webinars, certifications, and community engagement opportunities that strengthen both personal skills and organizational capabilities.

As you delve into these additional readings and resources, you'll discover that they are not only informative but also instrumental in cultivating a proactive cybersecurity posture within your small business. Each piece complements what you've learned so far, reinforcing core principles while introducing fresh perspectives relevant to today's complex digital landscape. Embracing this wealth of knowledge positions you as an informed business owner and a leader advocating for best practices in cybersecurity throughout your industry and community.

INDEX

This index serves as a quick reference to essential topics covered in this guide. Whether you are revisiting a concept or seeking clarification on a particular strategy or tool discussed earlier, you can rely on this index for easy navigation. Keep it close at hand as you further your understanding of cybersecurity practices tailored for small businesses.

www.ingramcontent.com/pod-product-compliance
Lightning Source LLC
LaVergne TN
LVHW022300060326
832902LV00020B/3187